By the same author

ON AUTUMN LAKE

THE COLLECTED ESSAYS

ON AUTUMN LAKE

THE COLLECTED ESSAYS

DOUGLAS CRASE

NIGHTBOAT BOOKS

NEW YORK

Copyright © 2022 by Douglas Crase

All rights reserved

Printed in the United States

ISBN 978-1-64362-143-2

Cover photo: Detroit Publishing Co., *Lake Ontario from the boulevard,
Oswego, N.Y.* [between 1890 and 1901]. Library of Congress.

Design and typesetting by Crisis

Typeset in New Caledonia

"There's a better shine," "How bright you'll find young people" and
excerpts from "Lake Superior" by Lorine Niedecker, copyright © 1985
by the Estate of Lorine Niedecker, reprinted by permission of
Bob Arnold, literary executor for the Estate of Lorine Niedecker.

"Rain Moving In" from *A Wave* by John Ashbery,
copyright © 1984, 2008 by John Ashbery, all rights reserved,
reprinted by permission of Georges Borchardt, Inc.

"A Hidden History of the Avant-Garde," copyright © 2011 by
Douglas Crase, reprinted from *Tibor de Nagy Gallery Painters & Poets*
by permission of Andrew Arnot for Tibor de Nagy Gallery, New York.

Cataloging-in-publication data is available from the Library of Congress

Nightboat Books

New York

www.nightboat.org

HOW EMERSON AVAILS

THE PROPHETIC ASHBERY

PREFACE

If there's anything to explain about this book it's that I never planned to write criticism and, no matter the appearance of the pages that follow, I never did. A critic, as defined by Randall Jarrell with more than a hint of irony, is someone who protects you from the bad poems you shouldn't let yourself read, and by extension, I suppose, from the bad art you should be careful not to see. One would have to read all the poets, see all the art, to be of any use in such a job, which means the critics must suffer the very exposure they warn the rest of us to avoid. I'd retreat from the task before it was even begun. The essays here must belong in some other category; they are appreciations or predilections, though to be truthful they were more like affairs of the heart, affairs of attention and intellectual desire, rather than criticism.

I didn't plan a life in literature, either. In college I toyed briefly with the prospect of switching from pre-law to the recently organized and optimistically named program in American civilization. My temptation was thanks to Wallace Stevens, whose insistent cadence I encountered in an elective during the second year. I went so far as to show poems of my own to the professor, emboldened, no doubt, because he wore boots, a leather jacket, and sometimes arrived for class on a motorcycle, all of which lent him considerable authenticity in the eyes of a college sophomore. This was the professor who tactfully advised me later that "poetry is an avocation, not a vocation." By then I was in law school, so perhaps he thought his advice would do no harm.

Another two years were required before I abandoned law school for good, a liberation I owe to the life-altering influence of heroes, including Stevens, and friends. Heroes and friends were to be the visible saints who supplied by their example the education I missed in school.

An education by friends, in my experience, is an education by enthusiasm and reproach. Nobody in their proud twenties wants to play the sedulous ape; but to adopt the passions of a lover or a friend, to try them on like clothes even if you must painfully outgrow them, has to be one of the most glorious paths to an advanced degree. The drawback to the curriculum is that it leaves blind spots. You can emerge from your education by heroes and friends lacking a certain conventional balance, partial for the rest of your life to a set of values acquired when you were the fool of love. I wouldn't have it any other way.

Still, I was surprised to discover from a trial arrangement of these essays that their strict chronology put a piece on landscape as first in the book. I shouldn't have been. Land use in America, urban and rural, was an early obsession. One evening at dinner in the apartment I shared with my partner, now husband, Frank Polach, our friend James Schuyler took a long look around the room where the books were stacked in piles on the floor. "Every book I see in this room has the word America or New York in its title," he gently observed.

If this was a limitation, it didn't bother me. I had been won over by Gertrude Stein's remark in her lecture "What Is English Literature?" that she was content not to know everything. In fact, she was more than content. "I know that one of the most profoundly exciting moments of my life," she said, "was when at sixteen I suddenly concluded that I would not make all knowledge my province." In an age of information overload, her wisdom is more thrilling by the day.

Within the province of my interests I seemed to narrow the focus even further. Whether this was by default or design is no longer important, but it did register as a conscious decision at the time. I wanted a life to be partial to; wanted to know things like the hedgehog instead of the fox, or, to pick a more vividly North American metaphor, I wanted to travel a good deal in Concord. I wanted this because I'd developed the idea from subjects in history and political science that knowing one thing in depth would make an emblem for knowledge elsewhere, that knowledge in all its diversity was nonetheless, in its internal density, complexity, and structure, isotropic in all directions like the universe.

Say you've decided to read all of a single author, as I did Emerson, or as Susan Howe must have done with Dickinson; read them as if no one had read them before, and only afterward consult the established critical writings on that author. You soon note that the writings generalize where they might be particular. They elaborate on their learning, impressions, and at times their prejudice, until it appears eventually they have substituted the elaborations for what the author actually wrote. Jarrell cautioned his readers to remember that the criticism of any age, even the best of it, becomes inherently absurd. Sometimes it's risible. And the conclusion is: if they got Emerson wrong, or Dickinson, how can I believe what they are telling me about Ashbery, or Niedecker, or the origins of the New York School?

On the other hand, if you travel much in Concord it tends to define you as a conversationalist. People get tired of hearing for the nth time about the depth of ice on your neighbor's pond while they are recalling to each other their favorite restaurants in Paris or paintings in Proust. No passion comes free of embarrassment. The advantage is, it directs your attention. The first articles I published were not about art and literature at all, but about the possibility of a new politics in the short, incandescent era between the Vietnam Summer of 1967 and the massacre of students at Kent State in 1970. My friends and I felt that possibility intensely; I imagined my heroes did, as well. Those articles, which appeared in the *Nation*, are too naive and dated for this book; but they remind me that essays as much as poems must believe themselves at the risk of embarrassment into being.

The result of running that risk was more essays than I expected to write. It would be satisfying to claim I had principles that informed the writing, but each occasion seemed to me an emergency of pure empiricism. Whatever habits of thought could be discerned were deduced only afterward. Foremost, in retrospect, was the need to reveal in public my affair with a writer, or an artist, who deserved new notice or a fresh appraisal. This would be less a principle than a sense of urgency, the objective being in each case to replenish in the present the community of heroes and friends, who, as I knew from experience, can alter careers and lives. Probably that's a truism, and I'm not the first to favor it. Robert Duncan closed his essay "Towards an Open Universe" by quoting to like effect the words of Alfred North Whitehead. "The communion of saints is a great and inspiring assemblage," wrote Whitehead, "but it has only one possible hall of meeting, and that is, the present; and the mere lapse of time through which any particular group of saints must travel to reach that meeting-place, makes very little difference."

It is said that poets in their spare time should write criticism, though there exists also the romantic notion that a driven genius has no time to spare and would never bother to write about someone else. Of course that is an aristocratic ideal, which degenerates in modern society to a dandy ideal and not a democratic one. Poets serve together in this project of cultural evolution, regardless of the resistance from those who are fearful of culture and evolution both. Literature is for the descendants of the fearful, too. It must be sent ahead to meet them, when they break free as I did and burn to catch up.

—D.C.

FOUR SAINTS

ON AUTUMN LAKE

It was convenient for John Ashbery, and dumb luck for me, that I was living in Rochester and could pick him up at the airport whenever he arrived from New York to visit his mother. Sometimes, because he didn't like to fly, he'd arrive at the bus station instead; but I could meet him there too. It was an arrangement from which we both might profit, he explained, not profit in the American sense but in a way best expressed if you said it in French, *profiter de*. And thus we began my unexpected education, a kind of improvised fellowship with visiting tutor and bonus bits of wisdom delivered in French.

John, as most anyone who follows poetry will know by now, was born in Rochester and raised on his father's fruit farm in the next county to the east; though he spent a lot of time in town, as much as he could, at the home of his maternal grandparents at 69 Dartmouth Street. His grandfather was no farmer but a cultivated professor of physics, and the young John had let his preference show. Perhaps it was auspicious that we were only four blocks from that Dartmouth Street house the night we met. The director of the Rochester Oratorio Society was hosting a dinner party, which included among its guests a handsome assistant to Aaron Copland who drove up from New York. John had hitched a ride, crashed the party, and was slouched in the doorway of the dining room when he caught my eye.

He was, to get this on record, sexy. He seemed intent on it. He was forty-five that autumn night (I was twenty-eight) and he looked as he does in the now-famous photograph taken a year earlier by Gerard Malanga on Eighth Street—full mustache, unruly hair, and a practiced

3

slouch that was part boredom and part come-hither-if-you-dare. Of course I hadn't seen the photograph, didn't recognize him, and would hardly have known a reason why I should. A friend identified him as a poet and supplied his name. With the instinctive opportunism you have when you're young—apparently I had it, anyway—I detached myself from the friend, approached the mustache, and inquired if he was *the* John Ashbery.

It was a cheap gambit, no sooner spoken than I realized from his expression of disarmed surprise how cruel the young opportunist can be. "Have you read my work?" he asked, while the light in his eyes darkened from split-second joy to caution. "No," I said, trying weakly to undo the damage. "But I will now."

Lucky for me that John, as many a young poet can since attest, was by nature generous. He smiled, if just enough to signal his satisfaction, and forgave me the slight. There would be further generosities ahead, although in this first instance I suspect he was already calculating, in the sense of *profiter de*, the ride he would request from the dinner party to his mother's house in Pultneyville, twenty-eight miles east of Rochester on the shore of Lake Ontario. It was late as we left the party, had been dark for hours, and I couldn't see much of the narrow Federal-style house (it's at 4188 Lake Road, known locally as Washington Street) where I dropped him off. He was swallowed by the night and I never expected to hear from him again. He called the next day.

A week later, after John had returned to the city, a copy of *Three Poems* arrived in the mail. Reading it, I must have held my breath from the first sentence to the last. If poetry should be as well written as prose then here was proof that the secret was to write it *as if* it were prose. Here was language in the shape of a quest, language that had

4

detached utility from the great quests of the Sixties and employed it as a means to continue in the wake of their defeat. It was a way to go on without hope, but without losing the feeling of hope. In 1972, with the war still unended and Nixon's re-election all but assured, the ambiguous resolve of *Three Poems* was the exact resolution a stalled intellect needed to hear.

I wish I'd told him that. Instead, when he asked how I liked the book I answered—and what imp of aesthetic cowardice prompted me?—that perhaps his previous book, written in lines that actually looked like poetry, was even better.

My luck held, not least because I had the car; and John, who in those days didn't drive, did like to go for rides in the country. In this he claimed to resemble his mother and quoted fondly her declaration, heard frequently when he was a child, that she was "a great *go-er.*" We became go-ers, too. We must have driven all over western New York State, stopping at antique shops, used book stores, fruit stands and general stores (where John insisted, to the consternation of the owners, on washing the apples he bought), parks, historical sites. Waterfalls. If these were pleasure trips for him they counted as field trips for me, made instructive by the exemplary way he indulged his interests and wasn't ashamed of them. He could spend hours looking through old postcards at the used book store in Springwater, a favorite; or, if not hours exactly, then certainly time enough to make us late in getting him back to Pultneyville.

Our rides were exhilarating, not only for the miles we covered but because his conversation, so habitually casual and good natured, was also fearless. Each ride was a rolling preceptorial. We were headed west down a long hill in remote Wyoming County the first time he quizzed me on what I'd been reading lately. I was deep into local history before we met, had spent days in the Rundel Memorial Library absorbing histories of the New York frontier, its penetration, the displacement of the Iroquois. I was anxious to know how you transform the local into something mythic. No surprise, then, that what I'd been reading was Charles Olson. To test my memory, or because he didn't remember any lines by Olson himself, John demanded an example. With my hands on the wheel and eyes on the road ahead, I retrieved a memory of "The Kingfishers" and began to recite. "When the attentions change / the jungle / leaps in // even the stones are split."

Immediately from the passenger side of the car came an explosion of triumphant scorn. "I always thought he had a tin ear!" exclaimed John.

Olson's was not the last of the established reputations to be trimmed for my benefit. Now that he'd liberated my interests, I could confess to John that I once attended a poetry reading at the University of Rochester. Friends in the English Department had said it would be a big event. So who was the reader? he asked impatiently. When I told him it was James Merrill he responded with a delighted sneer. "Oh, you mean the *Fabergé* of modern American poetry?"

John never insisted on being the sole poet you were allowed to admire. Not long after he sent *Three Poems* he embarked on a mission clearly designed to improve my library. *Freely Espousing* arrived, by James Schuyler, followed by the recently published *Collected Poems of Frank O'Hara*. To these he soon added *Hebdomeros*, Hesiod, and Raymond Queneau. If you hadn't majored in literature, as I hadn't, John's erudition was thrilling and his eagerness to share it, a revelation.

Gradually I discovered he did not know everything. He was rather a snob about classic American literature—he once admitted this—which must qualify as a blind spot when you think of it, since the man who could write "Daffy Duck in Hollywood" was enthralled by American comics, old movies, and popular culture. But when I ventured to say how cool it was that he actually grew up *by blue Ontario's shore* he didn't have a clue what I was talking about. I had to explain that this was the title of the grand poem in which Whitman summons the poets of the American future; so his being born and raised on that very shore made it seem Whitman had John in mind. At this he didn't sneer, but said nothing. Years later he took to reading Whitman and claimed that perhaps he'd been influenced after all.

But Whitman or no, there are numerous lakes and shorelines to be found in John's poems, and a persuasive list of examples to demonstrate how Rochester and its environs once lent their climate to his work. His poem "The Chateau Hardware" is in effect a greeting card from the place that formed him. Anyone who has lived beneath the gray skies of Rochester can acknowledge the truth of the opening line, "It was always November there." I loved this poem the moment I read it, a feeling that was intensified when John pointed out from the car the location on Monroe Avenue of the mundane hardware store that had provided the allusive title. In the rush of time, both the store and its sign—*Chateau Hardware*—were gone.

As our own days rushed by I was the lucky witness to additional scenes newly transfigured in his poems: the weigela that does its dusty thing in "Grand Galop," the cool downtown shadow of the bus station in "The One Thing That Can Save America." In the gap between the occasions and the poems I had a measure of the abiding concentration it would take to transform the local; and do it without the oracular pretension which, as I was discovering in the work of formerly favorite poets, might not age so well.

John wasn't the only member of his family with insight into his work habits and raw material. On Elmwood Avenue we drove by the vast Rochester State Hospital, an asylum for the mentally ill. One afternoon we saw patients assembled on the grounds, apparently for their exercise, which led him to recount how he and his mother had passed this same asylum and likewise seen patients brought outside for exercise. "Look, John," said his mother. "Isn't that sad? I suppose you'll go home and write a poem about it."

His mother's prediction was later repurposed and passed to me, as in a kind of inheritance. I had acquired a passion for the orchestral suite *Three Places in New England,* by Charles Ives, in particular its haunting third piece, "The Housatonic at Stockbridge." Because that piece is short I made a tape on which it repeated continuously, so I could listen while writing. John was aware of this fixation. One day we took the northern route to Pultneyville and at the town of Sea Breeze came to a bridge across the mouth of Irondequoit Bay. He turned to me and said, "I suppose you'll go home and write a poem called 'Irondequoit Bay at Sea Breeze.'"

His erudition was not always noble. We were invited to dinner by my friend Robert Sobieszek, curator of photography at George Eastman House and finally at the Los Angeles County Museum of Art. Bob was the expert who would be brought in to testify at the obscenity trial in Cincinnati that the photographs of Robert Mapplethorpe were art; but at this point his eminent career was still ahead. John posed a question about our favorite composers, to which Bob replied with enthusiasm that he'd been listening to some music that was really terrific,

the Brandenburg concertos by Johann—he pronounced the full name
—Sebastian Bach. John let out a punishing sigh. "That's like saying
you discovered the *Sistine Chapel!*"

My friend's face went slack and I was furious. Imagine if his beloved
grandfather had greeted John's childhood enthusiasms with derision.
But we were not children and that, perhaps, was the point. Art isn't a
doting grandpa, as John may have painfully learned, but a lover whose
escalating demands cannot be satisfied.

There would be other lessons that art was a jealous mistress, but
none more memorable than on the morning I arrived in Pultneyville
to pick him up for our first ride farther east along the lake. It was October, bright and chilly, and his mother, then seventy-nine, was raking
leaves in the front yard. She was not making much progress. She had
a scarf wrapped around her head and her nose was dripping. As John
came out of the house she said to him—and she had a voice that could
rise in a nasal whine to match his own—"John, if you were any kind
of a son at all you'd help your mother with these leaves."

John, his hand already on the car door, turned briefly back and
replied in exasperation, as though she should have known better,
"Mother, I'm a poet!"

No doubt he was right; though the example was stern, perhaps suspect, and hard to emulate. Sometimes there is nothing there, he once
remarked, but you have to proceed on the assumption that something
is, or you write no poetry at all. I got to see that proposition in action,
following yet another tour on blue Ontario's shore, when he sat down
with pen and a pad of yellow paper to write the poem "On Autumn
Lake." It isn't his greatest and it has an opening line that has always
made me cringe. Yet there are certain moments as well expressed as

if they were in French. By this time I'd written some new poems of my own that surely profited, in the sense of *profiter de*, from his suggestive taunt at Sea Breeze on Irondequoit Bay. He never said he liked these poems, only that they marked a breakthrough. So it privately took my breath away when he offered the yellow pad for inspection and I came to the freshly written lines:

> Turns out you didn't need all that training
> To do art—that it was even better not to have it.

In his last email to me, John recalled the longest trip we made together in the car. Then, early the Sunday morning of September 3, 2017, it was too late to reply. I'm glad he had the last word. I loved the man; and could be ready at a moment's notice to resume our rolling curriculum on autumn lake.

***LITERARY HUB*, 2020**

A VOICE LIKE THE DAY

Because my name appears in his poem "Dining Out with Doug and Frank," I should probably disclose that James Schuyler was a friend of mine—though of the two of us, Doug and Frank, it was Frank he really liked. Over the years this preference was our source, not of tension, but of new humor and affection. One August evening, when I was coming out of the building where Frank and I live in New York, I found Jimmy, as we called him, standing across the street with Raymond Foye and pointing up in the direction of our apartment windows. Kind as he was, Jimmy had a voice of abrupt authority, and on this occasion he summoned it to announce, "We are going up to see *Frank*." My surprised explanation that Frank was out of town gave him the perfect opening to reclaim his advantage: "I know." People who never saw the three of us together sometimes nervously suggest that "Dining Out with Doug and Frank" betrays a similar amusement at my expense. They do not need to be embarrassed. James Schuyler was arguably the most perceptive observer I knew, in person or in poetry, but it was perception without malice.

When Jimmy first showed us "Dining Out," I didn't like it. It was the fall of 1977, we were together in the sweaty single room where he was staying at 201 West Seventy-Fourth Street, and I remember thinking as I read the manuscript that although I could admit the glamour of poems about John Ashbery and Jane Freilicher, or Wystan Auden (and on a first-name basis, too), I did not understand what our names were doing in such company. We had met Jimmy three years earlier when he was fifty-one and we were both thirty and new to city life.

11

Could he now be making fun of us? But he never made fun of anyone I knew of, not in a cruel way. Gradually I came to understand that when he wrote about John and Jane and Wystan he wasn't name-dropping, either. To Jimmy these were real people and real people were the kind that counted. Readers of poetry are used to poems that are pumped up with references to Orpheus and Eurydice, to Bogart, and soon perhaps to Bart Simpson. Whether from education or exposure, a reader has some expectation of what these fictions signify, and it seems to be human nature to like poetry that invites us to bring our expectations to a poem and so to feel included when we get there. My own experience with "Dining Out" suggests that someone who brings such expectations to a poem that refers to actual persons, rather than culture heroes or movie stars, is apt to feel excluded instead. Imagine feeling included by fictions but excluded by real life. Yet this was exactly the perversion I was being encouraged to reconsider. It was not important I know who Doug and Frank were, only that as real people caught in real life they were representative, not of something unattainable, but of something I had all around me. They stood for "friends." They stand for you. When Jimmy put our names in that poem it was a way of saying what to him was always obvious, that we must treat our friends and ourselves as if we were the stars, unalterable and moving as the stars.

It was not long before Frank and I regarded Jimmy as our own moralist of the everyday. He didn't so much teach as exemplify, which is the way it should be, since even the wisest lesson soon sounds like drivel. I suppose in this case the lesson would reduce to something like being quick to love the world rather than waiting for the world to love us the way it seemed to do those stars on TV. Coming as we both did from religious and consumer traditions that train you to prefer a world that is always strategically somewhere else, Jimmy's was just the message we needed to hear. "You see, you invent choices where none exist," says his magnificent "Hymn to Life," and when I read that line in context, I recognized it as the adrenaline of a new responsibility. The exciting thing about knowing as well as reading Jimmy was to observe how his ethics seemed to emerge directly from the life around us. His ethics seemed earned—not scooped up from elsewhere as if our long civilization was a mere cargo cult in thrall to morally richer aliens, but earned—and from the simplest and most democratically available situations. One evening after dinner at our apartment he was admiring the pink cover Robert Dash had done for John Koethe's book *The Late Wisconsin Spring*. It was, he said, "a very fine pink." But Jimmy, I warned, Bob says it's the wrong pink. Jimmy regarded me silently for a moment, then in that voice of sudden gravity he said, "Only if you had another pink in mind."

We call it the everyday, when it is more likely that experience is the one thing that is not commonplace, the one source of the saving distinctions that give us lives. I have noticed how Jimmy's readers like to quote in this regard the first lines of "Letter to a Friend: Who Is Nancy Daum?" ("All things are real / no one a symbol"). But because the Jimmy I knew was so faithfully unpretentious, I always liked the blunter formulation, in a poem called simply "Mike," which went out of print with *Hymn to Life* and became available again in his *Collected Poems*.

Look out
the win-

dow cluck:

it's real,

it's there,

it's life.

In that unembarrassed view it might even be "theory" that dulls
one's capacity for moral response, while flowers and people and the
weather are worthy of the most careful attention. I remember how
Jimmy would sometimes turn to Frank, who was once plant information officer at the New York Botanical Garden, to verify the exact identity of a fruit or flower. The last request (though Frank had long since
left the Garden) came in the matter of "Yellow Flowers," a poem in
which a *Coreopsis* is distinguished by its sweetness. A fact checker at
the *New Yorker* had balked at this, as might anyone who noses up to
the *Coreopsis* on sale at the local florist. Jimmy was delighted, and
perhaps a little relieved, when Frank turned up a scented variety. Fairfield Porter, the master of painterly realism who had been in Jimmy's
judgment his best friend, believed an artist was someone who "distinguishes endlessly"; and the entries that Jimmy made in his journals
during the summers spent with the Porter family on Great Spruce
Head Island in Maine show him practicing distinctions of his own.
Some of these appeared in *The Home Book* and later in a chapbook
published by the Dia Art Foundation. "Differences from yesterday:"
begins the one dated June 27, 1968, "the overcast sky is streaked with
yellow, Isle au Haut is bluer, and, though only the most feathery of the
grasses sway, the surface of the water is crinkled and running."

Jimmy said he never wrote poems about Porter's paintings, but he
did admit in an interview with Mark Hillringhouse that he tried to

write poems that were *like* those paintings. The working principle seems to have been to register your attention, whether in paint or words, before it could be altered by your expectations of how things should, or, as Jimmy would add in the poem "Dec. 28, 1974," by your wishes of how things might, otherwise be. For me the date of that poem marked the beginning of an intense three-day course in what it would mean to pay attention in poetry. Jimmy, Trevor Winkfield (who would later edit *The Home Book*), Darragh Park (who was in many ways to take over from the Porters as Jimmy's chosen family), Frank and I were all staying as year-end guests of Bob Dash at his studio and garden—Jimmy loved gardens—in Sagaponack, New York. On December 28, while the rest of us came and went, Jimmy sat unbudging in a kind of genial secrecy and wrote "Dec. 28," complete with its now frequently quoted lines about saying things as they are, and its infrequently quoted but to me dearer lines about someone of a "frank" good nature whom you trust. On December 29 he wrote a poem called "'Can I Tempt You to the Pond Walk?'" in response to an invitation extended to him in those words by Trevor. And on December 30, prompted by an unwanted drama I had allowed to develop, he wrote the uncompromising, one-stun lines of "Growing Dark," a poem that went in and out of print but reappeared in the *Collected Poems*. In 1980, on an evening when I was out of town on work, Frank witnessed another demonstration of poetic attention. Jimmy had come for dinner, sat down to sign Frank's new copy of *The Morning of the Poem*, and just kept writing. An hour passed before dinner, reheated, was resumed as if there had been no interruption. Afterward Frank opened his book to find not an inscription but a love poem—to Tom Carey. Jimmy called the next day to ask that a copy be transcribed and brought to him. We never saw that poem in print. The aim of paying strict and immediate attention, as Porter once said in reference to Eakins, was to strike through sentimentality. It is possible Jimmy decided the poem he inscribed in Frank's book had not met this goal.

By the time the two of us knew Jimmy he no longer lived with the Porters ("Jimmy came for a visit and stayed eleven years," said Anne Porter) as he did from 1961 to 1972. Once, when he took a company of friends which included us to retrieve some books he had left at the Porters' house at 49 South Main Street in Southampton, New York, Anne Porter greeted us at the door by saying tenderly, "My, there are a lot of you." Perhaps she envisioned another lengthy invasion. Jimmy's friendships with John Ashbery, Barbara Guest, Kenneth Koch, and Frank O'Hara made poetry history. There is no doubt that his friendship with Fairfield Porter was itself a defining chapter in the American culture of the last half of the twentieth century, a friendship that enriched two arts. Frank and I have been able to count twenty-five paintings or sketches Porter made of or including Jimmy, and we have managed to see many of them. None is easily accessible, although the Whitney Museum of American Art does own *The Screen Porch*, a group portrait of Jimmy, Anne Porter, and the Porter daughters Katharine and Elizabeth, which ought to be permanently on display. In an article in 1960, Porter wrote, "To ask the meaning of art, is like asking the meaning of life: experience comes before a measurement against a value system. And the question whether art has any meaning, like the same question about life, may not be answerable at all." In the last lines of "Hymn to Life," proving once again that when great artists steal, they add rather than subtract, James Schuyler wrote, "May mutters, 'Why / Ask questions?' or, 'What are the questions you wish to ask?'"

David Kalstone described Jimmy's tone as perfect pitch, and I have wondered ever since what it is that makes it perfect. There are the deftly struck syllables themselves: you hear each note, he doesn't write with the pedal down. It is not surprising that Jimmy brought a taste for Fauré, Sisley, and Cather into our lives. His poems seldom say look at me, me and my feelings, pity me. They say let us look together at that, isn't that something?—what love really says in its focus on a third thing. There is no mockery in these poems designed to inform you of the poet's superior taste or virtue, no one-upmanship. When several of us were together Jimmy often sat to one side, though foursquare as he does in *The Screen Porch*. You felt as if you were at a Council Fire and any moment true wisdom might be heard, more indigenous and primal than any of the advisories currently to be procured from page or image, and when at last it happened it was as if the DAY had decided to speak. One afternoon we were all discussing favorite poets and the favorite I offered was Whitman. Somebody laughed, and in a tone so-phisticated people once used to indicate there was something embar-rassing about Whitman said, "Oh, you probably like 'Scented Herbage of My Breast.'" I went hot with shame, and knew I had to find a way out, when the Day spoke from the side of the room. "*I* think that is a beautiful poem," said James Schuyler. It was thrilling to observe how the tables could be turned, and whatever new shame I felt at my near treason was transmuted instantly into emulation of this man whose honesty had saved me from betraying myself and my heritage for the sake of feeling momentarily snobbish and correct.

To Jimmy it was apparently only natural to extend his honesty to times when, as he wrote in "Trip," he was "wigging in, wigging out," and recovering in psychiatric wards. This is an honesty that seems to astonish people. I am sorry that I, too, once felt it necessary to explain away his fortunes as if I were enhancing *him* and not proving myself sentimental and smug. Frank always said Jimmy was the sanest person we knew, and in the shape of a life's gratified attention, I think that was right. In his book on Fairfield Porter, John T. Spike quotes a letter Porter wrote describing Jimmy's first visit to Great Spruce Head Island in Maine.

> Sometimes I hear him typing, and often I hear a woodpecker and think it is he. He loves to canoe, and has been in the water, swimming slowly around for a time with a smile on his face, and remarking very gently after a bit, "Why Fairfield. It's the coldest thing I ever felt."

The distinguishing tone of the poet we knew, described so well in that letter, was the same both before and after the accidents of mood for which he sometimes required outside assistance. On first reading, Jimmy's honesty can lead readers to interpolate into some of his poems their own expectations of anguish, when of course he was writing instead to observe one more aspect of things as they are: his mental weather, before intervention by pity or by our expectations of what that weather should be. I wish I could say I visited him when he was in the hospitals. I went only once, in the company and at the urging of the loyal John Ashbery. It was before hospitals had become a daily round of life for urban young people and the experience frightened me. It was I, not Jimmy, who was afraid to keep my eyes and ears open. "The daffodils, the heather / and the freesias all / speak to me," he wrote from Payne Whitney, the psychiatric unit of New York Hospital. "I speak / back, like St. Francis / and the wolf of Gubbio."

There were conversations about his work that Jimmy and I never had, at least not in person. In 1985, I wrote in a review that he seemed to consider simile and metaphor inherently untrustworthy. In all *The Morning of the Poem*, excluding only its Payne Whitney poems, he seemed hardly to have needed the word "like" or "as," except in reports of what *others* had to say—Auden being distinguished as saying, "'Poets should / dress like businessmen,' while / he wore an incredible peach- / colored nylon shirt." In the *Collected Poems* the table of contents displays at a glance Jimmy's trick of distinguishing even the dates of his attention: "June 30, 1974" is an American ode, to happiness. The more Dickinsonian "I Think" addresses a day directly. Other traps for the attention are the distinguishing contrasts ("trees that make / it and the / trees that don't") and corrections ("Smoke streaks, no, / cloud strokes") set like decoys through the poems. When he does arrive on an analogy it is not the subject-to-subject kind that William James derided as bare likeness; it is a kind that slips its reader from the subject to a surprisingly apposite, on-the-move event.

> March is here
> like a granny
> a child doesn't
> like to kiss:

When I wrote in my review that Jimmy was scrupulous in his use of analogy I meant it as a compliment. Later I was not sure he took it that way. In a selection from his journals edited by Raymond Foye and first published in *XX!st Century*, I found this entry dated July 12, 1989:

Finishing up shaving just now, I was also, somewhere, in my mind, searching for an image of what Artie's return is like to me: what momentarily struck (so to speak) was, a bronze snowflake. No wonder there

19

are those who find my verse bereft of simile and metaphor. Just as well, it would seem. Still, I can both see and hear the clatter of those bronze snowflakes. Artie is maybe a little more like a bronze cruller.

I did not know Jimmy when, at the instruction of John Ashbery, I read my first Schuyler poem, "Hymn to Life," in the April 1973 issue of *Poetry*. I had not seen a poem like this before. In one racing moment it altered the boundaries of form, a search of the earlier *Freely Espousing* confirmed the experience, and the arc of innovation to be seen in the *Collected Poems* can still, years later, recall the pulse of those first encounters. Jimmy once defined art, in his poem "A Stone Knife," as a thing in which the surprise is that the surprise is always there. So it seems just right that a surprise found its way permanently into his *Collected Poems*, the result of an event in his publishing history that serves now to emphasize how unlikely innovation is, and how lucky we are to get it. This event was *The Home Book*, a selection of then fugitive prose and poems, some dating to the 1950s, which was assembled by Trevor Winkfield and published by Z Press in 1977. The mostly early poems from that volume must have threatened in the *Collected Poems* to make either an oblique appendix or an impertinent prologue. They were inserted, instead, between *Freely Espousing* of 1969 and *The Crystal Lithium* of 1972—a fluent, attractive solution that makes it appear, nonetheless, that they had constituted Jimmy's second book. They really constitute a kind of sidebar. It would be foolish to overlook them. The apt "Dreams," the buoyant "Things to Do," and the happily titled "Self-Pity Is a Kind of Lying, Too" all seem to reach Schuyler status; and as to the others, well, I like as much as anyone to see how even a master had to practice. The built-in surprise is that I now like better than ever to begin again with those great poems that first announced him as the poet *Schuyler*, no longer taking them for granted, but thinking as on the day I met them, Here they are.

Jimmy truly did advise Frank, while they were dining out without me at the since disappeared McFeely's, to "'experiment / more,' 'try collages,' and 'write / some skinny poems.'" It was example again, the best advice. The title poem in *Freely Espousing* is itself a variant of Jimmy's collage, a form he made so unabashedly capacious it could hold even the sputtering accuracies of "O Sleepless Night" in *A Few Days*. His incisive skinny-poem form is implicit at the outset in "Salute," waiting to culminate in economies like "So Good" and "Growing Dark." And the great experiment that Charles North has described as Schuyler's mighty line is already tested in the brief, enduringly beautiful "December," poised to take off in "The Crystal Lithium," approach perfection in "Hymn to Life," and pass perfection to a planetary vitality in "The Morning of the Poem."

> and,
> Most beautiful of all, on a long long lawn running,
> racing as whippets
> Are bred to do and leaping straight into
> Kenward's arms, who
> Casually closed them: quite an act!

These mighty poems and skinny poems are like nothing another American poet has done. They are events in the single dimension of space-time. Occupying little space, the skinny poems take more time; occupying much space, the mighty ones must move in record time. Each form insists on what it thus exaggerates, in a way to demonstrate that form itself was Jimmy's deep analogy—to experience. Fairfield Porter said that in the history of the arts an afternoon sensibility of reflection was common, but a morning sensibility of observation was unusual. Among morning sensibilities he included Sisley. Jimmy's poems, too, are like urgent morning experience. "The Morning of the Poem" awakens with the pressing need to urinate and ends more than a few hundred lines and forty-four pages later in the relief of doing so at last. In all that racing interval, you are not allowed to rest your attention even once on a familiar prosodic form, no thinking to yourself "oh, terza rima," or "in memoriam stanza." You are not allowed to relax in any comfort of what you already knew your experience to mean.

In his twenties Jimmy typed manuscripts as a favor for his friend W. H. Auden, and he used to tell us he had realized then that if poetry was what Auden wrote, he would never be able to write it. He wanted to write stories anyway. So thanks to one of those detours that life reveals as having been no detour, literature got a new kind of poetry that tropes on stories. Jimmy made some of his poems remarkably from stories themselves: "Wystan Auden," and that unassuming example from *Last Poems* into which the ruling tragedy of the postwar, perhaps post-revolutionary United States is compressed to a bursting nanosecond and held, "Over the hills." Likewise impressive was the genius of retained attention by which he could make stories do the work of the simile and metaphor I truly hope he never thought I missed. In the rushing tide of his mighty line, this genius is easy to enjoy, but overlook. There is a passage in "The Morning of the Poem" in which he actually likened the air of an overcast day to a man he has followed at the supermarket in order to get a better view, but who, when the poet reaches his goal, "was wearing / (I surmise) Jockey shorts (I curse the inventor of Jockey shorts)." In our largely predictable poetry this is a moment too tender to miss. It gets funnier as it goes along. If one aim of paying attention is to strike through false feeling to a better view of reality, then what an instruction it is when, having reached our goal, reality is still mediated. The day wears Jockey shorts. All told, the analogy lasts through thirty lines, and it ends by recalling what it was meant to represent: "This day, I want to / Send it to you." The reality Jimmy wanted us always to have was a reality still alive, the present he called in his poem "At Darragh's I" the *va et vient* of life.

I once told Jimmy that his lines in "The Morning of the Poem" looked like the *Epodes* in my paperback Horace and he seemed mildly amused but not much impressed by my yard-sale pedantry. One year I was offered the chance to teach creative writing and he asked what I was going to do. I had been asking myself the same question with rising anxiety, and though I see now that my solution mainly relieved my anxiety, at the time I believed it the mark of a new professionalism, so I said, well, this week they are going to write a sestina, and next a sonnet. Jimmy looked at me in astonishment and said, "I didn't know people still did that kind of stuff." Between the publication of *The Morning of the Poem* in 1980 and his *Selected Poems* in 1988 he made a few nearly invisible corrections in "The Morning of the Poem" itself, though I don't know if it was Jimmy or an editor who in the same interval corrected the text of that poem so the initial letters of each long line would be consistently capitalized. The *Collected Poems* reinstated the lax, inconsistent capitalization, which had to be once more corrected in subsequent printings. The point of the capitals had been to emphasize that these were not alternating long and short lines, not—despite their adventitious layout on the page—like epodes at all. They were single mighty lines due, so Jimmy insisted, to what was possible on his typewriter. This does not mean they were casually achieved. On one occasion Frank called to ask him for lunch and he responded, in that voice like the Day, "Frank, lunch is for dilettantes." He held out for dinner instead.

I used to wonder, and still do, if a receptive attention to "things as they are" is apolitical or, to put it more sharply, complicit. It was another question we watched Jimmy address, not theoretically, but directly from experience. When Frank worked at the Botanical Garden both his office phone and our phone at home were linked to the city's poison hotline. One night at dinner, Frank told Jimmy the story of an emergency call that came in regard to a Virginia teenager who, after a quarrel with his family, had gone into the yard where he deliberately picked, crushed, and swallowed some ornamental castor beans. Crushing them makes them poisonous. "Eight is a lethal dose. He / Picked ten." We never learned what finally happened. But it had not occurred to us to question whether the boy in Virginia knew he was dealing in real life until we found his story in Jimmy's "Morning of the Poem," distantly juxtaposed to another poisoning.

> I switch to *Mod Squad*: Adam Greer (played by Tige
>   Andrews) is being shot by almost invisible poison pellets:
> He passes out on the grass: will Peggy Lipton and Clarence
>   Williams III find out what the poison is in
> Time to obtain an antidote? It seems likely.

Of course, Adam Greer could not be allowed to die. But was the boy in Virginia confusing the unbreakable conventions of television with the frangible reality of his own life?

Pity the young Virginian.

People who fail to regard what is happening as real, who know their experience only through mass-produced metaphor, get hurt. I cannot imagine Jimmy preaching. Yet "things as they are" is perhaps the last antidote we have to organized informational thuggery. In Washington, D.C., the world observed once a succession of governments whose sense of reality was so infirm that they could waste whole nations, including their own, on behalf of an analogy to dominoes. Jimmy was in Washington while one of those governments occupied the city. It was before Frank and I knew him, but I take it he saw no dominoes. The city he did see was made of real things, and celebrating those, he wrote in the face of the deathly Vietnam War a masterpiece called "Hymn to Life."

Lawrence Joseph has identified in an essay the important lines in "The Morning of the Poem" that suggest how words refract as light. I had not thought before about these lines, though they seem now another way of saying that words are to Jimmy's poetry what color was to his best friend's painting. Words are how we see, they reveal or hide (which shows how erotic words are). The intellect, complained William James, is quick to get between real life and the persons living it; the best philosophies, he thought, would be those that try "to restore the fluent sense of life again, and let redemption take the place of innocence." It's too bad this sounds so old-fashioned. Even people who like to think about poetry sometimes object to a poet's stubborn intention to eat the cake and have it too, to know there is no unmediated object and yet call on the medium to get us all the way through to what we love. I think this willful naiveté, if that is what it is, makes pragmatism in poetry. Truth is an experience, and if by asking a question you get experience that works then you have read in that experience the truth. "May mutters, . . . 'What are the questions you wish to ask?'" By posing his questions in the structural renewals of his poetry, Jimmy, who on the surface of his sentences seemed so limpid and spontaneous, reveals himself to have been thinking long and hard about what consciousness can do. Perhaps this is why poetry like his is so hard to write. Go ahead and try it, as Ann Lauterbach has suggested. Try to present the light and you will encounter what Jimmy described in "Growing Dark" instead: "So / beautiful and / things keep getting / in between."

Frank and I saw too little of Jimmy in the years just before the stroke that snapped at his body's syntax on Friday, April 5, 1991. Darragh Park was unable to reach us during the weekend and John Koethe called from Wisconsin with the news late Sunday night. On Monday we went down to St. Vincent's Hospital in the Village where at Jimmy's room we found Darragh, Eileen Myles, Barbara Guest, Morris Golde, and Artie Growich. Jimmy had many friends, and in this week they would come, as many already had and others would in the days ahead, to be at his side. On Thursday, in the bright, nearly hot spring afternoon, I went to his room again. Along Eleventh Street and the other side streets up and down Greenwich Avenue, the pent-up Callery pears and pent-up youthful pedestrians had burst into bloom. Jimmy had not recovered his speech. Everyone who saw him during that week reported how he laughed. I offered descriptions of the scene outside, to which he responded with wide-eyed attention. A doctor came in and asked me to help lift him. Lift Jimmy! When we got him to a thirty-degree angle the doctor, Robert Cohen, said okay you hold him while

I get the stethoscope on his back. Jimmy was hefty and I am not, and when my arms began to shake Jimmy looked up at me and winked. Darragh came in. David Trinidad arrived as I was leaving. Darragh says that among the last to visit was Anne Porter. On this sunlit afternoon she wore and did not remove a raincoat, together with a net scarf that seemed to catch and hold about her head the light coming in from across the Hudson to the west. She brought out pictures of Katharine's children which Jimmy very much wanted to see, but by the time his glasses were located the pictures had been put away, and throughout the lengthy and unsuccessful search through her purse to retrieve them she addressed him in a strainless monologue. His eyes, says Darragh, never left her. Eventually she said, "The weather was so beautiful coming in today it reminded me of Fairfield saying the light in New York is the most beautiful in the *whole world*, though he'd never *seen* the whole world." James Schuyler laughed. He died the next morning, April 12, 1991, about six o'clock.

Jimmy's ashes were buried that fall at Little Portion Friary near Port Jefferson, New York, a retreat of the Franciscan, Episcopalian order in which Tom Carey had become a friar, and where, thanks to Tom, Jimmy had periodically found friends, the outdoors, and a place to write. The ashes, in something like a mylar Pringles chips can, were carried to a ragged clump of conifers and hardwoods on a hill above the friary where someone had scraped a trustingly amateur hole. I remember a chickadee that would not shut up, as people in turn left a handful or trowelful of earth to complete this final resting place that looked for all the world, as Jimmy might have invented it himself, like a backyard pet cemetery. Everyone who has loved his poems, who knew James Schuyler in person or not, must sometimes reflect on his influence and how it will gather as he would have liked. He *would* like, after all. The day after his triumphant, first-ever reading at the Dia Foundation in 1988, I encountered him on Ninth Avenue buying cat litter for Tom's, and now his cat, Barbara. When I asked in too effusive a manner how it felt to be a star he looked at me in disbelief and said, "It feels fine, Doug." Simon Pettet is editing his art criticism, Nathan Kernan his diary, and William Corbett his letters. Frank and I think frequently of the day—and in deference to Jimmy's own principles I should say that day had a name, October 6, 1978—when he said suddenly at dinner, "My shrink says you stop writing to punish your friends." He gave us a split second to consider this new secret weapon, then added, "I have not known them to suffer." In a rush of piety I would like to say, no, it's not true, for every possible Jimmy poem we don't have because he didn't live long enough, or because he started writing late, or because he had to rest, we do suffer. Except I see him look from across the room, and I can hear him speak like the Day, "Only if you had another Jimmy in mind."

POETRY, 1994

MAKE IT TRUE

By the end of 1965, James Schuyler had lived with the Fairfield Porter family for five of the eleven years he was to spend as a virtual member of the household. "On the whole a very pleasant & harmonious household" is how Porter described it in a letter to a friend. For Porter, these were the important years when he had begun to paint in the style that would make him the great painterly realist of his time. Schuyler, sixteen years younger, had yet to see his first commercially published book of poems and was coming to terms, meanwhile, with the mental illness he would bear recurrently thereafter. This disparity of circumstance in the two men—to outsiders it suggested charity—was redressed in the wit of their friend Frank O'Hara, who, as he and Barbara Guest drove past the Porters' home in Southampton, New York, turned to her and announced, "The éminence grise in *that* house is James Schuyler."

Now the years have turned wit to insight, because the publication of Schuyler's fifth collection, *A Few Days*, makes it abundantly clear that we have witnessed one of those great friendships between painter-and-poet equals which can enliven painting and poetry both, and enrich a national heritage. In an interview, the poet was asked if he ever wrote poems about Porter's paintings. "No," he said, "but I tried to write poems that were like his paintings"—a project whose result, to my ear, is a body of the most bracing poetry written in North America during the last quarter of the twentieth century. Just as Porter became the central figure for painters who believed in an art outside the Abstract Expressionist mainstream, so Schuyler has become for younger poets an eminent example of instruction outside the workshop, of a poetry to fit what he once called "the pure pleasure of / simply looking." Anyone who has read Schuyler knows, however, that "simply looking" can be more complicated than it sounds. More rewarding, too; his collection *The Morning of the Poem* won a Pulitzer Prize in 1981 and the title poem of his *Hymn to Life* is surely a contemporary masterpiece. But readers who are encountering Schuyler for the first time may be surprised, as they turn the pages from poem to poem, to find lines like these from "A Few Days":

> This coffee is cold. The eighteen-cup pot
> > like most inventions
> doesn't work so well. A few days: how to celebrate them?
> > It's today I want
> to memorialize but how can I? What is there to it?
> > Cold coffee and
> a ham-salad sandwich? A skinny peach tree holds no
> > peaches. Molly howls
> at the children who come to the door. What did they
> > want? It's the wrong
> time of year for Girl Scout cookies.

Now, if poetry is almost incredibly one of the effects of analogy, as Stevens said it was, then what is remarkable about such lines from Schuyler's poem is the near total absence of analogy in its ordinary sense. Where are the similes, where are the words *like* and *as* that usually identify what we think of as descriptive writing?

The absence of those words is especially notable whenever a fashion for analogy overtakes our writers, or momentarily awes the critics. Of course, the temptations of the practice are not new. Stevens cited as an example Virgil's attempt to persuade us in the *Georgics* that farmers forget their worries in winter the way sailors adorn the poop with garlands when their ship reaches port. It works, observed Stevens, only if you think about it, and by that time you have lost interest. It lacks the discipline of "rightness." Schuyler came close to the same formulation himself ("it's / the just rightness that counts," he once wrote), and he seems as a result to consider analogies inherently untrustworthy. In the whole of *The Morning of the Poem*, he was so scrupulous in the employment of similes that they were confined to lines quoted from other people, or to a group of poems written while he was a patient at a mental hospital. Not once in the whole book did the word *like* or *as* occur in the poet's own free voice.

But look what he can do without them. In the few lines set out above—the ones introduced by the cold coffee—he has painted in the apathetic beauty of a whole suburban paradise by the technique of letting the things in the picture reveal themselves through their own actions. We come to distinguish the coffee pot because it does not work, the dog because it howls, and the season of the year because it isn't Girl Scout cookie time. The impression is of things left tactfully alone, to stand forth naturally, and there could hardly be a more loving technique. In the long run, maybe it's true you can't make poetry without annihilating the boundaries between the loved thing and your green thought of it. But a poetry that emphasizes distinctions, rather than analogies, is one way a poet may at least *try* to postpone the consumption in words of the very thing whose distinctive loveliness is what moved him to praise it in the first place.

That transitional meantime is unquestionably where Schuyler's best poems reside, and he has all but patented a number of seductive devices to get you to join him there. The trick is to involve you in the act of making distinctions as you read: "the cornflowers (or are they / bachelor's buttons?) stand." You choose the species and perhaps the flowers are real. Read on, and be beguiled by the possibility of real weather, real places, and actual people, too: "if / you hold your breath and make a wish," we are told, "you'll meet Virgil Thomson in the elevator." All this speciation is enlivening in itself. It is also a setup, because when the poet *does* deploy one of those analogies whose absence you've started to take for granted, the surprise can be liberating and swift. No one else has had Schuyler's genius for likening objects or attitudes to surprisingly apposite events.

> the sun is off the balcony,
>   the air is cool
> as one of Barbara's kisses, which don't make me feel
>   I turn her on.

The cumulative effect is of a poetry that wants always to be on the move. For a moment, you could almost believe we might be restored via poetry to the comings and goings of life, where our knowledge of reality is made in the tissue of time. It is a triumph of Schuyler's style that his poems seem to bring that possibility within reach, a triumph admired among poets along the whole spectrum from the Poetry Project in Manhattan to the departments of English in California.

Yet there is more to poets and poetry than technical achievement, and the Schuyler style implies a question that is rarely asked about our poets. Do they write poetry out of boredom and dissatisfaction with the world, or out of their love for it? When you consider the popularity among poets of the various prescriptions for altering their lives, for

making things new or making them strange, then it is logical to conclude that a large proportion must believe the world is either hiding
secrets or inadequate. By contrast, it would take a poet who believes
the world is both lovely and fully on display to assert, as Schuyler does
so bluntly, "I have always been / more interested in truth than in imagination." To a poet like that, reality would be the one thing that is *not*
commonplace, and it would stand to reason that life cannot fully be
lived until the reality is faced without embarrassment or flinch.

> "Oh shit," she said,
> "I stepped in some doggy pooh." Worse things could happen
>   to you. Meeting a
> man-eating tiger in the street, for instance.

It's an unmistakable voice. In an age when people are increasingly
cowed into euphemism, James Schuyler is stalwart for those realities
that link every one of us.

Stalwart, but not thumbing his nose. Instead, his poetry seems to
offer its lessons in a spirit of almost democratic charity. All of us, for
example, must have had the experience—if only to a slight degree—
of moments when our bodies insist so strongly on misperceiving reality
that we can't correct the inappropriate moods that have been induced.
In "A Few Days," one of the days in question is distinguished by the
poet's anticipation of a long-awaited dinner party. When he gets to the
party, however, things go wrong. Although he is taking Antabuse to
keep from drinking, and thus meant to ask for coffee, he has asked for
a drink instead. The mistake is inexplicable even to him. And yet he
"faces it out," accepts the drink, and the result is a predictable disaster
reflected immediately in the poem itself.

How could the lesson be clearer? To misperceive is to suffer, and

33

to say the wrong thing has *physical* consequences. If a single misstatement is an injury, then a collection of such injuries can be fatal: euphemism, disinformation, hype, and, yes, analogy—these are waystations on the road to death. I am putting the lesson at its grimmest, when it is one of Schuyler's characteristic charms to say the most serious things in diverting ways, as witness "The Fireproof Floors of Witley Court."

> Put to the test in a fire
> the firemen could not extinguish
> the fireproof floors
> failed to distinguish
> themselves and are no longer
> really to be trusted
>
> Visitor to Witley Court
> enter at your peril

Seen like that, it is just plain practical to learn to love reality.

The trouble is, the project does not get any easier. "Things should get better as you grow older," writes Schuyler, "but that / is not the way." The way, instead, is that at age sixty-two his life is increasingly restricted to the space of his room in the Chelsea Hotel with its view of West Twenty-Third Street, a street that "hasn't got much going for it." In such a diminished condition, not unlike the one that waits for everybody, even a poet might find it difficult to go on making fresh distinctions. "The morning / passes," he begins at one point; it passes —how?—"like an elephant in no stampede." One gets the exasperation of this, and also the humor. Maybe even the heroism. If the poet does not have the physical range he had when he accompanied the

Porters annually from their winter home in Southampton to their summer place in Penobscot Bay, he will still tell the truth—about what? About the balustrade outside his window, his assistant Tom and his unrequited love for same, the birthdays of absent friends, and the commonly enjoyed possessions (the moon, television) of those who live in isolation in New York. Yes, he implies in a lovely elegy on the death of his mother, the recipe for approaching death is to be an "old truth-teller," nothing smoothed over, right to the end.

In the world of public relations, which is a large part of the world we live in now, there is a well-known piece of advice to the contrary. You are not here to get it right, so the saying goes, you are here to put a spin on it. Engagingly put, this is the habit of mind that gives us preachers who can say that abortion is like the Holocaust, an attorney general who claims that affirmative action is like slavery, a president who tells us the mercenaries in Nicaragua are *like* the Founding Fathers. James Schuyler has struggled all his creative life against the temptation to impose this kind of spin on things. As a result, despite his years of diminishing prospects in the Chelsea Hotel, and despite the diminishing constitutional prospects facing his country as a whole, here is a poet who can write that he is still free.

> Yes, everything gets more
> restricted, less free.
> Yet I am free, one of the lucky ones. . . .

Lucky for us, as well. Because James Schuyler remains for poets, and everybody else, an unbowed reminder of what it means for the language to continue free, and of what a high calling poetry really is.

THE NATION, 1985

THE POET'S SO-CALLED PROSE

Even if we know what poetry is for, what do we make of a poet's prose? Especially when it's the taxing syntax of Marianne Moore. Imagine 462 prose items packed into six hundred pages, picture them dense with "independence of the subjunctive, and many another select defect" (the phrase is hers), then picture them denser still with her famously relentless quotations and you will understand if I answer my question by quoting (the habit is catching) from one of her best-known poems. "It is a privilege to see so / much confusion."

Except what looks like confusion turns out, when you find it in the full expanse of this poet's so-called prose, to be revealing if not clear. Credit the editor, Patricia Willis, who included in the *Complete Prose of Marianne Moore* just about every prose item Moore ever published, and presented it in sober, though sensibly adjusted, chronological order.

It is not what Moore would have done. The poet who in 1967 excluded "only" 120 poems from her *Complete Poems* left us no reason to think she would be less willful with her prose. In *Predilections*, she linked reviews together to form essays, and mixed those with other pieces in a way to suggest that serene institution, a poet's essays—the detached, the Olympian reflection on matters aesthetical. In *A Marianne Moore Reader* she emphasized a more extroverted prose (a piece from *Vogue*, one from *Harper's Bazaar*) and, fitting her late image as the Mary Poppins poet in a tricorn hat who once threw out the first ball of the season at Yankee Stadium, even included over the objections of her editors the correspondence with Ford Motor Company in which she proposed archly inappropriate names for the product Ford was to market later as the Edsel. The *Complete Prose* corrects both screwball caricatures by a method the poet herself applied to individual poems and essays, a method she called—though she was quoting someone else, of course—an "accuracy of abundance."

As Moore practiced it, this meant you might first learn what was *not* in abundance. "Certain of Marsden Hartley's stark austerities not here, are preferred by us to some that are," she wrote in a 1925 review. There were no diaries or letters in the *Complete Prose* [a selection of her letters has since appeared separately]. And there was not much in the way of memoirs, though we did get a sparkling if decorous account of her tenure as acting editor of the *Dial*, present at the creation of modernist American poetry. She was "our saint," said William Carlos Williams in retrospect. "She is one of the angels," said Wallace Stevens before he had even met her. She's a "hysterical virgin," said Hart Crane when she was meddling with his manuscripts.

She was also the most engagingly original of the great modernist poets born in the United States. Her first poems appeared in 1915— the same year as "The Love Song of J. Alfred Prufrock" and "Sunday Morning"—and one of them, "To a Steam Roller," started out like this:

> The illustration
> is nothing to you without the application.

Thus began, as Eliot pointed out a few years later, a brilliant use of "the curious jargon produced in America by universal university education." Today, this college vernacular has been so fully integrated into the American tradition that if you found those lines from "To a Steam Roller" lying around loose somewhere you might think they had been dropped by Ashbery or one of his acolytes. But in 1915 nobody had written poetry this way before. "I want to know," wrote Ezra Pound in a letter, "whether you are working on Greek quantitative measures or on René Ghil or simply by ear (if so a very good ear)."

It was a good ear, one of the best. And Moore put it to work not just in her poetry but in a distinctive criticism that likewise answered to what the ear hears, as well as what the eye sees. She once remarked that anything she wrote in prose, whatever its purpose, would really be an essay. Apparently she was right, because the five kinds of criticism preserved in the *Complete Prose* are distinguished not so much by form or quality as by length. There are essays of about five pages, reviews of two or three pages, page-length comments from the *Dial*, brief mentions from the *Dial*, and blurbs. The complete blurbs. And even these are little essays, as in the one for Hugh Kenner: "Entertaining and fearless, he can be too fearless, but we need him."

Since it was mostly criticism, Moore's prose doesn't reveal what Pound was anxious to discover, the source of her breakthrough poetics. But it does corroborate her poetics in ways that make it easier and more pleasurable to read her poems. Easier, because it provides access to the nonconformist sentiments that were otherwise disguised or unexpressed, including a statement of the young poet's belief that it's the *accented* syllable that is boring, while what we call the unaccented syllable is not. And more pleasurable, because it adds to the allusive resonance (in Poundian terms, the subject rhyme) of favorite poems. One of these favorites, for just about everybody, is "The Steeple Jack."

Dürer would have seen a reason for living
in a town like this, with eight stranded whales
to look at; with the sweet sea air coming into your house
on a fine day. . . .

Moore herself stretched the resonance of this poem when she told a student that the eight whales she had in mind had been stranded either in Sheepshead Bay—apparently she couldn't quite remember —or Brooklyn Harbor. But Dürer? In the *Complete Prose* is a comment she wrote for the *Dial* in praise of an exhibition, then at the New York Public Library, of prints by Dürer. "His mere journeyings are fervent," she wrote, "to the Dutch coast to look at a stranded whale that was washed to sea before he was able to arrive." All this time, then, the word Dürer has been a subject rhyme: for the conjunction of fantasy and detail we associate with his work, but also for fervor in research, and our own fortunate "accessibility to experience" (whales, in this case), which the poet would celebrate in another poem that she titled simply "New York."

Of course, if it's true that life consists in what you are thinking about all day (Emerson said it was) then this poet's prose also represents a life of the mind of Marianne Moore. In a single month the *Dial* carried one review, one comment, and three brief mentions, all by Moore. And because she was so deeply involved with the fortunes of Eliot, Stevens, Williams, and the rest, it represents likewise a life of modernist poetry in the United States, from its inception with Pound to its capitulation to Auden. Moore wrote nine reviews of Eliot, six of Williams, three of H.D., and five of Stevens. *Eliot*: "he seems to move troutlike through a multiplicity of foreign objects." *Williams*: his work is marked by "a concise, energetic disgust, a kind of intellectual hauteur which one usually associates with the French." *Stevens*: "Mr. Stevens is never inadvertently crude; one is conscious, however, of a deliberate bearishness." *Cummings*: "a kind of verbal topiary-work." *H.D.*: "actuality . . . being lost in the sense of spectacle." *Pound*: "To cite passages is to pull one quill from a porcupine."

Moore is sometimes cited as authority for a gentle, descriptive criticism in which the real opinions of the critic are indiscernible, to say nothing of his or her standards. "I have been accused of substituting appreciation for criticism, and justly," she wrote in 1958, "since there is nothing I dislike more than the exposé or any kind of revenge." You may take her at her word that the motive was never revenge. But in the accurate abundance of her prose her victims may not have known the difference—as when she made fun of the novelist Maxwell Bodenheim for his unexamined attitudes. "The writer's attitude of pronouncement," she wrote, "reaches its apex in the statement made by one of his *dramatis personae*, that there is zest in bagging a woman who is one's equal in wits; the possibility of bagging a superior in wits not being allowed to confuse the issue." And here in its entirety is her preemptive strike on the school of poets to be known later as The Fugitives.

Chills and Fever, by John Crowe Ransom (Knopf). Unrewarding dissonances, mountebank persiflage, mock mediaeval minstrelsy, and shreds of elegance disturbingly suggestive of now this, now that contemporary bard, deprive one of the faculty to diagnose this "dangerous" phenomenon to which one has exposed oneself.

The strike failed. But it does illustrate how deeply she was engaged in the campaign to create and consolidate a modernist aesthetic in U.S. poetry.

To regard the prose as primarily a concordance, however, or a life, would be to imply that a poet's prose is only ancillary to the poetry. This is a familiar assumption, predicated on the notion that poets should leave the business of criticism to those who are in it as a business, and sometimes on the notion that poets just can't think. But Moore, joyously quoting Eliot quoting Pound, actively believed that criticism and poetry were not exclusive ("'They proceed as two feet of one biped'"). Perhaps they were not even separable. Criticism, she wrote, inspires creation. More than that, "a genuine achievement in criticism is an achievement in creation"—her own prose being the case that proved her point, if not quite in the way she meant. Her reviews, and her essays ostensibly on poetics (these have enchanted titles like "Humility, Concentration, and Gusto" or "Idiosyncrasy and Technique"), don't offer recipes that explain poetry so much as they offer further examples of what goes on during poetry—Moore's poetry, to be exact. In the way that *Democratic Vistas* is more Whitman, or *The Necessary Angel* more Stevens, so the prose in the *Complete Prose* is more Marianne Moore.

No surprise, then, to find it as recalcitrant as the poetry. Moore is well known for saying that "one should be as clear as one's natural reticence allows one to be." It is easy to be amused by this, but it was not mere perversity on her part. For a woman who had embarked on an aesthetically exposed life for which there were few, if any, feminist models in her country, style was serious business. Style was not the result of freedom. It was the instrument of freedom.

When an artist is willing that the expressiveness of his work be overlooked by any but those who are interested enough to find it, he has
freedom in which to realize without interference, conceptions which
he personally values.

And if this sounds closeted, remember that we are talking poetics
not politics here. When she was twenty-seven, Moore could be found
at a Pennsylvania fair climbing onto the roof of a portable outhouse,
there to reattach a women's suffrage banner after an opponent had
ripped it down. No, her reticence was designed to induce you into letting her proceed, until it was too late to do anything but catch up with
her. Or, as she put it in one of the irresistible redefinitions that wait to
be isolated from her prose: "Poetry is an unintelligible unmistakable
vernacular like the language of the animals—a system of communi-
cation whereby a fox with a turkey too heavy for it to carry, reappears
shortly with another fox to share the booty."

It seems only natural that the way Moore organized her prose was
likewise designed to share the booty, not to mention the burden, with
the reader. "The objective is architecture, not demolition," she wrote,
indicating that she knew very well what we were likelier to think. Yet
her essays "Henry James as a Characteristic American," "Abraham Lin-
coln and the Art of the Word," and the earlier "Sir Francis Bacon" do
finally reveal their architecture in paragraphs the way her poems reveal
their architecture in stanzas. What appears at first to be an overturned
file of quotations turns out to be a stanzaic arrangement in which the
quotations probably do more work by virtue of reassociation and an-
tithesis than they did in the original. It can't be a coincidence that her

first professional review was built on the conceit of suggesting to T. S. Eliot how he might *rearrange* his just published book of poems.

Readers (and I am one of them) who have been upset by Moore's notorious revisions of her poetry will recognize that she was following a similar impulse in the rearrangement of quotations in her prose. In fact, given the examples and dicta to be found in the prose, we may have to consider that the poet knew exactly what she was doing to us. "It may be true," she once admitted, "that the author's revisions make it harder, not easier, for hurried readers; but flame kindles to the eye that contemplates it."

There's a decidedly spiritual tone to that defense, a tone that recurs so frequently in her prose that I suspect Moore saw her rearrangements and revisions as means to detain the mind— otherwise rapt with commerce—for decidedly spiritual ends. To rearrange a subject is truly to contemplate it. It is one thing in a review or an essay to express opinions, because opinions are easy to come by and much like everyone else's. Most of the time they *are* everyone else's. It's another thing to rearrange, because choices are both morally and technically interesting, with the added chance of being original. That was the added chance she was always ready to take, and (in the rearranged words of another) she lets us know exactly why. "The 'ability to be drunk with a sudden realization of value in things others never notice' can metamorphose our detestable reasonableness and offset a whole planetary system of deadness."

If deadness was the evil, the salvation was idiosyncrasy: the "indigenous gusto," as she wrote in praise of Auden, which makes a good poet "unable to be dull." The problem is, salvation doesn't matter much if it's for poets only—a decent, realistic judgment that was implicit in Moore's once famous statement to the readers of *Seventeen*: "Example is needed, not counsel." In fact, if you examine the screwball image of her later life in this perspective it doesn't look screwy, after all, but exemplary. Like her poems, like her tenure at the *Dial*, her public prose and public activities were examples of how the Americans might contemplate the startling details of their own existence: the St. Louis Cardinals or the Camperdown Elm in Prospect Park, the "impassioned emancipator" M. Carey Thomas of Bryn Mawr or the then middleweight medalist Floyd Patterson, even the art of individual dress. Just think of the effect on the readers of *Women's Wear Daily* who learned under Moore's byline that "Whatever the cut, width, or foot, the wearer should be able to step with assurance—as Dante says, like a crane—'come una crana.'"

So this woman who was among the first of poets bemused by "plain American which cats and dogs can read" went on in her prose and life to demonstrate what a Dürer would do with the mix of fantasy and calculation to be seen in ourselves. As she said of one modernist colleague, "In his modestly emphatic respect for America he corroborates Henry James' conviction that young people should 'stick fast and sink up to their necks in everything their own countries and climates can give,' and this feeling for the place lends poetic authority to an illusion of ours, that sustenance may be found here, which is adapted to artists." This was no jingoist or isolationist attitude. Already in her time she had seen how it was sublimely moral. A people who don't think themselves worth saving aren't going to care much about the rest of the world, either. "The thing is to see the vision and not deny it," she wrote; "to care and admit that we do."

In a lifetime of seeing, caring, and not denying, Moore was so spirited and yet so careful of hyperbole that she has earned the right to the corrective last word. Although she meant it in praise of a very different stylist, it can be applied reflexively, and with equal justice, to the *Complete Prose of Marianne Moore*: "But the book is a triumph, and all of us, that is to say a great many of us, would do well to read it."

THE NATION, 1986

A SCHUYLER BALLADE

It was December 28, 1974, when I watched James Schuyler writing a poem. I didn't realize it at the time. Frank and I, along with Jimmy, Trevor Winkfield, and Darragh Park, were all at Robert Dash's place out on Long Island for the holidays. That afternoon, while the rest of us came and went, Jimmy sat there with paper and pencil in a kind of prominent, genial secrecy. When I found out later that this day with us in it had been just right for a poem, it was a revelation.

> We are immersed in beauty, but our eyes have no clear vision.
> —RALPH WALDO EMERSON

> The days slide by and we feel we must
> Stamp an impression on them. It is quite other. They stamp us
> —"Hymn to Life"

> The supreme virtue here is humility, for the humble are they that move about the world with the love of the real in their hearts.
> —WALLACE STEVENS

> a never before seen liquefaction of the sun . . .
> Unbelievable, unwanted, and as lovely as though someone you knew all your life
> Said the one inconceivable thing and then went on washing dishes.
> —"The Crystal Lithium"

Perhaps indeed the efforts of the true poets, founders, religions, literatures, all ages, have been, and ever will be, our time and times to come, essentially the same—to bring people back from their persistent strayings and sickly abstractions, to the costless average, divine, original concrete.

—WALT WHITMAN

Look out
the win-
dow
cluck:
it's real,
it's there,
it's life.
—"Mike"

Q: How do you feel about the waking day, how do you handle it?
A: That's a hell of a big question [laughs].
—INTERVIEW WITH MARK HILLRINGHOUSE

I Think

I will write you a letter
June day. Dear June Fifth
—"I Think"

Experience in its immediacy seems perfectly fluent. . . . Its difficulties are disappointments and uncertainties. They are not intellectual contradictions.

—WILLIAM JAMES

An expression of the immediacy of experience—for what else is the namelessness of everything—is proper to poetry and natural to photography.

—FAIRFIELD PORTER

Q: Did you ever write poems about his paintings?
A: No, but I tried to write poems that were like his paintings.

—INTERVIEW WITH MARK HILLRINGHOUSE

After years of calling him Jimmy, we learned he would rather we had called him Jim. But what of all the Porters that Frank and I were making pilgrimages to see: "Jimmy in a Black Rocker," "Jimmy and Liz," "Jimmy and John," "Jimmy and Leaf Cart," "Jimmy with Lamp," "Jimmy" (not to mention "Iced Coffee" and "The Screen Porch"). In these paintings, Jim already looked the way Jimmy would look on December 28, 1974, the focus of a poem.

Life is a series of surprises. . . . I can know that the truth is divine and helpful; but how it shall help me I can have no guess, for so to be is the sole inlet of so to know.

—EMERSON

the Japanese cherries

Bust out into their dog mouth pink. Visitors gasp.

—"Hymn to Life"

Knowledge of sensible realities thus comes to life inside the tissue of experience. It is made; and made by relations that unroll themselves in time.

—WILLIAM JAMES

> If you've ever been in a car
> that was hit by a train
> whang
>
> —"Stun"

Knowledge is what you know and how can you know more than you do know.

—GERTRUDE STEIN

> and later
> a hunk of scrap iron
> just there on the turnpike
> for no reason
> flies up and
> whang
>
> —"Stun"

In the poem "Elephants," after five stanzas of beautiful description of the elephant and his mahout, Miss Moore suddenly backs off and remarks . . .

As if, as if, it is all ifs; we are at much unease

thereby giving dramatic expression to one of the problems of descriptive poetry . . . . But it may be noticed that although full of similes, and
such brilliant ones that she should never feel the necessity of complaining, she uses metaphor rather sparingly and obliquely.

—ELIZABETH BISHOP

and who was it
who in the Café Montana told,
In all seriousness, that the triumph of Mrs. S.,
future Duchess of W., was that
"They say she's a circus in bed." I like to
dwell on that, the caged lions
And the whips, ball-balancing seals, "And now,
without a net . . ."
—"The Morning of the Poem"

So long as we deal with the cosmic and the general, we deal only with
the symbols of reality, but as soon we deal with the private and personal
phenomena as such, we deal with realities in the completest sense of
the term.

—WILLIAM JAMES

"Sodomy in the first degree; sodomy in the second
degree: sodomy in the third
Degree": what's that all about?
—"The Morning of the Poem"

The sea-shore and the taste of two metals in contact, and our enlarged powers in the presence, or rather at the approach and at the departure of a friend, and the mixture of lie in truth, and the experience of poetic creativeness which is not found in staying at home nor yet in travelling, but in transitions from one to the other, which must therefore be adroitly managed to present as much transitional surface as possible,— these are the types or conditions of this power.

—EMERSON

Life is in the transitions as much as in the terms connected; often, indeed, it seems to be there the more emphatically.

—WILLIAM JAMES

          So under lilacs unleaved
Lie a clump of snowdrops and one purple crocus. Purple, a polka-dotted
Color little girls are fond of: "See my new dress!" and she twirls
On one foot. Then, crossed, bursts into tears. Smiles and rain
      —"Hymn to Life"

Good taste is not essential, and it is often a brake on energy. . . . Energy is a bridge to whatever is essential.

—FAIRFIELD PORTER

     Energy! The sun sucks up the dew; the day is
Clear; a bird shits on my window ledge.
      —"Hymn to Life"

My parents were visiting New York, and Frank and I took them around the corner to McFeely's for dinner. In came Daniel Halpern with a small group that included Stephen Spender. They sat at the next table. Unaware of our presence, Halpern produced *The Morning of the Poem* and read aloud the whole of "Dining Out with Doug and Frank" while Spender looked around at the restaurant where the dining out occurred, looked even, from time to time, right into the eyes of Doug and Frank. What would you have done?

> Art is as mysterious as nature, as life, of which it is
> A flower.
> —"Hymn to Life"

> The path of things is silent. Will they suffer a speaker to go with them?
> A spy they will not suffer; a lover, a poet, is the transcendency of their
> own nature,—him they will suffer.
> —EMERSON

> grabbed
> a cart, went wheeling
> Up and down the aisles trying to get a front view of
> him and see how he was
> Hung and what his face was like. But when I reached
> my goal he was wearing
> (I surmise) Jockey shorts (I curse the inventor of
> Jockey shorts)
> —"The Morning of the Poem"

He judges not as the judge judges but as the sun falling around a helpless thing.

—WALT WHITMAN

> And now the sun shines
> down in silent brightness,
> on me and my possessions,
> which I have named,
> New York.
> —"Moon"

Gusto, in Smart, authorized as oddities what in someone else might seem effrontery.

—MARIANNE MOORE

> "The genitalia
> of plants we regard
> with delight; of animals
> with abomination; of ourselves
> with strange thoughts" (my own
> remind me of a ruby-crowned kinglet
> —"Gray, Intermittently Blue, Eyed Hero"

Continuous transition is one sort of conjunctive relation; and to be a radical empiricist means to hold fast to this conjunctive relation of all others, for this is the strategic point, the position through which, if a hole be made, all the corruptions of dialectics and all the metaphysical fictions pour into our philosophy.

—WILLIAM JAMES

> So
> beautiful and
> things keep getting
> in between.
> —"Growing Dark"

At last I wrote something I thought was really good, only to realize I had stolen it direct from Jimmy. When I confessed, he had this to say: "Take it, Doug, it's free." In this country! Free.

> in which
> the surprise is that
> the surprise, once
> past, is always there:
> which to enjoy is
> not to consume.
> —"A Stone Knife"

DENVER QUARTERLY, 1990

NOTE ON NIEDECKER

Sometime late in 1962, in a tiny log-sided house on the banks of the Rock River in Wisconsin, a poet who had no phone sat down to write an ode to her newly acquired pressure pump. "I've been free / with less," she wrote—"and clean." The poet was Lorine Niedecker (say NEEdecker), and the principle she was expressing was put to work as triumphantly in her poetry as in her life. In the 1930s she had been grouped with William Carlos Williams and others among the Objectivists. But perhaps it's more helpful now to locate her work simply in reference to those two cranky and glorious traditions of American poetry, long lines or short lines. The long-liners tend to be expansionist, transcendental; the short-liners isolationist and reductionist—theirs is the prickly demurrer from boosterism, and Niedecker ranks with the most independent among them. Observed Basil Bunting in tribute: "No one is so subtle with so few words."

Subtlety likes movement, and the danger for any short-line poem is that it will just sit still. But a Niedecker poem does not sit still. It is kept moving by the poet's scrupulous attention to transition: from word to word, line to line. In an uncollected verse play of 1936 she included a character who speaks fondly of "exquisite tether and release"—a phrase to describe her own technique as well. Consider the little poem about her lost granite pail, a justly famous work that is not too slight to invite comparison with Elizabeth Bishop's villanelle "One Art." In its third line ("Think what's got away in my life"), Niedecker tethers her poem to a conventional emotion, though she has used an unconventionally lovely expression to do so. Then, in the fourth line ("Was enough to carry me thru"), she offers a transition to release the tether and put the poem back in motion. Unexpectedly, loss carries you through. And there might be the end of it, except *carry* is hesitant with a tether of its own, the heft of that lost time lifted on its handle once again. The transitions harbor the surprise and this is how the subtlety enters in.

It is that way with life, too. By insisting on transition in her poems, Niedecker was insisting on lived experience as an alternative to the thrall of acquisition that customarily passes for life among the Americans. "O my floating life—," she wrote, "Do not save love / for things / Throw *things* / to the flood." The people honored in her poems—Jefferson and Black Hawk, Audubon and Darwin, unnamed but unbowed women like herself—these were people whose originality stemmed from the simple but radical act of paying attention to realities no one else was bothering to see. It will be our turn to respond with attention when Niedecker's selected poems is published later this year. If I had the chance, I would nominate it for every honor in poetry that her country can bestow.

POETRY PILOT, 1986

FREE AND CLEAN

Not long after Lorine Niedecker died, on December 31, 1970, her husband recalled that when she first told him she was a poet she whispered it. "Later on," he said, "I got the devil bawled out of me when I told somebody in a tavern that my wife was a writer. She didn't want it known. She was bashful." They were married in 1963, when Niedecker was sixty, and had recently built a small house on Black Hawk Island (not an island but a peninsula in the Rock River just above Lake Koshkonong), the place in southern Wisconsin where the poet was born and where, despite interruptions, she kept returning to live throughout her life. It was in the front room of this house that her husband spoke to a reporter: "After she left, I thought, 'Who is she? And what was she?'"

His questions have not been properly answered yet. Because Niedecker married so late, because for many years before that she lived alone on the river in a cabin with no indoor plumbing or telephone, because her primary link to the literary world was her thirty-nine-year correspondence with Louis Zukofsky, while her other correspondents were also Objectivist poets or their admirers, and because we didn't know enough about her otherwise, a largely sentimental image took hold where the answer to her husband's questions ought to be. According to this image, she was the American bittern of poetry, a Thoreauvian Bashō who somehow got reincarnated female in the upper Midwest but adjusted to the accident with Objectivist therapy. She crafted poems of nicety and discretion and made them, we have been told, of language "whittled clean." They were poems the more emphatically discrete for the silence in which they were said to be contained.

This image is about to come unstuck. For years you couldn't get a Niedecker collection anywhere and then there were two of them, sufficiently different to demonstrate how truly inadequate our understanding of this poet has been. One was a selected poems, *The Granite Pail*, edited by Cid Corman. The other was a complete poems plus creative prose, *From This Condensery*, edited by Robert J. Bertholf and since superseded by Jenny Penberthy's edition of the *Collected Works*. Corman put together a seductive selection unencumbered by notes or textual variants; some of its pages are almost unencumbered by words, since *The Granite Pail* is the Niedecker planted in silence, the orthodox version up to now. Bertholf, by contrast, counted more than four times as many poems in his collection; sometimes he counted them more than once. Working with the poet's surviving manuscripts he delivered in *From This Condensery* a Niedecker that was rangy, turbulent, and troubling as well.

Maybe no one was more surprised than these editors, because the result of their contrasting presentations is a disagreement over Niedecker's intentions and methods which amounts, ultimately, to a disagreement over her achievement as a poet. The issue was joined in what is probably her best known poem.

> There's a better shine
> on the pendulum
> than is on my hair
> and many times
> . .   . .
> I've seen it there.

Even by itself, which is how Corman prints it, this is a complex performance. By itself, it is a subtle reflection on life's vanity, say, on the cycle of personal fate. But when Niedecker first published the poem in 1936 it wasn't by itself. It was third in a series, "Mother Geese," arranged among other poems predominantly concerned with cycles of a more inclusive sort—the economic and political cycles whose reality was vivid during the Depression years when "Mother Geese" was written. As an expansion of context the arrangement is so effective that when the last line of the sixth poem tolls

<blockquote>lost, our land, forever.</blockquote>

you are likely to hear how *this* pendulum was attached all along not just to the ticking heart but to a ticking economy too.

So much for the discrete poem. In a manuscript note (included among the "Notes" in Bertholf), Niedecker observes of another poem that "these phrases that look forward and back are fascinating to do but I suppose there's a limit." A limit, that is, unless you can arrange the poem within a series where poem as well as phrases look forward and back. It's a distinguished strategy, ever since Whitman. The trouble is that Niedecker rearranged her work continually in this manner, until at the time of her death a single poem might exist in several versions, in more than one position among the manuscripts, in a sequence and on its own. On the evidence of *The Granite Pail*, which moves smoothly onward with no hint of options, Corman must believe that what Niedecker required was a good editor. Bertholf was inclined to let the manuscripts have their own way, the result being that *From This Condensery* was thick with confusing variants and near outright repetitions. It's impossible to say how many of these Niedecker intended to clean up. Not all of them perhaps, since way back in 1955 she had concluded—as if in anticipation of Jennifer Bartlett or Steve

Reich—that "a recurring thing, for all but the apathetic student, is never the same."

The irony is that Bertholf left so little out of his edition then chose to call it *From This Condensery*. The phrase comes from one of Niedecker's least satisfying and more self-regarding poems, but its elevation was probably inevitable since it echoes the Poundian and then Objectivist notion that the poet's job is to condense the raw material until she has revealed the discrete poem waiting at its core. Of course Niedecker would sometimes borrow this expression; it isn't easy to find the right metaphor for how you make metaphors. But what is equally clear is how much she was aware that her own methods differed from those of her correspondents, and that this difference would not be recognized for some time. In the poem "Otherwise" she has turned for sympathy to a likewise idiosyncratic practitioner, Gerard Manley Hopkins, addressing him as "Dear friend," and getting in along the way an unusually irreverent pun on the name of the master condenser, Ezra Pound.

> the scanning's plain
> but who will veer
> from the usual stamp and pound
> Other work?—I've not yet found
> the oak leaves' law . . .

Maybe she hadn't codified it, but in her poems Niedecker returns frequently enough to "the law of the oak leaves" to indicate that here was a principle she meant to follow in poetry.

Good enough, but aren't we just out on a limb with another metaphor? Better would be to watch the poet in action, and if you were patient with the perversely unindexed *From This Condensery* there would be times you could almost see a poem take shape. One persuasive example is in "Crèvecoeur," a poem based on *Letters from an American Farmer*. Bertholf prints the initial prosy piece in which Niedecker has entered two lines that seem only recently harvested from her reading. "Astonishing how quick men learn who serve themselves. / At night the fireflies can be caught and used as a reading / light." But when this harvest reappears in a more obviously finished poem ("To Paul now old enough to read:") the transformation has been dramatic.

> Read Crèvecoeur and learn fast
> the firefly, two pairs of wings
> and a third to read by
> disappearing.

Shorter by three words, this is hardly a condensation. The poem has expanded, burgeoned almost, the way an oak leaf takes up its mineral facts and unfolds from the bare branch. "True value," this poet has written elsewhere, "expands."

As it turns out, the leaf metaphor was not wholly Niedecker's own, no more than the condensery. Hopkins had described "the law of the oak leaves" in his journal, July 19, 1866, and she would have seen the phrase there. Oak leaves also show up in the first sentence of Zukofsky's 1931 brief for Objectivist poetics; he later remarked in a letter to Niedecker that to prepare for a poem you must wait for the fact to die out and come back like a leaf on a branch. Surely she knew the sources of her metaphor. Just as surely, there were bound to be differences in what it would mean to her. At home on the Rock River her father had been a commercial fisherman who sometimes took his daughter along to seine for carp on the lake and river. "I spent my childhood outdoors—" she remembered, "redwinged blackbirds, willows, maples, boats, fishing (the smell of tarred nets), twittering and squawking noises from the marsh." It was a world of natural reality too sensuous for her ever to leave.

> My life
> by water—
> Hear
>
> spring's
> first frog
> or board
>
> out on the cold
> ground
> giving

There was also the world of words, and Niedecker acknowledged in particular the influence of her mother, every day "speaking whole chunks of down-to-earth magic." It must be too trite to say that poetry provided the theater where she could mediate the tug-of-war between her father's magic facts and her mother's magic words. Yet in the earliest poem made available by Bertholf, a poem first printed in her high school yearbook, this tug-of-war between reality and words is already Niedecker's subject. It was still the subject a year before she died, when she observed in a letter to Corman how a poetic method was successful if it suggested "the reality that may get inside us and fill the subconscious of the future!" If this is what she understood from Zukofsky about the fact coming back like a leaf on the branch then we have in Lorine Niedecker a magnificent example of how good poets turn influence to—it's irresistible—misprision.

Misprision, "devoted treason," is the infraction partly illustrated by the poem set off in the preceding paragraph. Yes, those short lines and tripartite divisions are reminiscent of certain earlier poems of William Carlos Williams, who once counted Niedecker along with Zukofsky and himself among the original Objectivists. But the alliteration, the assonance, the near rhymes—the sheer insistent rhythm—these add up to a sensuousness you may rarely associate with Zukofsky or even Williams. And because she could deploy this sensuous magic without getting burned, a skill she had begun to perfect in "Mother Geese," Niedecker could take on subjects sometimes thought too hot for modernist poets to handle.

> How bright you'll find young people,
>   Diddle,
>   and how unkind.
> When a boy appears with a book
> they cry "Who's the young Einsteind?"
> Einstein, you know, said space
> is what it's made up of.
> And as to the human race
> "Why do you deeply oppose its passing"
> you'll find men asking
> the man with the nebular hair
>   and the fiddle.

Sophisticated in its ambiguities, lucid as a nursery rhyme, this poem is also distinguished by something that makes it highly unusual in recent poetry. You can memorize it. Because of its music you may even want to memorize it: a poem about anti-intellectualism and the nuclear arms race which works because it's so subversively joyful. It also works because, as with the pendulum poem, Niedecker fitted it into a series that greatly expands its context. This series, "For Paul," was addressed to a talented child of six as a sort of premonitory guidebook to the grimly magical outside world, a *vade mecum* as concerned with questions of public and private virtue as if Anne Bradstreet had returned to bequeath a state-of-the-art version of her *Meditations* to the children of a very altered commonwealth. It was as tender as Whitman, but as sharp in places as Lowell and as angry as *Howl*. "I've never felt the times to be so dark," observed Niedecker to Zukofsky, "so ignorant as these."

Begun in 1949 shortly after the Soviet Union detonated its first atomic bomb, and written for the most part in the early 1950s, "For Paul" was to be an arrangement of more than fifty constituent poems in eight groups. It was published in parts but never as the composite work the poet first intended. Corman prints a few of the poems individually but without mention of the dismantled series. Bertholf attempted a restoration, which should have ranked as the biggest surprise and triumph of *From This Condensery*. Unfortunately, he was no match for the manuscripts. He never settled on satisfactory versions of later groups in the series and failed to recognize the missing fifth group altogether. Even mutilated, however, "For Paul" could be briefly glimpsed in its position as a central work of Niedecker's career, a rich example of her redemptive talent for subtle, resonant, and even humorous transitions.

It may seem devious in a review to praise transitions since you can't easily quote one. But transition is nonetheless the element that imparts their unimpeded grace to Niedecker's late and finest sequences: "Lake Superior," "Darwin," "Paean to Place." Each of these demonstrates how poetry is enlivened during those moments it looks both forward and back. How different that turns out to be from the Objectivist ideal, at least as expressed by Zukofsky, that no verse could be called a poem unless it conveyed "the totality of perfect rest." For Niedecker, accustomed by her river to fluxes of flood and silt, humans themselves were a transition and their cultural evolution likewise a transit of fact as it leafs into words. So nothing could be more important than this unrestful evolution where we in fact *make* our lives and which is, so poets must hope, the project of poetry.

Until now, Niedecker's engagement with the project hasn't received enough attention. A reviewer in the *Times Literary Supplement* once asked, "Why have the critics been so slow?" One answer is that even critics may transmit unexamined attitudes. In Britain in 1969 a critic noted that the complexity of Niedecker's writing was "hidden under feminine ease." In the United States in 1972 another said of her work that "the concerns are always close to home and personal in ways peculiarly feminine." So you may be surprised to learn from Bertholf's introduction that Niedecker worked two years for a Madison radio station and another six for a national dairyman's journal—eight years in that most modern of occupations, the information industry. When she abandoned it in 1951 she quoted William James's famous remark that we are in for a new, worse dark ages now that the press supports illiteracy with such an enormous literary organization. But Niedecker went even further, noting how this organization "protects and is protected by that other and still more expensive organization, war. I'd found that a job does not necessarily sustain life."

> I worked the print shop
> right down among em
> the folk from whom all poetry flows
> and dreadfully much else.

Niedecker was thus a dropout in 1951, before that strategy became current in the 1960s and long before the present decade when her example must seem all but incomprehensible to her countrymen. Feminine *ease*? For twelve years she lived without plumbing—among the Americans! And when she finally had to sink a well and install a pump, she wrote, "I've been free / with less / and clean."

Free and clean, but wasn't she—*frei aber einsam*—lonely? I doubt it. We will know more when we see her letters to Corman due this fall from Duke University Press. According to excerpts published some years ago she once wrote, "I can't enter into social meetings . . . since I housekeep—plural:houses—and write and read and walk and sew and sing at the top of my voice when folksy records are being played on the phonograph." In the familiar photo by Jonathan Williams, now on the back of *The Granite Pail*, she has always looked a little cornered. Not the least revelation of *From This Condensery* is the picture taken by her neighbor Gail Roub of a candid Niedecker sizing up the country from her vantage point on the Rock River. In time this new image will overtake the previous one, if only—well, the relevant words are in

Niedecker's "Thomas Jefferson," drawn from that once admirable figure's address to his eldest daughter on the subject of her future happiness.

> To daughter Patsy: Read—
> read Livy
>
> No person full of work
> was ever hysterical
>
> Know music, history
> dancing
>
> (I calculate 14 to 1
> in marriage
> she will draw
> a blockhead)
>
> Science also
> Patsy

To which there's not much to add, except—Read Niedecker, Patsy.

THE NATION, 1986

NIEDECKER AND THE

EVOLUTIONAL SUBLIME

Poetry is words: though when I think of the Whitman who found he incorporates gneiss, the Stein who says anybody is as their land and air is, the Stevens who locates mythology in stone out of our fields or from under our mountains, then I have to admit that the sublimest American poetry has always read to me as if it would rather restore, or even realize, its desire for a wealth outside words, a wealth that is wild outside the human voice. That is what I always liked about it. It is what I liked at once about Lorine Niedecker's "Lake Superior," that spare ferropastoral of a poem in honor of the rock and mineral wealth

Iron the common element of earth

for which the human species is just another mode of transport. I also have to admit that what I like about our poetry may be exactly what makes it so alien to other readers. I remember vividly the disapproval of a British reviewer who once noted that the heroes of "Lake Superior" seem to be rocks, not men, and went on to judge "repellent" this same bias, this same extra-species deference, that I read as honestly sublime.

The sublime is a term that does not come unembarrassed into American discourse. But sublime doesn't have to mean ultimate, and there is no inherent reason why a mention of the sublime has to be less practical, say, than a reference to the lyric. The sublime, too, ought to describe itself in traditions, and in the poetic practices implied by those traditions. In England the poetry of the egotistical sublime took shape, and probably impetus, from its tension with the social order. The poet, as Wordsworth was careful to add in the 1802 Preface to the *Lyrical Ballads*, was an individual who nonetheless spoke in a community: "the rock of defence for human nature," to use his exact words, who "binds together . . . the vast empire of human society." In America, Emerson left the binding—and the ego—out of the sublime. The poet, he wrote in the 1844 essay of that name, is one who apprises us not of personal wealth, but "of the commonwealth." Emerson, too, was careful with words, and I suppose it is almost diagnostic that he would reject words like empire and society, and, with Wordsworth's prior example in mind, identify the poet's material as a commonwealth instead. Because at its most reductive

Iron the common element of earth

the commonwealth is the land.

That line I have quoted twice is Niedecker's, of course, from "Lake Superior." The poem itself appeared complete in England in 1968, then remained for all practical purposes unavailable in the United States until its publication seventeen years later in *The Granite Pail* and *From This Condensery*, those two very different collections of Niedecker's work. Even today the poem can come as a surprise to readers who encounter it for the first time in the *Norton Anthology of American Literature*, where its inclusion has been both just and a little ironic. As another apprisal of the commonwealth, "Lake Superior" extends a tradition that seems peculiarly American: it's a tradition we honor only partway. For the truth is, when our poets start telling us about gneiss, or land and air, when they locate their story in stone or, as Niedecker does, in rock, I think we are likely to allow them the trope but not likely to believe they are saying what in fact they just said. They and their poems are made of land and air and rock. People who read poetry have always been alert enough to entertain the trope while avoiding the notion itself as sentimental, romantic, or worse, perniciously near to nationalism.

Get them away from poetry, however, and today's readers are also alert enough ecologically to know that their own identification with the environment isn't ipso facto proof of direct-mail mysticism or gang nationalism. In 1945, twenty-one years before she began work on "Lake Superior," Niedecker had written to Louis Zukofsky that she was reading Diderot. "This is what I could have used long ago," she reported, "alongside Engels and while I was wondering what Emerson was getting at. Elements for awhile before we again become, if we ever do, another mass. Time is nuttin in the universe." It's a summary formulation, but it is hardly repellent. On the contrary, it reminds me agreeably of the presence in Wisconsin in those years of another commentator on the earthly commonwealth, one who sat down in his university office in Madison shortly before Christmas 1941 to write an article, "Odyssey," which would appear the next summer in *Audubon* magazine, and later as one of the now famous sections of *A Sand County Almanac*.

> An atom at large in the biota is too free to know freedom; an atom back in the sea has forgotten it. For every atom lost to the sea, the prairie pulls another out of the decaying rocks. The only certain truth is that its creatures must suck hard, live fast, and die often, lest its losses exceed its gains.

The writer was Aldo Leopold, one of the inspiring saints of contemporary environmentalism. He was also a consultant to the Federal Writers' Project, which became the Wisconsin Writers' Project and produced in 1941 the WPA guide *Wisconsin: The Badger State*. On the Project staff, although she didn't contribute directly to the guide itself, was Lorine Niedecker. She was living in Madison at the time.

The speculation is hard to resist. But nobody needs to propose a biographical connection when the attitudes are in print themselves. The excerpts from Niedecker's letter and Leopold's article imply, whatever their immediate genesis, a shared, recognizable desire for a wealth where, as Whitman so perfectly put it, every atom belonging to me as good belongs to you—and you don't have to be clear whether the atom is currently in the biota or not. Both excerpts imply a recognizable faith in a commonwealth whose abiding satisfactions might rest in the irrepressible transit of earth into life and back again. This is, indeed, what Emerson was getting at. In the awesome last paragraph of "Nature" (the great essay, not *Nature* the book), Emerson invoked the popular idea of the sublime—the doctrine of the immortality of the soul—in order to replace it with the sublimer reality of an evolving earth. "The reality," he says there with stunning concision, "is more excellent than the report." It is a concision "Lake Superior" seems ready to confirm.

Desire can hardly be the lengthened invention of one individual, not even Emerson. There must be some persistent urgency that makes poems like "Lake Superior" recurrently useful to a certain strain of the American psyche. Harold Bloom has described how poems emerge from the struggle with their precursor poems, poets from precursor poets. In that New World where the poet's subject is the commonwealth, I think there are other precursors who raise as provocative an anxiety. These are the discoverers. One sign of how much anxiety they provoke is that we know better than to call them discoverers, and are up and willing, centuries after the fact, to take sides over whether they were malevolent predators or just evil ones. In terms of the poetic tradition, though, they were unarguably and unforgivably first. First to relate on the record their apprisals of the commonwealth, of Lake Superior, as in the process its riches were betrayed.

Niedecker began to write her own "Lake Superior" in 1966, following a summer vacation with her husband, Albert Millen, which took them in his Buick from Milwaukee to Green Bay, along Lake Michigan's northern shoulder to St. Ignace, then from Sault Ste. Marie westward around the north shore of Lake Superior and on into the northern Minnesota lake country where Millen had been born and raised and where the Mississippi has its source. The notes Niedecker made in reference to this trip have survived. Condensed into some thirty typewritten pages, they refer not only to the geology of the vast territory she and her husband crossed ("Traverse des Millens!" she once called it) but also, and extensively, to the precursor explorers who got to map it first. This is more than a figure of speech. The Jesuit explorers, "black robes" like Father Marquette, did in fact make the earliest accurate maps of the Great Lakes, including a famous one from around 1680

Through all this granite land the sign of the cross

which was first to represent the upper Mississippi, and on which the mission sites were marked, as is granite on geological maps today, by crosses.

But notes or no, it would be wrong to imagine that the figures named in Niedecker's poem are so recondite that she or her compatriot reader should need an encyclopedia to be aware of their historical significance. Radisson, most famous of *coureurs de bois*, was in his late twenties when he and Groseilliers became, in the words of the old Wisconsin *Guide*, the "first white men to penetrate beyond the Great Lakes" into Wisconsin and Minnesota. They were to be remembered in classrooms there as Radishes and Gooseberries. Marquette was thirty-six when he left his mission at St. Ignace and went with the twenty-eight-year-old Joliet to look for the Mississippi. His memorials include a mural in the Milwaukee Public Museum which depicts him standing in his canoe, face upturned and hands aloft in devotion, as three converts paddle him to destiny. Even Schoolcraft, mineralogist, ethnographer, and U.S. Indian Agent, twenty-seven when he made the journey most likely referred to in the poem, is no stranger. His pioneer, if misguided ethnographies led Longfellow to place an Iroquois hero, Hiawatha, forever in the Lake Superior territory of the Ojibwa enemy—a taunt that survives today in countless reminders, including in Schoolcraft County the Hiawatha National Forest that Niedecker and her husband drove through as they proceeded into Upper Michigan and on toward Schoolcraft's agency house, still standing, in Sault Ste. Marie.

Those are Niedecker's precursor explorers, and it is probably no surprise that she has named the ones whose journeys, taken together, just about circumnavigate her native Wisconsin. No surprise, either, if their journeys have in common that each was first to open Wisconsin and the surrounding region to yet another kind of plunder: furs, lead, copper, iron, souls, and ethnographic pelf. It is all a fascination and it is all grotesque. In the names of counties, forests, towns, at markers along the road and monuments in the parks, you walk in on a kind of Primal Scene, the transgression by which you were engendered, and nobody tells you to look the other way. In Wyalusing State Park in Wisconsin, where Niedecker and Millen stopped on an earlier trip in 1963, there is even a monument to that very symbol of extinguished commonwealth

Did not man . . .

mash the cobalt
and carnelian
of that bird

the passenger pigeon. Anywhere in North America the anxiety of this kind of influence must be broadly the same. Beautiful as the land still is, and mine, it should not have happened this way. As far as the commonwealth is concerned, every one of us must know it would be better if we had never arrived.

Along with the contrition, however, goes the complicity, because who wouldn't want that adventure, to stand there first, to look on Eden with a wild surmise? "We weare Cesars," wrote Radisson, "being nobody to contradict us." In this regard, I think it is fair to say that Niedecker associated the lingering wildness of Lake Superior with a desire for unopposed poetic immortality. She gives herself away in a letter to Gail Roub, the neighbor who took what is perhaps the most memorable photograph of her, home at Black Hawk Island on the Rock River. Niedecker was afraid his photo was too candid, not enough like those of Cather and Dickinson, which were, she wrote him, "perfectly calm & beautiful—they belong with Time, you might say." Then without a pause she added, "There are some timeless, smooth rocks up around L. Superior. Schoolcraft, by the way, called that lake 'the blue profound.'" It is a totally believable association, especially when you remember that Whitman invoked his bards of the future also on a great lake, not by Superior's but by blue Ontario's shore. Then as now, the problem for a bard of the commonwealth was this: you have to believe your country wants you, just as it spurs desire if your partner feels it too. Like Radisson, you have to believe there is nobody to contradict you.

When the contradictions are strong as the desire, the only way out is the sublime. This is the escape route to poetry which today's readers may recognize better as repression, followed by emergence into a language where, from then on, you are on your own. Intuitively, you might suspect that a procedure that helps to deal with literary origins could help with the origins I have been suggesting as well. The evidence to support the intuition is right there in "Lake Superior," as Niedecker removes her precursor explorers one by one from the land and identifies her hopes for her unconscious directly with the geology itself. We also have her own testimony as it appears in the vacation notes, where it follows directly her description of the eons-long itinerary of a pebble in this Great Lakes country that was once, after the lava and before the glacier, covered by a sea.

> The sea went over and left me dry, parched for knowledge! The feeling of being a part of all this. How?—the body, the unconscious. Let us sing, as they say in church.

Later there was to be still further evidence of Niedecker's unspoken designs on her predecessor discoverers, and on the priestliest of them, too. When she initially finished "Lake Superior," in October 1966, it did not include its present section on Marquette. That was a separate poem. Another year would pass before she decided to bury Marquette in *her* Lake Superior, over which she, not he, has risen. In the month when she must have been making this decision she wrote to Cid Corman, reported a visit to Wisconsin's Door Peninsula, and signaled her motives in what seem now, even if ironic, the least controvertible of terms. "The whole north country, I'm completely absorbed in it, I'm buried and rise again!"

A redemptory intent like Niedecker's shows up in much of American art. Today it erupts frequently into environmentalist prose, with results that are sometimes lamented as the nature writer's one note, Wonder. But scoffing is easy, and wonder is only a spell the writer casts in an attempt to transform loss into some kind of enduringly positive sustenance. In 1947, when that monument to the lost passenger pigeon was dedicated in Wyalusing State Park, the occasion was commemorated by another article from Aldo Leopold—this one, too, reprinted in *A Sand County Almanac*.

> For one species to mourn the death of another is a new thing under the sun. . . . To see America as history, to conceive of destiny as a becoming, to smell a hickory tree through the still lapse of ages—all these things are possible for us, and to achieve them takes only the free sky, and the will to ply our wings.

Redemption, it needs to be said, is not the same as nostalgia. When it is desired by one species for the others, or for the land as a whole, it really is something new under the sun. Perhaps it is the one cultural achievement, though the price was dear, which might be the glory yet of human presence: a passionate deference to the organic and inorganic commonwealth that cannot otherwise speak for itself. In the meantime, and as demonstrated once more by Niedecker in "Lake Superior," this same deference has already become the identifiable, continuing attitude of the tradition we should call, not the egotistical, but the evolutional sublime.

Attitude takes style, and a likely style if you are reaching for the sublime is hyperbole, or exaggeration. The Aldo Leopold quotation is an example of hyperbole. Sometimes, though, the sublime seems better served by hyperbole's mirror image, abbreviation, or litotes. This was the choice posed so movingly at the beginning of John Ashbery's *Three Poems*.

> I thought if I could put it all down, that would be one way. And next the thought came to me that to leave all out would be another, and truer, way.

Niedecker, as we know, chose leaving out. In all of "Lake Superior" there are but 393 words, and to reach that total you have to include the subtitles. The paradox is how much the poem gets in by leaving out.

The impulse to concision must strike some readers as an impairment. Based on Niedecker's example, I would sooner argue that "leaving out" is the freedom you fight for when you can no longer bear the received deceit of the sentence, the connectives and prepositions that accumulate with the weight of irredeemably inaccurate history. One strategy is to go ahead and employ all the syntax of the sentence while staving off disgust with a strong dose of irony. This will cease to work, however, if you have come to fear irony as just one more accent of fraud in the prison house of prose. In that case, the sentence becomes a temptation to avoid, a temptation I think Niedecker acknowledged as her own when she made her otherwise too famous comment, in a letter of 1968: "Koch, Ashbery—there but for the grace of God and Louis Zukofsky go I."

Niedecker's response, at its most pronounced in "Lake Superior," was to scour the sentence as if to sand, the way the glacier scoured the Lake Superior rocks. Her style became in this way a cognate for the evolutional attitude: primal elements in evolving arrangements. Even words—since as proofreader at *Hoard's Dairyman* she worked for six years in what she once called a "print shop," where agate (it is also a color, iron-oxide red) might mean a size of type—

> in my mind
> between my toes
> agate

even words are a kind of sand. Words are for rearrangement, much as the history of Lake Superior has been the evolutionary rearrangement of its minerals by lava, sea, glacier, and human industry: the whole Lakes Basin being in this way a kind of sand lake. Thus the poet never misses Sand Lake

> I'm sorry to have missed
> Sand Lake
> My dear one tells me

we did not

We watched a gopher there

because she is an example of it. As are we all, who, following the land treaty at Prairie du Chien in 1825, moved like a boom of gophers to dig, mine, and rearrange the earth all over Wisconsin and—the gopher state—Minnesota.

Niedecker's rearrangements have redemptive ends. If you treat words like sand, stories by their constituent elements, perhaps you can incorporate the contradictions that created you, embody them enough to leave the land clean again on its surface for desire. Of this hope there is no more resonant example than the Radisson section of "Lake Superior."

> Radisson:
> "a laborinth of pleasure"
> this world of the Lake
>
> Long hair, long gun
>
> Fingernails pulled out
> by Mohawks
>
> > > (The long
> > >
> > > canoes)

The British reviewer I mentioned at the outset (it was Donald Davie) read this section as only potentially pathetic, an attempt to win for Radisson a pity that he, as predator in someone else's land, did not deserve. But Radisson's fingernails had not been extracted in punishment for his incursion into Wisconsin. They were extracted during an earlier eighteen-month captivity that began in 1652 when he was taken, as we would say, *hostage* from the outskirts of Trois Rivières, in Quebec, where he lived. He was at most twenty years old. Seven years would elapse before he and Groseilliers first penetrated into the Wisconsin country he called "a laborinth of pleasure," and another nine or ten before, in England in 1668–69, he wrote those words themselves. Niedecker has reversed the chronology. She has reversed it as if to insist on the preeminence of desire. Knowing already of pain, her Radisson speaks only of pleasure. Without claim of pity he speaks, through her arrangement, of the wonder of desire for the dominant X of earth.

There was more. Radisson and Groseilliers astonished Quebec by returning from their Lake Superior voyage at the head of 360 long canoes—the parentheses in the poem make (the long canoes) even look like downriver canoes—so laden with furs that they saved the economy of New France. The two were fined, the furs were confiscated, Groseilliers was jailed. They had gone without a permit. Nor would Paris take seriously their discovery that Hudson Bay could provide a better route for the fur trade. Unrepentant, the partners tendered their expertise to London

Gulls playing both sides

and, fatefully for New France, the Hudson's Bay Company was born. There would be further instances, too, of Radisson gulling and being gulled by rival sides. Still he speaks only of pleasure. The wonder of desire for the country is how it supersedes the state. The wonder of Niedecker's style is how this "discoverer" now discovers our wisdom and follows, none to contradict him, our desire.

Although "Lake Superior" may at first seem spare of words, Nie-decker can be wide and generous within a single one of them. Some-times she practically harmonizes with herself. Readers who recall her lines from another poem about "the very veery"

> We are what the seas
> have made us
>
> longingly immense
>
> the very veery
> on the fence

will know where I got that idea. The veery is a thrush that actually does sing in harmony with itself. A bird's syrinx is capable of more than one note at a time, and the veery takes advantage of this ability to pro-duce an unusually allusive, yet one-"word" song. An example of like effect in "Lake Superior" occurs in Niedecker's description of the Schoolcraft expedition as it proceeded west along the south shore to old Fond du Lac at the end of the lake, and on into

> the redolent pondy lakes

of northern Minnesota. Schoolcraft made his first such trip in 1820 as the Americans belatedly arrived, flags flying, to take possession of the area. He went along as mineralogist. But anybody who reasons by syl-lables, and knows how carefully Niedecker avoids redundant ones, might hear in the syllables I just quoted a reminder that in another six years Schoolcraft will make the trip again, as U.S. Indian Agent this time, to oversee the treaty of Fond du Lac

pon dy lakes
fon du lac

by which the Ojibwa will sign over "the right to search for, and carry
away, any metals or minerals from any part of their country"

Iron the common element of earth

to the United States. In one widening note, Niedecker avoids the
monotony of wonder to harmonize wonder with its human cost. She
has been, like the veery, immensely concise.

Whitman told us the effect of true poets was to bring people back from
their sickly abstractions to the divine, original concrete. From the moment I discovered "Lake Superior" I thought it just right, therefore,
that Niedecker went for her material directly to the place she calls in
the poem "true source park." It seemed an especially skillful phrase
for the divine original concrete outside the human voice, except it was
even more skillful than that. Niedecker was singing two notes at once
again. Her "true source park" turns out to mean also its opposite, the
literary source—the human source, for that matter—of reality.

When Schoolcraft finally located the pondy lake in Minnesota
which is the source of the Mississippi River, he named, or rather renamed it Lake Itasca. The word Itasca is not Ojibwa or Dakota, the
two contenders for an indigenous naming. It is a neologism invented
by Schoolcraft himself from the three middle syllables of *veritas caput*,
signifying "true source." Millions of tourists have now walked across

the Mississippi without getting their feet wet, at, inevitably, Itasca State Park. Niedecker and Millen stopped there in 1966, having driven on from Lake Superior. It is all a fascination, it is grotesque, and sometimes it is a kind of farce. At roadside markers, in parks, you stumble in on the inventive transgressions by which you were engendered— *veritas caput*, can you believe?—and nobody tells you to look the other way. Surely Niedecker must have meant the true true source: rocks, minerals, gneiss. Just as surely, she meant also that there is a deception at the very fundament of true source park, and the deception is language, literature.

Sweet deception. Throughout "Lake Superior" runs like a canoe the shadow of Schoolcraft's unexpected progeny, *The Song of Hiawatha*. The first poem I remember hearing (in my grandmother's voice) was *Hiawatha*, and hearing it like that how could anybody forget the insistence of it?

> By the shores of Gitche Gumee
> By the shining Big Sea Water

Today I know of course that Longfellow, drawing chiefly on Schoolcraft's *Algic Researches* and multivolume ethnography, was drawing on material in some cases about as indigenous as the word Itasca. I know Longfellow even compounded the iniquity

> Beauty: impurities in the rock

by adding willful misrepresentations of his own. The question is whether to be indignant over the cultural impurities that have preceded us onto the land, or to think of them as, of all things, beauty. The slightly paradoxical answer of "Lake Superior" seems to be that literature is beauty as long as it leads you to true source park, and back. People forget, in their fresh indignation against Longfellow, the function *Hiawatha* itself once performed. It led imaginations inland, away from sickly abstractions to the lakes and woods. It was among Aldo Leopold's favorite books. In fact, the South Shore journey

> as if Life's—

which has really been repressed in "Lake Superior" is Hiawatha's. If you were another Harold Bloom, you might be justly gratified to point out that Hiawatha's first quest westward along the shore of the lake was to locate and defeat his own precursor, his father. In the ensuing struggle, the weapon Hiawatha picks up

> The smooth black stone
> I picked up in true source park

is fatal Wawbeek, the black rock. The battle will end as a draw, but what hasn't ended yet is the task Hiawatha took up on the spot, given him in his father's words:

> "Go back to your home and people,
> Live among them, toil among them,
> Cleanse the earth from all that harms it,
> Clear the fishing-grounds and rivers,
> Slay the monsters and magicians. . . ."

Now that I'm grown and know how to cringe, I can admit that this thrilling passage was grade B property at best. But to the extent it reveals Longfellow's motives (he sounds like an emerging eco-activist, his Hiawatha a Greenpeace warrior), he wasn't such a drip after all.

84

Besides, what if you could convince him of his errors? He is unlikely to fix them now.

The only way to cleanse the earth of the old *Hiawatha* is to write a new one. The point isn't whether Niedecker knew Lake Superior was the shining Big Sea Water, though of course she did. The point is that she expected us to know. Given the allusive concision of her style, she would never have to bring this knowledge to the surface. Treating words like sand, she could return the literature of Lake Superior to its constituent physics in which every atom belonging to me, belongs to you. In "Lake Superior" you can almost feel the land *wanting* you again, feel the reciprocal desire to make poetry

> The smooth black stone
> I picked up in true source park
>
>   the leaf beside it
> once was stone

from unmediated contact with matter. Emerson thought poetry a kind of second nature, like a leaf from a tree. Zukofsky, too, would employ the analogy. So the leaf that once was stone is, in Niedecker's litotic harmony, also a poem. Reduce your precursor errors to their constituent elements, and poems can be made again, not of words, but stone.

In a land where poems are made of stone, and rock, there could be no more stupendous region for Niedecker to visit than the Lake Superior country, where uplift and glacier have exposed the oldest rock on earth. A great knob of this rock that was "superior" in strength to the ice

> And at the blue ice superior spot
> priest-robed Marquette grazed
> azoic rock

rises west of the town named for Marquette on the lake's south shore, a result of the Laurentian orogeny that formed the granite of the Canadian Shield three billion years ago. The north shore is all such granite. In the whole Lakes country the glacier left no rock that is not at least 280 million years old. It is a place to sense evolution at its most powerfully telescoped. Even the fossil record is gone, scoured off by the glacier. You stand on trilobites. Iron was discovered on the Marquette Range in 1844, almost pure, among the last elements to have been manufactured in some anciently distant star before it shed its mineral wealth into space, and set the course for eventual human contact along *le lac supérieur*.

It's no wonder, in such a country, if "*voyageurs* crossed themselves" and "Chippewas threw deermeat," and no wonder either if a poet in the tradition of the evolutional sublime

> Why should we hurry
> home

should feel strangely at home. ("Maybe as rocks and I pass each other I could say how-do-you-do to an agate," noted Niedecker as her trip began.) In the essay "Nature," Emerson seems already to have described the place.

We come to our own, and make friends with matter, which the ambitious chatter of the schools would persuade us to despise. We can never part with it; the mind loves its old home: as water to our thirst, so is rock, the ground, to our eyes, and hands, and feet. It is firm water: it is cold flame: what health, what affinity!

From the mind's old home there would be scant reason to hurry back to a world so predictably inferior.

On the other hand, if inanimate matter equals stony rest then there's no reason to hurry to *that* home, either, or hurry it along—not when we are so desirably lively now. Of course life is not good enough for everyone, I know. Critics who find the evolutional tradition alien seem largely to be repelled because it doesn't provide immortality (or is it the discipline of damnation they miss?) for the individual soul. The pique is more evident if they are criticizing not Emerson or Whitman but an easier target like Robinson Jeffers, and can disguise their animus as taste. Yet the poets in this tradition will continue by definition to apprise us of a commonwealth that is indeed without revelation. In North America, nature has revealed no special exemptions for the human race, no single truth. The continent itself is True Source Park. Or, as Emerson responded in exasperation when someone tried to settle an argument by citing the other world, "Other world? there is no other world; here or nowhere is the whole fact."

Niedecker's deft gift to this tradition is that she will not let her excursion into its sublime end in mere grandeur. She offers her poem, but on the condition apparently that the sublime make room for her own disabused tenderness toward the most expensive, precarious component of evolution, the human one. The Sand Lake she missed in "Lake Superior," or didn't, is a case in point. It is not a lake in Ontario as once identified in the *Norton Anthology*. The *Norton* took her spelling literally and forgot how ruthless Niedecker can be with an unwanted syllable. Sand(y) Lake, as the westering itinerary of her poem itself implies, is in Minnesota, the site of the Sandy Lake trading post where in late 1850 the Ojibwa bands of Wisconsin were directed to receive their annuities. The United States had already ordered the Ojibwa removed permanently to Minnesota, and the idea now was to delay the distribution of their annuities until the increasingly bitter winter forced them to remain there. As many as four hundred died near Sandy Lake or

> Why should we hurry
> home

trying to walk back home into Wisconsin. A century had elapsed since the once expansionist Ojibwa, themselves, had forced the Dakota from a village at that same Sandy Lake.

To a man, the explorers who preceded Niedecker at Lake Superior treated the land as theirs for the taking. Radisson didn't call it a laborinth of pleasure for nothing. A modernized version of his *Voyages* gives you an idea of what he had in mind. "What conquest would that be at little or no cost, what labyrinth of pleasure should millions of people have, instead that millions complain of misery and poverty?" In a sense the land took Radisson, as agent, instead. His very name, Pierre, means stone. Orimha, his adopted Mohawk name, meant stone. Marquette sought to raise souls up to life everlasting, made contact instead with pre-lifeform, azoic rock, and, after his converts in homage had carved the unresurrected meat from his bones, was born again in the name of the Marquette Range as iron ore, rock. Schoolcraft couldn't believe nature had created a scene of such magnificence, as he put it in his *Memoirs*, "merely to look at." A mineralogist tapping away with his hammer, he was known to the Ojibwa as Paw-gwa-be-ca-we-ga, Destroyer of Rocks, which reveals on their part a certain prospective irony since Schoolcraft is gone and rocks are still here. Anxious to extract the wealth and take it "home," Niedecker's predecessors never got the news

                    Why should we hurry

that this is home—iron in our blood, a transit of minerals ourselves, and necessarily native in the larger transit that "Lake Superior" will describe in accents of the evolutional sublime.

By the time Niedecker and her husband made their trip around great *Kitchigami*, in 1966, it seemed clear that the once invasive American population would continue to treat its commonwealth with no letup of contempt. "Often on the trip the stones that had a shine turned out to be bottlecaps," reports Niedecker in her notes. On the Minnesota shore, at the first port south of Gooseberry (né Groseilliers) Falls, the Western Reserve Mining Company was into its eleventh year of shedding slag straight into the lake, a rapture of industrial vandalism that wouldn't end until 1980. As a direct result, the western floor of "the blue profound" is covered today in asbestos sludge—and I think anyone who reflects on the severity and permanence of such violence might justifiably demand to know how it could happen in a land where the evolutional sublime is the tradition I have been making it out to be. The patient, unworn answer is that in this species we die miserably every year for lack of the news we could find in poetry. And the news in American poetry has yet to reach people who still, against all the available evidence, regard humans, not rocks, as the heroes of this earth.

The more intimate question posed by "Lake Superior" is whether the news is at an end. Can an evolutional earth ethic help an urban population to fashion human selves and achieve human connectedness in a time tectonic with cultures, and commerce, and claims? Offered multiple panoramas on tape, in travel, on film, who really could care about pebbles, orogenies, stone? Maybe it's too obvious to say. In such a time, more especially in such a place, the land is the one thing that people who can't afford vacations in Europe do have in common. When Niedecker retells in "Lake Superior" the story of Joliet, ex-priest, fur-trader, adventurer, native Quebecois

> At Hudson Bay he conversed in latin
> with an Englishman

she projects our necessary cultural dexterity as if to say, the new world has always been like this. When she presents the figure who proceeded onto the austere lake

> Schoolcraft left the Soo—canoes
> US pennants, masts, sails
> chanting canoemen, barge
> soldiers—for Minnesota

like a spectacle out of Hollywood, bearing blandishments of the sort the White House basement might devise, she projects our image-daft innocence as if to say, the new world was always like this.

Niedecker liked language and she was fond of the corruptions that might make it momentarily, transitionally indigenous. Soo, for example, is the funny way Michiganders say Sault (as in Soo Saint Muh-REE), but the pronunciation was made deeply serious when applied to the strategic Soo Canal. "The North is one vast, massive, glorious corruption of rock and language," she observed in her notes. "People of all nationalities and color have changed the language like weather and pressure have changed the rocks." She enjoyed the story she recounted in a letter to Corman of how Schoolcraft on expedition was greeted from shore with shouts of "bosho!"—a noise made locally to signify *bonjour*. Read it against these rich corruptions, and Niedecker's "Lake Superior" seems all the more in profound contrast. Her style seems by its immense concision to say what her subject matter likewise says, that on this linguistically promiscuous and overwhelmingly talkative continent the self will not be composed of language only. It is also composed

> wave-washed and the rains
> did their work and a green
> running as from copper

of the mute things we look upon, the unspoke beauty of them. Desire may even equal just that percentage of things we feel as yet to be unspoke. And that true source, where every atom belonging to me as good belongs to you, is perhaps the one ultimate connectedness at last possible for the democratic individual.

Wordsworth, in the 1802 Preface, used the word *human* eleven times, each time favorably. Emerson, in "The Poet," used it only once, and then to denote a limitation to be escaped. Poets, he wrote, must unlock at all risks their "human doors" and be caught up instead into the life and thought of the universe. "Man is made of the same atoms the world is," he would write in a later essay. "When his mind is illuminated, when his heart is kind, he throws himself joyfully into the sublime order, and does, with knowledge, what the stones do by structure." So Aldo Leopold was securely in the tradition when he introduced into our ethics a phrase that has become almost scriptural: thinking like a mountain. Niedecker, in turn, could coax you into thinking like Lake Superior. On Lake Superior not one human culture exactly fits. Maybe none ever will. In the meantime the promise of her brave pastoral is that the poetry of the evolutional sublime will continue to arrive, bringing its news, to set desire free for a wealth that is yours

> Inland then
> beside the great granite
> gneiss and the schists

clean through to the oldest rocks in the world. There, thinking like Lake Superior, you might even regard it the least repellent, most promising of poetries that could realize rocks as the last "laborinth of pleasure" humans have got. Pleasure: because they have no sympathy unless it's propagated by that.

RARITAN, 1992

HOW EMERSON AVAILS

HOW EMERSON AVAILS

He was ready to encourage us wherever it might count, and even a partial record will suggest his success—and stamina. "With the Kingdom of Heaven on his knee," observed Emily Dickinson, "could Mr Emerson hesitate?" Yet for much of the twentieth century it was possible to ask if his own works weren't fatally dated. It was possible, that is, until the moment in 1984 when John Updike made the question securely obsolete by asking it in the *New Yorker*, a forum to demonstrate how timely Emerson had again become. Soon you could see the name Emerson used to brighten the book reviews, like Foucault, or Derrida, or Virginia Woolf. I even saw, in my college alumni magazine, remarks by a sophomore who referred in passing to his "Emersonian self" as if that needed no explanation, as if he had used a world-class signifier to disclose one of his more desirable attributes.

It was not the first time Emerson had been used this way. His *Essays* were once in everybody's hands and everybody's thoughts. You could find them in John Muir's hang-nest at Yosemite, in Nietzsche's pocket, or in bed the morning of January 18, 1895, with Marcel Proust. Given the impact of that previous distribution, its impact on art and society, I think the renewed attention to Emerson could hardly be more significant. It means the scholar, not just the American Scholar, will be less easily disinherited. It means we have the luxury to worry that the inheritance might become an embarrassment of riches, that we might actually make an authority of this writer who in his first published sentences equated biographies, histories, and criticism with sepulchres, and asked, "Why should not we also enjoy an original relation to the universe?"

Exactly, why shouldn't we also? If the textual Emerson, too, now stands with the great apparition, the nature that "shines so peacefully around us," then the recourse is to inquire, to what end is Emerson? The inquiry has been put by some very smart critics and philosophers. What I'm proposing is that you and I inquire, as poets, how Emerson avails.

"Avail" was one of Emerson's favorite words, a good word to use on him because it implies that he is not just a theme park to wander around in, but a transitive, updatable input for poetry. He would have liked that, or that's one way to read his hope in that last sentence of his essay "Experience."

> and the true romance which the world exists to realize, will be the trans-
> formation of genius into practical power.

His genius, our power: it was no imaginary romance. In fact, there's a whole procession to testify how his genius has availed. There was Whitman, who said he was simmering until Emerson brought him to a boil. There was Frost, who said never forget Emerson. And there was Gertrude Stein, who said "and I said there was Emerson, and there was Hawthorne and there was Edgar Poe and there was Walt Whitman and there was, well, in a funny way there was Mark Twain and then there was Henry James and then there was—well, there is— well, I am."

We could cite the evidence at length, although trails of influence, like money trails, seem often to leave the impression that writers are exchanging something on the sly. I think it's more honest than that. In his book *The Selfish Gene*, the evolutionary biologist Richard Dawkins suggested a word for ideas and phrases that are replicators in cultural evolution the way genes are replicators biologically. By analogy, and with a root as in mimesis, he came up with memes. From what I know about poets and writers, "memes" makes at least as much sense as saying that mature poets steal. Steal implies intent, but when you end up hosting powerful phrases isn't it because you can't get them out of your head? There are countless memes, replicating in our poetry this way, which can be tracked to Emerson.

My own prejudice is that when so many poets host memes from an identical source it raises the presumption that the source is another poet. The problem is, most of the influences you can trace to Emerson aren't from his verse but from his essays. Or maybe it isn't a problem, but a clue. Because all you have to do is ask whether the essays are really poems, or contain hidden poems, to take possession of the Emerson that is truly there.

> Vast spaces of nature, the Atlantic Ocean, the South Sea,—
> Long intervals of time, years, centuries,—are of no account.
> This which I think and feel underlay every former state of life and
>   circumstances,
> As it does underlie my present, and what is called life, and what is
>   called death.

That is actually not Whitman, even if it does sound so much like "Crossing Brooklyn Ferry." And of course I've cheated to show that you can demonstrate how Emerson's essays are like poems just by setting them as poems. Those lines are from "Self-Reliance," and the lines that follow in that essay are better known, more beautiful.

Life only avails, not the having lived. Power
Ceases in the instant of repose: it resides
In the moment of transition from a past to a new
State, in the shooting of the gulf, in the darting
To an aim. This one fact the world hates,
That the soul *becomes*. . . .

But the prosody isn't the point. The point is, when you set Emerson's words this way the lines themselves reveal how someone can love the essays even if they refuse to come clear as criticism or philosophy. They don't have to come clear, not as poetry.

Emerson has a reputation for memorable images and analogies, partly because that's what he said good writing consisted of. "Wise men pierce this rotten diction and fasten words again to visible things" is just one way he put it. So which are the visible things in "Life only avails"? There is a thing called power and one called a moment of transition, a gulf, an aim, and states both past and new. Talk about abstract diction.

Yet that is finally how Emerson's power is conveyed, in a diction that doesn't fasten words to things so much as it lets ideas loose in sounds. Those roomy vowels in *Life only avails* (even roomier as the *l*'s stretch them out) are vowels that make space and time in the very pronouncing of them, enough time for you to reconnoiter his typical inversion. Did he mean "only life avails" or life but avails only? *Life only avails*, is what he writes, and listen to how it reverberates over the lesser vowels that are rushed aside: "not the having lived." These measure the inutile, flip side of life, and there's no way to pronounce them expansively. It's not an image, but sounds that make the idea of this line, the constricted syllables of past tradition being blown away by the hosanna at the beginning and that sforzando coming at the end: *Power.*

This is not to say you won't find in Emerson plenty of things: "swine, spiders, snakes, pests, madhouses, prisons, enemies"—though even this list is trying to vaporize into abstractions. Which pests or enemies? These are less things than enabling images. They permit you the liberty of moving on to visible things of your own, and liberty, yours and his, is something Emerson is scrupulous about. In the essay "Nominalist and Realist" he writes that the world is so full of things it's good you can't see them all. If you could you would be immobilized.

As soon as the soul sees any object, it stops in front of that object.

He doesn't mean just paused. He means transfixed, taken prisoner. This is the ex-minister who wrote elsewhere that every thought, even every heaven is a prison. Translate into poetic practices and you see why he so seldom beats you over the head with some x-is-like-y analogy. Powerfully good or bad, an image can bring you to a stop.

The analogies Emerson prefers are the kind that emphasize how you can get free of one heavenly prison and enter the next—how something moves, becomes, how it avails. And if, in the face of the world's hostility, the idea is to keep your soul becoming, to keep it on the move, then we have a clue as to why Emerson's real poetry is in the essays and not so much in his verse. Because if the soul stops in front of an object, it may also stop in front of a rhyme.

In an early lecture on English literature Emerson came close to saying he admired George Herbert, for example, in spite of his rhymes. After conceding that Herbert's poetry was initially "apt to repel the reader," he went on to propose that its thought nonetheless had "so much heat as actually to fuse the words . . . and his rhyme never stops the progress of the sense." In a later lecture he claimed that the finest rhythms of poetry were yet unfound, "compared with which the happiest measures of English poetry are psalm-tunes." It was March 5, 1842, in the Library of the New-York Society at the corner of Leonard Street and Broadway. Here is what else he said.

> I think even now, that the very finest and sweetest closes and falls are not in our metres, but in the measures of prose eloquence which have greater variety and richness than verse.

Then he added, "In the history of civilization, Rhyme may pass away." If that sounds familiar I don't have to tell you who was in the audience in Mannahatta that day.

What's significant, of course, is not whether traditional or nontraditional form is better. That's not an argument poets should want to settle. What's significant is that Emerson's distrust of rhyme points, like a shadow to the sun, to what he thought poetry was for. It was liberty, liberty of perception: "The senses imprison us, and we help them with metres as limitary,—with a pair of scales and a foot-rule and a clock."

The paradox was that while meters might infringe on your perception they offered one liberty that prose withheld, the freedom to tell the truth. For the rest of what was said to the twenty-two-year-old Walter Whitman and the others in New York that March day was that rhyme might pass away, but it would always be remembered as a "privileged invention possessing . . . *certain rights of sanctuary.*" It seems inevitable in hindsight. But if your problem is to invent a form that permits you that liberty to perceive which belongs to prose, together with that privilege to speak which belongs to rhyme, you do what Emerson did. You invent the prose-hidden poem.

So what is the truth a lapsed minister, an aspiring poet, cannot put into ordinary prose? You can't tell mother, father, wife, and brother flat out in prose that the tropes, the metaphors of their society are a prison. You might say it, but you can't tell them, because logic is powerless against their metaphors. "I fear," wrote Emerson when he was only twenty, "the progress of Metaphysical philosophy may be found to consist in nothing else than the progressive introduction of apposite metaphors."

Today, we've had whole literatures and philosophies to point to our imprisonment by trope, and language, and media prime time—so much pointing you have to wonder if this fascination has become *our* apposite metaphor of the hour. But Emerson did more than point, and it would be interesting to know how he would proceed against the metaphors of today. We know his pleasure was to subvert trope with trope. Of society, far more a male club then than now, he focused back on it the anxiety that male bonding is supposed to alleviate in the first place. "Society everywhere is in conspiracy," he wrote (and we have learned to supply the italics), "against the manhood of every one of its *members.*"

Of getting rich quick, too often called the American Dream, he labeled it a "bribe." Of gender vanity, he wrote (and here the italics are his own) that there is "in both men and women, a deeper and more important *sex of mind.*" Of divine absolution, he simply referred us to a divinity closer at hand. "Absolve you to yourself, and you shall have the suffrage of the world."

I would like to say these examples amount to recombinant memes. I can certainly say along with Charles Ives that Emerson, in his essays, was "lighting a fuse that is laid toward men"—and I could hardly say it better, except to add that it was laid toward women to the same impolite effect.

So where, as poets, does that leave you and me? If the old metaphors are blown away it leaves us right where Emerson wanted us, in the position of having to choose metaphors, turn tropes, that express our own original relation to the universe. It's a heresy that may seem too much to ask, and there were times in Concord he must have thought so, too. "Despair is no muse," he wrote in his *Journals*, a formulation that makes you aware of the extent to which Emerson's so-called optimism is a strategy for writing: self-help for poets.

In life he had plenty of practice. When his five-year-old son died, in 1842, Emerson lost his first and, as far as he knew then, his only son. "I am and I have: but I do not get," is what he would write in "Experience" two years later, "and when I have fancied I had gotten anything, I found I did not." He had not even be-gotten a biological future for the name Emerson. "Never mind the ridicule, never mind the defeat:" he continued bravely, "there is victory yet for all justice." But what kind of victory can compensate for the failure of heirs to carry your name in the world? You can still beget memes named Emerson.

> and the true romance which the world exists to realize, will be the transformation of genius into practical power.

Considering how he left us face to face with the universe, we could use some of that practical power. Because no matter how good you are with words, it's hard to turn new tropes until you newly perceive, and the redemptive power of the trope will be proportional to the redemptive power of the perception. This is bedrock poetics, and it is this ratio that was behind Emerson's consistent emphasis on the eye-ball, on vision: "We are never tired, so long as we can see far enough." The implication is that how you manage your perception will determine how much energy there is in what you write, which does sound like the start of a self-help course for poets.

My guess, though, is that the course will seem compromised in its first lesson, *Nature*. You are probably not convinced by Emerson's analogy that the poet who turns nature into tropes is like the savior who rides in triumph into the holy city, an analogy which, taken to its conclusion, can only mean that salvation itself depends on the tropes you mount. We don't make big claims like that for poetry. There are a lot of bat-boy ideologues and vigilante divines in public life, and they make claims. But among poets and scholars there still flourishes the notion that poetry makes nothing happen and can be written accordingly. I have a hunch that if Emerson were around he would see that as a metaphor for *our* imprisonment.

Chances are, the tropes you turn on nature do support salvation. When Emerson was reading astronomy in 1833, he noted in his journal that "God has opened this knowledge to us to correct our theology & educate the mind." Yet more than 150 years later, when the space shuttle *Columbia* had exploded and slapped into the Atlantic Ocean, the best the president could do was to paraphrase a naive sonnet. The astronauts, he said, had "slipped the surly bonds of earth and touched the face of God."

Forget the face-touching part and it is still unbearably dissonant. What can it mean to refer to the surly bonds of earth? Bonds not slipped at all, by the way, since gravity brought the astronauts and their cabin into contact with the surface at 200 miles per hour. And what is surly about the bonds that hold the atmosphere, that make this planet the only breathing, protected paradise we know, and keep it from becoming, for instance, Mars?

You're wondering if I'm really serious, if it matters that an ill-managed president broadcasts a piece of mimetic vandalism grabbed up by a speechwriter. But tropes that make the earth unlovely make humans that do not love the earth. If theirs is the species that also has the bombs, or just the subdevelopment rights, then I think poetry has quite a lot to do with salvation. You don't have to be so impersonal about it, though. "For the value of a trope," or so Emerson left the issue, "is that the hearer is one: and indeed Nature itself is a vast trope, and all particular natures are tropes."

Clever enough. Except it still leaves for us the problem of nature, which as a source of poetry can seem like one painful anachronism. Walking in the Walden woods, the woods he owned, Emerson thought nature was "sanative," a remedy for everything false in human culture. It was a standard by which inconstant culture could be measured, retroped. But who can study nature now, except with a broken heart? There's that hole in the ozone, isotopes in the reindeer, and a mile to the west of Emerson's woods are the waters of the Sudbury River, which flow into the Concord River, go under the rude bridge that arched the flood, join the Merrimack and pass Plum Island into the Atlantic—all this after taking the outflow in Ashland, Massachusetts, of a little tributary called (of all things) Chemical Brook. That is where the river received the mercury, lead, chromium, cadmium, arsenic, trichloroethylene, nitrobenzene, and chlorinated benzenes that have made its contamination, according to the EPA, permanent.

Emerson thought there was nothing, except losing his sight, no calamity that nature could not repair. A mile from where he stood, nature cannot even repair itself.

It's no wonder, considering what has been done to North America, if the American Scholar would rather contemplate frescoes in Italy than benzenes in Massachusetts. And yet what were American scholars up to in 1837 but Italian frescoes? Or Emerson would have had no subject for his famous talk. The difference is that they complained the continent was too empty, too untouched for art, and here I am complaining it's too full and too messed up. But since they felt despair because nature was too empty, and we feel despair because it's too full, is it possible the fault is not in nature but in despair?

> The ruin or the blank, that we see when we look at nature, is in our own eye. The axis of vision is not coincident with the axis of things, and so they appear not transparent but opake.

He never said it was easy to perceive what nature was about. "It is easier to read Sanscrit," is what he did say. But you and I have this advantage, that somebody tried the axis of vision once before, and left us records—essays—on how to proceed.

A peculiar thing about the *Essays* (and another way they are like poems) is their titles: titles that don't reveal the subject so much as they disguise it. Of these, none has been less forthcoming than the most famous one, "Self-Reliance." Partly as a consequence, there is no masterpiece in our literature that has been more capriciously maligned. Emerson does insist on liberty, it's true, while the world seems to offer endless illustrations that humans can't always live up to liberty. Why this should make anyone feel smug is beyond me, but it does. More than one person of letters has felt compelled to note how irrelevant "Self-Reliance" is to a wiser culture that recognizes the errancy of the individual as opposed to the steadfast guidance of . . .

But that's just it. No two agree on what the alternative authority is, though each must have one in mind, even if, too bad for the other, it's not the same in both cases.

Of course, there is creative reading as well as creative writing. Because, despite its title, the famous essay is not really about the selfish self at all. On the contrary. If we are to have our original relation to the universe, then the self, the one with the instilled appetites and the learned desires, this self must stand aside—which makes sense when you remember what the problem was. The ruin that we see when we look at nature is in our own eye.

So if not the self, who do we rely on? Like any poet, Emerson suggests his answer in a writerly way, by qualifying his terms. Not halfway through, and he has renamed self-reliance as self-trust, in order (while reminding his reader that trust has a fiduciary meaning) to ask "Who is the Trustee?" It is, he writes, "that science-baffling star, without parallax."

No parallax: so it appears never to change position, even though he described it at the outset as flashing from within. You can see Emerson liked riddles, since the light that never changes position, yet is carried hither, thither, and elsewhere within you, is our "common origin." Instructed, as we are supposed to be, in the dimensions of our cosmic inheritance—in the starbursts that deliver the elements that twist themselves up into things that replicate—we can better appreciate the justice of his answer, our common origin. It's a meme he elaborates at length.

> We first share the life by which things exist, and afterwards see them
> as appearances in nature, and forget that we have shared their cause.

Nice, but. Taken to its logical conclusion what does it mean? That you put your trust as a poet in the Big Bang?

Intelligent people like to think intelligent thoughts, not wacko ones, so those people will be happy to see the word "cause" in Emerson's sentence. "Cause" will remind them of nineteenth-century Idealism and its has-been philosophers, and if Emerson was like those philosophers then his sentence must be a has-been, too. No wonder he believed a thought was a prison. Because what his words really add up to is a sentence that wants to release you where it will, just like poetry. So what if we forget philosophy and read "Self-Reliance" as natural history?

We apparently do share, in DNA for instance, the life by which things exist. We apparently do share in the maintenance of the biosphere, although for centuries we thought earthly things were natural appearances instead of dependents in a common cause. Here is Emerson's sentence in its place.

> In that deep force, the last fact behind which analysis cannot go, all
> things find their common origin. For, the sense of being which in calm
> hours rises, we know not how, in the soul, is not diverse from things,
> from space, from light, from time, from man, but one with them, and
> proceeds obviously from the same source whence their life and being

also proceed. We first share the life by which things exist, and afterwards see them as appearances in nature, and forget that we have shared their cause.

What fascinates me in those lines is the assumption, made in slow and equal iambs, of equal status among the five reliers in the one consortium. Being human doesn't separate you, not from things, from space, from light, from time, from man. With a list like that, the mind reaches farther back than DNA. Far enough to raise the question again. What are we supposed to do, rely on the Big Bang?

Well, we *were* looking for an original relation to the universe. And the Bang does promise a new twist on the axis of vision, especially if we could perceive our rights to be but co-equal in evolution with those of space, of time, of light, of things.

Emerson let self-reliance in for a lot of trouble when he wrote on the lintels of his doorpost, *Whim*. People have come out of the woodwork on account of *Whim* to condemn him for everything from bran flakes to poets who lust after the Big Bang. What they are really condemning in the process is your liberty as a poet to perceive. "Thoughtless people . . . fancy that I choose to see this or that thing," he writes, beginning one of those qualifications you learn to keep reading for. "But perception is not *whim*sical, but fatal." I added the emphasis, because the secret of "Self-Reliance" is that it proposes no whim, but a release of objectivity: the objectivity to honor facts as perceived from the axis of our common origin. In that case your perception itself is a fact, "as much a fact," reports Emerson, "as the sun."

The catch is what happens when the soul sees a fact. It stops in front of that fact. The soul stops and, to adopt the figure of "Circles," it is encircled. Lucky for us if our Virgil knows an escape. "The way of life is wonderful:" he explains, "it is by abandonment." Brilliant as your perception was, the thing to do is abandon it.

Maybe this won't sound so frivolous if you consider what we've learned from quantum physics about the uncertainty of measurements. Heisenberg's uncertainty relation is taken in popular terms to mean you can't measure simultaneously the momentum and the position of any particle, though this is apparently not quite right. What you can't know simultaneously are the average of many momenta and the average of many positions for any particle. To know one average completely you would have to abandon completely your measurement of the other.

Heisenberg argued that you could not draw moral or practical analogies from quantum nature. Niels Bohr argued that you could. To an Emersonian self like mine it seems inevitable. For example, if as a poet I measure for pollution at Chemical Brook, then I will perceive either more or less pollution. If less, I will be gratified by the better fit with our fashionable metaphor, ecology. If more, I will be in pain, my axis of vision out of whack with the axis of things.

But what if I were to abandon ecology and measure instead by that lesson from our common origin?—evolution. From the first contamination of protons after the Big Bang to the chlorinated benzenes in Chemical Brook, the project of the universe seems to have been to make big molecules and mix things up. Given the record, you might wonder if humans aren't specifically here to mix things up, if we shouldn't as poets write that Chemical Brook, for degree of evolution, was never so beautiful as when it ran with a trichloroethylene sheen.

Maybe that's what he meant in *Nature*, about how sordor and filths will no longer be seen.

I agree it's a perverse perception and I am duly embarrassed. Embarrassed enough to be the example for his second remedy for encirclement. In order to write, you not only abandon your first perception, you must abandon yourself to love of the new one.

People don't regard Emerson as a lover, but he was a lover at least once or he couldn't use love as the standard for how far you have to go in order to write. Think of love as the time when we forgive ourselves all embarrassment, and later never remember that we were ridiculous, but only that we were in love. If, in the act of writing, you turn Chemical Brook into a freshet of the new Eden you could stop in embarrassment or keep writing and go all the way. After all, "Life is a series of surprises." Or so begins in delight that passage from "Circles" which is one of his most beautiful and ends, after he has discharged his "hoard" of knowledge, in a relief of wisdom.

> The simplest words,—we do not know what they mean, except when we love and aspire.

Turn that sentence around and it says, to love is to know what words mean. To perceive is to know what words to write.

Today you may be justly suspicious of any presumption in favor of new perceptions, as if anybody needed more of them, as if they didn't crowd in on us already from film, TV, from printed things and things unprintable—so many of them, there are days the world seems nothing but rumors, everything less and less for real. Yet it's largely due to our present experience of data overload that Emerson's complaint in "Experience" can sound, not fatally dated, but as modern and postmodern as our own.

All things swim and glitter. Our life is not so much threatened as our perception. Ghostlike we glide through nature, and should not know our place again.

It isn't fair. You follow all his self-help counsel and he informs you at last that experience will undo your perceptions, once by denying them outright and again by not being true enough to have ever made them real.

A measure of how this troubled Emerson himself is that "Experience" is the most overtly organized of his famous essays. Eight parts, though if you subtitle them according to his own summary, the essay is actually seven parts plus a coda. You will find his summary in the initial sentence of that coda, and discover there that he puts part four—"Surface"—right at the essay's center, ever more clearly the focus than it seemed before. In the essay's first three parts Emerson names those sensations, all too real, that conspire to deny our best-begotten perceptions. In the last three, he counters with generalizations to mend or embrace the denials. Nowhere does he suggest that the generalizations are good enough, say, to make up for losing a son. "The amends," he writes elsewhere, "are of a different kind than the mischief." But the structure reveals how hard he was trying, and how compelling this makes the resolution he has balanced there in part four on "the equator of life, of thought, . . . of poetry." There, in a kind of purgatory between the inferno of sensation and the paradise of generalization, his solution is to "add a line every hour, and between whiles add a line." His solution is to write.

To say inferno, purgatory, and paradise comes close to accusing

Emerson himself of hosting some famous memes. He once noted that he would use Dante as his textbook if he ever taught writing, so my speculation isn't wild. Of those three beasts Dante confronts after he wakes, lost in midlife, it is the wolf of envy that finally destroys his hopes. Predictably, or so Virgil tells him, because envy lets no one pass and you must take another way. In the first sentence of "Experience," Emerson likewise wakes, is likewise lost in midlife, and having suffered the death of his son he, too, has an envy to confront: his martyrdom has been insufficient, the griefs of others are more romantic than his own.

Not martyred enough. On one level this sounds like some vestigial religious envy of those who have suffered more than we have. At the level of Emerson's concern it is envy of those persons—those systems, even—who have *perceived* more than we have, seen all the data in the world or, worse, seen through it all. It is especially envy of data itself. And it's to counter this romance of envy that he offers at the end of "Experience" what he calls the true romance. Turn the genius of your own perceptions into practical power. "Thou art sick," he writes, not mincing the word, "but shalt not be worse, and the universe, which holds thee dear, shall be the better."

I'm not sure how the universe will be better if everybody sits down tomorrow and writes a poem. It's possible, if the project of the expanding universe is to evolve, to become something else, then the more memes, the more poetry, the better. What I want to know, especially since I thought the anthropic cosmos was a conceit peculiar to the new cosmology, is whether he really believed the actual, physical universe would be better.

Eight years after "Experience" was published, Waldo Emerson, then only forty-nine, lamented in his journal that just when you get to be a good writer you get old. Your physical energy has begun to fail. Then he reminds himself that whatever he has already perceived and written was thanks to the universe, and thanks to the universe he, and any of us after, may write again.

> In you, this rich soul has peeped, despite your horny muddy eyes, at books & poetry. Well, it took you up, & showed you something to the purpose; that there was something there. Look, look, old mole! there, straight up before you, is the magnificent Sun. If only for the instant, you see it. Well, in this way it educates the youth of the Universe; in this way, warms, suns, refines every particle; then it drops the little channel or canal, through which the Life rolled beatifically—like a fossil to the ground—thus touched & educated by a moment of sunshine, to be a fairer material for future channels & canals, through which the old Glory shall dart again, in new directions, until the Universe shall have been shot through & through, *tilled* with light.

Like nature as he hoped nature could be, it was Emerson's motive that is revealed as sanative, a remedy for what is false in our culture. As an incitement to write and a guide for doing so, it is unbeatable. It indicates now, and will indicate deep in the twenty-first century, how Emerson avails.

DELIVERED TO THE LITERARY ROUNDTABLE,
ACADEMY OF AMERICAN POETS,
NEW YORK, JANUARY 13, 1987

A BRIEF HISTORY OF MEMES

LEAVES OF GRASS

In the history of civilization, Rhyme may pass away.

—EMERSON

Rhymes and rhymers pass away; poems distill'd from poems pass away.

—WALT WHITMAN

WALDEN

We think our civilization near its meridian, but we are only at the cock-crowing and the morning star.

—EMERSON

The sun is but a morning star.

—HENRY DAVID THOREAU

CIRCUMFERENCE

There is no outside, no enclosing wall, no circumference to us.

—EMERSON

My Business is Circumference.

—EMILY DICKINSON

SONG OF MYSELF

I am not careful to justify myself.

—EMERSON

I celebrate myself.

—WALT WHITMAN

PRAGMATISM

Life only avails ... it resides in the moment of transition from a past to a new state.

—EMERSON

Life is in the transitions as much as in the terms connected.

—WILLIAM JAMES

THE MAKING OF AMERICANS

Men resist the conclusion in the morning, but adopt it as the evening wears on, that temper prevails over everything of time, place, and condition.

—EMERSON

It is hard living down the tempers we are born with.

—GERTRUDE STEIN

HARMONIUM

Money, which represents the prose of life, and which is hardly spoken
of in parlors without an apology, is, in its effects and laws, as beautiful
as roses.

—EMERSON

Money is a kind of poetry.

—WALLACE STEVENS

THE POET

He is the true and only doctor; he knows and tells; he is the only teller
of news.

—EMERSON

It is difficult to get the news from poetry yet men die miserably every
day for lack of what is found there.

—WILLIAM CARLOS WILLIAMS

TRADITION AND THE INDIVIDUAL TALENT

It has come to be practically a sort of rule in literature, that a man, having once shown himself capable of original writing, is entitled thence-
forth to steal from the writings of others at discretion.

—EMERSON

Immature poets imitate; mature poets steal.

—T. S. ELIOT

FLOW CHART

Our moods do not believe in each other.

—EMERSON

But no one, of course, ever trusts these moods.

—JOHN ASHBERY

WEATHERMAN

You don't get a candle to see the sun rise.

—EMERSON

You don't need a weatherman to know which way the wind blows.

—BOB DYLAN

1987

NATIVE GENIUS

A good question for critics is what difference they make to poetry. Not what poetry gets appreciated, depreciated, or taught, but what poetry gets written. It is not a frivolous question. Think back to Emerson, whose critical advice to writers ("do your work and I shall know you" is what he promised them in "Self-Reliance") laid the foreground for both *Walden* and *Leaves of Grass*. The example is so luminous you might take it as predictive: the best criticism works less by constraint than by liberation.

Yet if those are the ingredients the proportions turn out to be complicated, and the critic Richard Poirier devoted much of his career to exploring how the complications run, and why. In the process he was having a pertinent good time. He could never resist pointing out that Emerson's initial formulation of his advice was *do your thing*, meaning that the phrase was no sixties anomaly, after all, but a trope so fully tenured in our literature that it remains a precedent from which no American thinker, writer, or critic can be honestly free. Even Emerson seemed to feel its constraint, as in the essay "Compensation" where he produced this stern variant: "Do the thing, and you shall have the power: but they who do not the thing have not the power."

At issue in Emerson's advice, of course, is not your willingness to follow it, but how to identify what *thing* a writer has to do. On this issue, Poirier meant to make himself a guide. In his books on Frost and Mailer, in his essays in *The Performing Self*, he sought to turn attention from preoccupations with theory toward an appreciation of what actually goes on in writing, the performance of it, traced out in words. In *The Renewal of Literature*, he directed attention to the writer's performance ahead of time, beginning in the blank, untexted space where genius shelters before its works can be written. How would "genius" (a word he attempted to rescue) respond when ensnared in the very language it must use to even imagine a new expression? From his lifetime of reading, Poirier concluded it would respond with antagonism, sport, and a reflex rejection of hand-me-down tropes and assumptions—including assumptions of its human selfhood—in order to assert its own priority.

Thanks to poststructuralist vocabularies, the prospect of rejecting the human self may no longer seem paradoxical. What might have startled you in conversation with Poirier was to discover this prospect relocated to the work of those he identified as the Emersonian "contingent," meaning Emerson, William James, Frost, and Stevens—a proactive cohort he later expanded to Stein and Ashbery, while holding it open to further writers likewise prepared to do their thing. It was Poirier's claim that the characteristic thought of this contingent not only anticipated that of prominent theorists (he specified Derrida, Foucault, and Lacan) but offered a better alternative. "To put Foucault next to Emerson," he wrote, "is a provocative way of reiterating that Emerson's writing makes claims on us to which we have not yet sufficiently responded." He was especially disappointed—annoyed might be a better word—by the insufficient response of his own circle of intellectual friends, a circle that orbited loosely that center of gravity represented by the *New York Review of Books*. But the writers he had named in his contingent were not exactly forgotten figures. So I think we are entitled to wonder, as his intellectual friends no doubt *did* wonder, just what he was complaining about. His answer was more provocative than his initial assertion. There could be no adequate response to the Emersonian component of American literature because that component has been suppressed.

Strong word, suppressed. And yet, think how frequently we were urged by certain of Poirier's friends to attend to various endangered national literatures, then ask yourself how often we were urged (by the *New York Review of Books*, for example) to reclaim our own authentic Emerson. There was a time, within the memories of modernists Pound, Moore, and Eliot, when the slight would have been inconceivable. Two years before the twentieth century—when Moore was ten years old and Eliot nine—the remarkable John Jay Chapman observed that he did not need to enumerate Emerson's works. "They are in everybody's hands," wrote Chapman, "and in everybody's thoughts." Maybe you will assume that the works faded from attention because their author had become irrelevant, a stuffy moralist. But if your impression of Emerson derived from Eliot ("Upon the glazen shelves kept watch / Matthew and Waldo, guardians of the faith") then you were in for a surprise when you met the subversive philosopher-critic—anything but a guardian of any faith—who was reintroduced by Poirier. Emerson, he wickedly explained, was allowed to be "a pervasive presence, but he has not been allowed to *be* Emerson."

Let Emerson be Emerson, and you begin to understand who might have an interest in suppressing him. Imagine a literary founding father who labeled capitalism a "bribe," referred to the Bible as "the phraseology of some old mouldered nation in another country in another world," and objected to literature itself because "it exists." That, in Poirier's opinion, was the real Emerson, an indigenous threat to established power—and power knew it. Witness the little papal bull on the humanities, *To Reclaim a Legacy*, which was issued by Ronald Reagan's Secretary of Education, William Bennett, while he was still installed at the National Endowment for the Humanities. Predictably, the legacy that this secretary wished his country to reclaim did not include his country's greatest writers. It was a legacy handed down, instead, in the pieties of one Matthew Arnold, the loyal subject of a foreign monarchy. Poirier wanted you to think seriously about that. The erasure by political authorities of an entire national tradition, followed by the imposition for purposes of social control of an alien tradition, would be called, if we saw it in any other country, suppression.

In the United States, of course, one could still get at the books. This was an Enlightenment subtlety that made the Emersonian writers inconvenient, not just to political but to literary power—particularly inconvenient, in Poirier's estimation, to the rise of modernism as exemplified by Eliot. Throughout the Emersonian literature runs the marked conviction, after all, that the display of learning, the conspicuous consumption of culture, is not the same thing as knowledge. Yet modernism—consider *The Waste Land* or *Cantos*—pretends effectively the opposite. Since Emerson's essays were in everybody's hands when Eliot was growing up, the best weapon he could level against them was condescension. Subsequent writers he could simply deny. Poirier was always delighted to recount how Eliot feigned surprise that there was no edition of Stevens available in England, where Eliot himself, as editor at Faber & Faber, should long since have published it.

Poirier came close to suggesting outright modernist malevolence. This was probably for effect. He did mean to emphasize, however, that his Emersonian writers threatened to subvert the power of many a critic, and, once again, power knew it. The irony is that the success of his argument turned largely on the arrival of those offshore criticisms that were eager to humble the common adversary, but for whom the liberation of our indigenous Emersonianism was surely an unintended side effect. Because the poststructuralists, too, liked to think of themselves as subversive, they would train American readers to look for just the kind of resistant, perplexing densities that Poirier located in his indigenous pragmatists. A traditionalist might console the readers for being perplexed. The postmodernist protested the perfidy of language itself. Poirier's charge was that neither went far enough to appreciate what the densities were really doing. "Let the experience be perplexing," he advised; it is the closest we can come to an experience of genius, before it is netted by language, still doing its unmediated thing.

There was something epochally diagnostic in that advice. The literary era we once knew best was fueled by its intimations of immortality. Now that the soul is not a soul, those intimations supply an ever-wheezier motive for a poet's metaphors. But if you followed Poirier and his writers into their dense perplexities you might read there the oncoming intimations of a whole new literary era. I am putting the critic out on a limb, where in fact he was happy to go. Because the logical conclusion of his argument was this: it is not their intimations of individual redemption but of unselfed genius—an evolutionary potential not restricted to the individual nor perhaps to any one species—which have made some very perplexing works of our recent literature so powerfully affecting to their readers.

Poirier didn't cite Ashbery in this context, but there was hardly a better example of a writer whose work was both so moving to its devoted readers and so frequently assailed by its critics for lack of clarity. "If we take meaning to refer to the possibility of shared discourse," clucked one critic in disapproval, then Ashbery "eliminates meaning." Poirier insisted you judge the value of such disapproval not on its face but prospectively. *Judge the criticism by the writing you haven't yet written.* One doesn't need to be a writer to wonder how genius could materialize if, just as it reaches for expression, we hand it a language of "shared discourse" instead. What could be newly described in terms already agreed upon? Nothing but a reality, as William James once complained in memorable disgust, which has been already "peptonized" and cooked for our consumption. The reader who will entertain a writer's reach for the reality that is not yet peptonized may get intimations of unselfed genius the way earlier readers got theirs of immortality—intimations that justify the mind that reads and render it, just as in the nineteenth century, actually sort of thrilled.

Poirier never meant to propose that the more perplexing a poem the more thrilling, period. It should not be required of readers that they be pleased with the grimly adversarial, and Stevens was right to specify what a poem must do: it must give pleasure. Somehow, genius must *pleasurably* decline to comply, a charm it most typically accomplishes, according to Poirier, "by the covert allusiveness of troping." Now, trope is one of those terms that has swept its rivals from the field —remember metaphor and simile?—and if you ever thought a definition was in order then Poirier was your man on that account alone. "Troping," he wrote, "is the turning of a word in directions or detours it seemed destined otherwise to avoid." So a trope can be local, like Thoreau's groaner about his bean field in *Walden*: "I was determined to know beans." Or it can be global, the way *Walden* as a whole troped on the tradition of the New England salvational journal, including the one Emerson was keeping, but not keeping *to*, himself.

No *Walden*, then, except for that day in Concord when Emerson mobilized the jealous genius in Thoreau by asking if he, too, kept a journal. Not until he engaged the tradition could Thoreau trope against it in a way to show it up, while yet furthering it along. As a result, *Walden* became a prefiguring example of that resistance via compliance that was a familiar concept, apparently, to readers of Foucault. But according to a delighted Poirier you didn't have to read it in Foucault. You could have heard it in Boston on December 9, 1841, from the thirty-eight-year-old Waldo Emerson.

> For as you cannot jump from the ground without using the resistance of the ground, nor put out the boat to sea, without shoving from the shore, nor attain liberty without rejecting obligation, so you are under the necessity of using the Actual order of things, in order to disuse it; to live by it, whilst you wish to take away its life.

It is common wisdom, of course, to opine that the poet cannot achieve freedom until he or she submits to form, a wisdom that nonetheless fails to explain why the greatest of American poems have not been in handbook-compatible form. There are stunning exceptions— Frost's sonnet "The Oven Bird," Bishop's villanelle "One Art"—and Emerson's insight helps us to realize why they *are* exceptions. In the United States the actual order of things is too recent to have encoded itself contemporaneously in the traditional sonnet or villanelle. The American poetry that is liveliest, and lives the longest, is poetry that tropes on the forms in which the actual order has actually encoded. So Emerson in his *Essays* troped on the sermon, Thoreau on journals, Dickinson on the hymnal, Stevens on the law brief, and Ashbery on the postgraduate vernacular.

Those are the kind of speculations that Dick Poirier seemed born to provoke. They represent what clearly exhilarated him about his Emersonian contingent: its radical desire to disuse the actual order of things in words. Nothing but writing, he thought, not art, music, politics, or dance, "can teach us so much about what words do to us and how, in turn, we might try to do something to them which will perhaps modify the order of things on which they depend for their meaning." Thus he identified the pragmatic instrumentality that made the Emersonian impulse a worthier alternative, in his view, to "the incipient hopelessness" of theory, of Foucault.

Modifications don't stir people, however, the way calls to action do. So it was easy to be disappointed by Poirier's insistent effort to keep literature from becoming a weapon (he would have said casualty) of a partisan agenda. The genius of literature, he believed, was disinterest; and he was always happy to cite Emerson's claim to be speaking "in the interest of no man & no party, but simply as a geometer of his forces." That was a memorable claim, no question. It was so memorable that once you have seen it in place you will remember vividly why it was there. It was Emerson's justification, entered in his journal during the grim Civil War year of 1862, for the geometry of forces he had just recommended against the South: the "forcible subjugation of the rebel country," to be followed by a Reconstruction that should "go down to the pan" and "turn on a jewel." No wonder the New Critics, who were at first mostly Southerners, wished Emerson to oblivion. Geometer of forces?—in whom the motive for metaphor was pretty strong. For that matter, Poirier betrayed a motive of his own. He frequently noted that works of genius advance in ways subversive of their rhetoric. And though he was amused by the prim intentions of manuals like *To Reclaim a Legacy*, he himself meant to reclaim for readers and writers their authentically radical American legacy.

America, to borrow the title of a poem by Frost, is hard to see. It is especially hard to see if we don't look beyond its surface glitter to our long literary foreground. Yet Poirier's contingent—Frost, Emerson, Stevens, Ashbery—aren't they hopelessly compromised by the establishment history of bankers, judges, CEOs, politicians, and preachers whom they resemble in both color and gender? Genteel critics will sometimes plead, because the United States is big, supposedly young, and has no settled ethnicity, that we must tolerate an absence of literary tradition until the country *becomes* a country. One critic suggested a timetable of a thousand years. But genius should not be so patient, and a prominent genius who wasn't was Gertrude Stein. Fat, brainy, Jewish, lesbian—she had good reason to complain of her country yet nonetheless asserted her inheritance like this: "The United States is just now the oldest country in the world, there always is an oldest country and she is it, it is she who is the mother of the twentieth century civilisation." Poirier took his time in coming to appreciate Stein, but when he arrived there he recognized at once that he shared with the author of *The Making of Americans* a central insight. The texts were making the Americans. It was his own brand of genius to make those texts newly visible by making it intellectually dramatic to read them again. In those texts, poets who have not yet written will find an actual order worth troping on, even as they wish to take away its life.

THE NATION, 1987

LINES FROM

LONDON TERRACE

January 1, 1987: At precisely midnight when the firecrackers began to go off I looked out the bedroom window toward Times Square and, better than fireworks, saw Ursa Major standing on her tail directly over the Elliott-Chelsea Houses. The year starts in the cool, unstartled stars, as we are in fact in Ursa Major as it disperses, opening out to Deneb or beyond.

January 5: Right-to-life is a metaphor adopted by the deathliest people. Does nature believe you have a right to life? HIV does not think so, nor do the businessmen manufacturing bombs. The nation, likewise, is a metaphor for something that has long since ceased to exist in terms of active power, or virtue. It is a market, yes, to multinational corporations but it is not their nation. It is a source of subsidy for the defense industry, but it is not what they defend. It is not there.

January 17: I took Frank to the airport this morning & stopped off at Achkinkesacking on the way home: a hawk at the landfill, the pond frozen over, song sparrows in the stiff dead weeds along the causeway. And in the flats the most beautiful male shoveler, there in that once desolation. Looking flat to the sun, his head is black; looking out of the sun, green; & half into the sun, purple. The eye always yellow— & that chestnut flank. He seemed to follow me. Colder than shit, & the landfill very busy with dumpsters.

One difference between you and the modernists, you and the critical wisdom, should be gratitude. Those brief moments, the intimations of a world in ecstasy—for them you are grateful and hold on to them. You are not going to deny them because they don't happen every day. But the others, the "realists" who still like to make fun of the sixties, say, are as little boys who, having been disappointed once, aren't going to let you catch them being disappointed ever again. They deny even their first experience of ecstasy its reality. Rather than being grateful for having seen, they curse sight because they can't have it whenever they want it, all the time. Who is being naive?

January 18: Snow all morning, and wonderful. From Weehawken you could not see across the river. I went looking for our hawk, because it irritated me all night I wasn't sure which one he was. No surprise, he was in the same tree. My stopping brought a second observer in a van. Hard to tell at first: but a third car scared him off to a different tree, and there in the January light, the thick snow light, was the rufous tail. I thought if I stayed watching him long enough somehow Frank could see him, too.

January 19: Another thing you can't do is characterize, much less condemn, whole generations. When Vietnam came along, they called a whole generation selfish, spoiled, because it would hold them and their country to their revolutionary word. *Our* leaders (as if leaders were wanted) being assassinated & discredited has left *them* in control, even to this day; and what have they done with that control? They have presided over the dismantling of liberty, industry, the dollar, foreign trade, the phone service, railroads; they have pillaged, destroyed & vandalized—they the most aggressively selfish and spoiled generation ever set loose on this country—& have left to us and to our children a diminished estate & fateful downward mobility: the first generation since the Revolution to face such inescapable diminishment. The Second World War was a war America could not choose to ignore, but it has been a disaster in aftereffect for all that was once called American: for the land, for American virtue, for democracy, for the future, for American antimilitarism, for what was once called American independence. What we have left is an internationalist superstructure of economic and cultural privilege which can now seek only to pacify or suppress the Liverpools, Manchesters & Boltons it has left behind all over the United States, the Scotlands & Irelands & Haitis it has left behind on lands where Emerson & Louis Sullivan imagined lions of the West instead, where Whitman could imagine a place (in Ohio!) where the perfect personalities without noise meet. Can you say poetry is not to be read against this radical disappointment?

January 31: More taxis spotted: Gist Cab, Godspeed Taxi, Random Cab, Puddle Taxi, & the driver—honest—was taking a piss.

February 3: I locate those of our generational persuasion from birthdate 1939, when the first volunteers left for the Canadian RAF, to 1946, when the draftees came home. Hence: Frank Bidart, Pinsky, McMichael & Hass, Ann Lauterbach, Susan Howe & Marjorie Welish, John Koethe, Paul Hoover & Vicki Hearne.

February 6: With Marjorie I was too happy to agree: it is not America as a trope for renewal and resistance that I love and want to protect. What I want to protect is America herself, the very body of her: arms, legs, swell & dip—goldenrod hills of her. It is this body that has been exploited and ravaged and vandalized by those who think of her only as an abstraction. Not the trope, but the real sunswept tilth of her— never to be ignored, to be sidelined, to be exterminated again.

February 10: I am a populist, though we're all so awful, because I know one of us is just like me.

March 2: People! and I am as dislocated as an animal that has been picked up out of its path, & when replaced must cower & turn around five times to find out where it was.

April 7: Donald Davie reviews W. C. Williams the way Fenton did Ashbery, as though poetry were a game to be played in a zero-sum society, in which the poet sees a certain role or position open up & shrewdly fills it. One would like to hear what Williams would say about the Englishness of that.

April 19: Poetry is the moment we are free. It does not devalue or inauthenticate poetry if in other moments we are not free. In the moment you are a transparent eyeball you experience true freedom, functionally true while it is happening. If the freedom is not made universal, this is no fault of the poem but a condition of fate: we will die, there is no permanent freedom ever. But to say freedom in poetry is no good because we can't always be free is like saying sex is no good because we can't always be doing it. If you cannot have sex, have as much as you can. If you cannot be free, be as free as you can.

April 24: They say hyperbole is when the language strains against the realities that constrain us: every time I, for instance, return my argument to "America."

May 20: There are professors who believe the Royalists to form a continuous part of our tradition—to *be* our tradition—which is not only ahistorical but a kind of literary betrayal. The first Emerson, Emerson's great-great-great-great-grandfather Thomas, was in Ipswich [Massachusetts] in 1638, so soon after the publication in England of George Herbert's poems that, gee, maybe he didn't have time to pick up a copy before he left.

May 28: This morning in Clement Clarke Moore Park, in the first

Gleditsia: a yellow warbler, singing madly, and a northern parula driven off by the yellow. Then the parula alone in the second Gleditsia, now singing himself.

May 29: Why not an *evolutional* imperative? So act, and so write, that the rule by which you operate could be adopted universally without obstructing the process of evolution. Thus jetties, which obstruct the evolution of a beach, violate the evolutional imperative. Thus nuclear explosions on earth, which return time and matter to a more primitive state, violate the evolutional imperative. Thus prejudice, which obstructs the progress of a democracy of options, of the evolutionary increase in mobility evidenced by living things. Drunkenness, which obstructs the advance of thought into lonely places to make them less lonely. In a way, psychoanalysis—at least too transfixedly pursued—violates the evolutional imperative. Oppressions of all kind violate it. Rhyme and antique meter and sestinas and sonnets violate it. The universe expands, and whatever seeks to stop the expansion violates this imperative. Thus specism, which denies the planet as a field of action to any but one species, violates the evolutional imperative; likewise all the concomitants of specism, the specist prejudice against abortion, birth control, homosexuality, and a decent, self-chosen death.

May 30: The reason it takes so long is: I reason by syllables.

June 1: You wouldn't ask an English lawyer to try your case in American law because he knows English law, yet we ask the English critic to judge American poetry because he knows *English*.

June 8: The task is to preserve American prophecy from the long reach of European eschatologies. There is no somewhere from which our conduct will be punished or approved, no elsewhere that is superior to this *here*. There can be no appeal, no forgiveness from Europe or extraterrestrial beings or even the Universe. On Earth we are functionally alone, just as the Americans were. That is why their experience still avails.

June 9: The John Winthrop kind of liberty has been exhumed by the new neos, and the flacks and sourpusses have begun bawling about the need to surrender personal liberty in service to the community. Even the Supreme Court's perfidious Hardwick decision may, in the back of the judges' putative brains, seem to them to express such deference. But the experience of the American wilderness has shown that civil insistence is not enough. The evolutional purpose of community is to set free the individual, otherwise everywhere trapped in Nature and in nature's true totalitarian commune, death.

June 26: At lunch at the Sazerac House on Wednesday, I: "No one will dare to say the word 'impeach' until some institution calls for it." Marjorie: "Or some logo."

**TAKING NOTE: FROM POETS' NOTEBOOKS,
A SPECIAL EDITION OF *SENECA REVIEW*, 1991**

THE LEFTOVER LANDSCAPE

"Facts become art through love," wrote Kenneth Clark in *Landscape into Art*, but who can freely love the landscape now? Clark's prediction, already in the mid-twentieth century, was that no artist could. Landscape painting was an act of faith in nature and it would continue to decline as the faith disintegrated. Truly, he explained, "we have even lost faith in the stability of what we used hopefully to call the 'natural order'; and, what is worse, we know that we have ourselves acquired the means of bringing that order to an end." An artist, he observed, cannot escape from such an idea.

The trouble is that ideas, even of the apocalypse, seem never to survive the crossing quite intact. If the American faith in nature were only eighteenth-century reasonable, or nineteenth-century romantic, then our appreciation of landscape should run down with nature as clock or expire with nature as sanative influence. But somewhere along the way nature got hitched up with democracy in the American mind. Think of *Democratic Vistas* (even the title connects them), in which Whitman returns again and again to the notion that the two are joined. Democracy, he writes, is "in some sort, younger brother of another great and often-used word, Nature, whose history also waits unwritten." Only democracy had anything like nature's scale. Even the lessons to be drawn were similar. "As the greatest lessons of Nature through the universe are perhaps the lessons of variety and freedom," he announced, "the same present the greatest lessons also in New World politics and progress." The scale and the evolutionary direction went together in an abundant landscape that was, like the imagined frontier, an area of total possibility.

Whitman said he could conceive a community, in running order, where "the perfect personalities without noise meet." It is one of his most touching moments. "I can conceive it," he repeated. "Perhaps even some such community already exists, in Ohio, Illinois, Missouri, or somewhere, practically fulfilling itself." Given a map dotted with Oneidas and New Harmonies, maybe this wasn't an original vision. But what about us? What can we conceive? Ohio, it seems, has finally taken care of the notion that it could harbor a community where the perfect personalities without noise meet. And the liberalism of total possibility likewise appears compromised in a country that has found its once boundless West to be a world of limits to the end of it. The lesson of nature is no longer variety and freedom; it is fragility and dependence instead. And as nature becomes the environment it affects its little brother, democracy. While one looks more fragile and rare so does the other, and together they take on the scale of an earthly trust. It is an accurate perception, this not-quite apocalypse, and as an idea about nature why can't it find landscapes all its own of fact and love?

Knowing Ohio isn't infinitely perfectible, knowing despite Ronald Reagan's protestations that it's no longer possible to "vote with our feet," perhaps we can pay attention to what we've got left. In a letter published shortly after his death in 1975, the late Fairfield Porter said he agreed that this country had not been loved enough. "I agree, but I would put it differently," he wrote. "I think this country has been taken too much for granted, the country geologically, botanically as well as its creatures, all of them. From this it follows that no one pays attention to it." Of course from Porter's paintings we know *he* paid attention to it. And my reflections on the subject were prompted by the recent work of two other painters who have likewise paid attention, Eugene Leake and Robert Dash.

Dash makes large painterly acrylics of Long Island's potato fields (he lives immediately next to one), *Phragmites* reeds, semirural roads, roof lines, and telephone poles. Leake makes large painterly oils of Maryland's horse country (he lives in a spacious farmhouse there), whitewashed fences, barns, and rolling pastures. From the cities it would be easy to protest that most of America doesn't look like either of these favored places anymore, but the truth is that much of what's leftover does. Besides, this must be the way many of the less-favored would *like* to look, or we wouldn't have suburbs. No matter how tucked away the country's ideal vistas, they continue to be among its essential drawing cards.

The irony is that the very Americanness of some landscapes can make them problematic. "America," as Frost put it, "is hard to see." So I was not surprised to hear someone say of a painting at Dash's recent show at the Fischbach Gallery in New York that it made him think of a cover from the *Saturday Evening Post*. I suppose that's an indictment if you loathe not only the politics but the climate and vegetation of your country. More likely it was the sound of an American twisting in embarrassment. Should we really like something so much about ourselves? But Kenneth Clark was right, painters do paint their Dedham Mills from love. And if the Dash painting in question, *Sagg Main, Spring Shadows*, comes courageously close to the *Saturday Evening Post*, that's because it starts from love of the same real things: a dog, a farmhouse, a girl riding off on a bicycle down the road. Much of art is the struggle to make emotion less embarrassing. Camp brings love down to size, kitsch turns it rancid, but an artist somehow refines what was merely endurable until it becomes a surprise to be enjoyed. In our case, if it still has an American stir about it, that is a measure of its success.

Because *Sagg Main, Spring Shadows* could not have been painted in any other time or place, it was something of a surprise to see it. In a painting that works, recognition does come as a surprise, just as in a poem that works the beauty of the words comes from their unexpected ways. Anybody who has ever delighted in the way the yards spread out as you are leaving a small country town will know roads like the one Dash has painted. But the surprise of the painting is space. The horizon—I almost want to call it "the frontier"—is entirely occupied and closed. In the foreground is an overhanging barrier of branches. The format is even vertical; but in spite of this the vista seems long and wide. Gertrude Stein explained America by saying there was more space where nobody was than where anybody was, and that is what made Americans different. Although there is less of our national elbow room all the time, perhaps the sense of it will persist with greater tenacity in the culture precisely as it vanishes from the landscape. In *Sagg Main, Spring Shadows* it survives by means of one patch of sky contained between telephone wires. To me, the genius of the painting is in its attention to this persisting sense of distance in an otherwise lessened American space.

Eugene Leake has also been painting vistas to recognize, and also with a twist. The foreground of his *Pastures* delivers your attention immediately to the horizon, from which it returns forward over green hills that honestly beg to be called Jeffersonian. There are horses in the middle distance, the same whitewashed color as the fence behind them. The scene might have begun as a picture of Whitman's nagging vision: "Far, far, indeed, stretch in distance, our Vistas! How much is still to be disentangled, freed!" The surprise is in the fence. Close to one-third of Leake's recent paintings have featured the fence, and a number of others hint strongly at its concealed presence. "I paint what I see," he will tell you, pointing to the fences that approach and leave, up and down the rolling hills. But in many of his fence paintings the subject doesn't approach or leave: it stretches broadside across the painting as if to remind you of what a fence really is, a barrier. The frontier is closed. The vista may stretch far indeed, and there may be no way to lose sight of it, but it can't be reached. Leake says he is interested in "how far back I can go when there isn't really any space there at all." I don't think it bends his words too much to say that he, too, is paying attention to the question of distance in a lessened space.

There is an American anxiety about the land, a worry that even if we examine it geologically, botanically—inch by inch, as Porter recommended in his letter—we will still be fenced off from the spirit of the place. The anxiety is met with a bravado that eventually obliterates what we are unable to inhabit. Whitman called it "beating up the wilderness," and it is still no conquest. The vista in Leake's *White Barn* is reduced by the scale with which a corner of his barn and studio, complete with propane tanks, dominates the left foreground. The generous landscape beyond the barn might be only the yard of advancing commerce. But somehow, as if at the last moment, it escapes out of reach beyond its fences, while remaining so clearly in view it is hard to adjust to its refusal to be possessed. It's as though we were rebuffed by the object of our keenest appetite.

I suppose reality is always intransigent, especially when you try to build it from compounds as intractable as nature and democracy. Emerson must have had this in mind when he spoke of the "odd jealousy" of the poet who cannot get near enough the object. "The pine-tree, the river, the bank of flowers before him, does not seem to be nature. Nature is still elsewhere." So it may be a logical development of our history that the desire to soothe this odd jealousy runs more insistently in the stir of things these days. We have organic kitchen gardens and backyard nature preserves, all designed to get us closer to intransigent nature. The paintings of Neil Anderson, on view at Fischbach in September 1975, were perfectly on target. Each provided a botanist's-eye view, straight down and enlarged, of the forest floor. Dash's *Sagg Preserve* affords a face-to-face encounter with a swamp. Perhaps the country *is* going to be courted inch by inch.

Dash is not a painter of nature's more ostentatious moments. Although he lives near the ocean, I can't remember seeing it head-on in any of his pictures. If there are moments of transition they are the accustomed ones—a shower over the Shinnecock Canal, the last train of the season, tennis players changing position for a serve—moments that accord without complaint to the logic of some implied order, whether the unseen ocean, the pageant that has just gone by, or the rules of the game. In such scenes, he creates an ecology in which even a car or a telephone pole may occupy its appropriate evolutionary niche. (If we are to believe his paintings, Long Island must have the most beautiful telephone poles in America.) This is not the impassively reasonable natural order whose loss Kenneth Clark lamented, nor is it the environmental holocaust. It's the frangible ecological order working at its precarious loveliest. Although it is common to hear people express the sentiment that the environment would be better off without humans and their machines, the truth is it can no longer do without us. Not until this revised vista is perceived can we be placed in our territory without obliterating it, and become truly naturalized citizens of the country we can no longer vote ourselves out of with our feet.

Nature, thought Emerson, has been loved because there is no citizen. "The beauty of nature must always seem unreal and mocking, until the landscape has human figures, that are as good as itself." But to be good as nature itself might surprise him as something entirely other than he had in mind. The current lesson of our PCB-ridden, perforated biosphere seems to be that what is good in nature is what doesn't transcend its limits. The painter Raoul Middleman observed of Leake's paintings that a figure will sometimes interrupt to give them human scale; but the figure in Leake's *Blue House* looks as though it had been reduced instead to a natural scale. Likewise, the citizens of a Dash landscape are neither more nor less apparent than the organic and inorganic things around them. His ambition, says Dash, is to paint the figure outdoors "as commonplace as a bone," and in the tennis painting *Georgica Association No. 25*, he has done just that. To reduce the human figure to a natural ordinariness is to show how it could be indigenous at last, how it might move in the environment as well as an animal built to live there.

Fairfield Porter had a similar genius for making the figure as ordinarily there as the rest of the landscape. It showed up especially in *Girl in the Garden*, which was among the watercolors shown at Brooke Alexander Gallery six weeks after his death in 1975, and in *Anne in the Doorway*, a large oil among his last works shown at Hirschl & Adler the following spring. Porter counted both Dash and Leake among his artist friends. He once shared a studio with Dash in New York and he stayed at Leake's home during visits to the Maryland Institute of Contemporary Art (of which Leake was president for more than ten years). All three were skilled in composition, and what Frank O'Hara wrote of Porter—that he did not wish to *be* nature but to pursue its imitation through composition—could have been written later of Leake or Dash. "Composition is a function of the sensibility," explained O'Hara, "an 'agreement for cessation of hostilities' between oneself and nature." If that is true, then the motives as well as the effects of composition should be very much in line with an emerging perception of the country as an earthly trust.

Perhaps it's a coincidence that Dash and Leake both live in landscapes that vanish as they paint them, vistas in the path of the developer. But I don't think so. From Dash's studio, you can watch the construction of yet another Hamptons "cottage" smack on the shore of Sagg Pond, a shore that has been the artist's favorite subject for many years. To reach Leake's studio from Baltimore you cross a narrow bridge over the Loch Raven reservoir, where you can see a wider, high-traffic bridge under construction alongside. Of his valley Leake told me, "It is doomed." Sadly, there aren't many of us who are innocent of the destruction. Leake and Dash paint landscapes that will make people want to visit, as I visited both, proving how we are drawn to such places to make their doom inevitable. The end is the more devastating because Leake's Harford County and Dash's South Fork are landscapes of the rich. If the rich can't afford to preserve the land unspoiled, it's logical to expect that there is no one who can.

In November 1975, while Leake's landscapes of Maryland were showing at the Green Mountain Gallery in New York, the Sunday *Times* published a commentary about an indictment then facing the Maryland governor. If there was corruption in Maryland, the writer concluded, it was due to the overwhelming temptations presented by the land. Suburbanizing pressures, especially from Washington, D.C., had made development the all-but-irresistible adventure of ambitious

140

men throughout the state. So the American vista, which, as one is accustomed to believe along with Whitman, brings out the best in us, also brings out the worst. People who are thinking of preserving a remnant of the space that fashioned us, or thinking only of their personal Waldens, may find themselves in time facing this unpleasant dilemma.

Of course, paintings are not going to save the country if the developer's price is right, despite the energy with which Eugene Leake or Robert Dash attends the details. There are no innocent encounters to be had with a nature so fragile it requires human protection. "Aesthetics is what connects one to matters of fact," said Porter in his letter. "It is anti-ideal, it is materialistic. It implies no approval, but *respect* for things as they are." It's an aesthetic one might properly admire, this attention that responds to the vanishing facts as they are, with—of all things—love.

PRESENTED AT THE SEMINAR "PAINTING AND POETRY OF THE SOUTH FORK," SOUTHAMPTON COLLEGE, SOUTHAMPTON, NEW YORK, AUGUST 6, 1976

AN OUTSIDER'S

INTRODUCTION TO EMERSON

One reason Emerson is so persistently central, why his essays can still unsettle and arouse, is that he wrote with his transparent eyeball focused on the space we would come to occupy. I mean the actual physical space. It's true that we have seen what he could not, the first photograph of Earth taken from the outside—and in generous moments I suppose we may even regard that photograph as token of a perspective new in history, the edge and advantage to date of all evolution. So it should be something of a surprise to return to his *Essays: First and Second Series* and find on their opening page an analogy that insists on such a perspective while you read: "As the air I breathe is drawn from the great repositories of nature, as the light on my book is yielded by a star a hundred millions of miles distant, . . . so the hours should be instructed by the ages and the ages explained by the hours." It's a beautiful analogy, active, complex, and—the part I like best—advanced as self-evident. Here, more than a century before *Apollo 8* or the Gaia hypothesis or Spaceship Earth, Emerson is practically saying you have a right to think like a planet.

This is not how we are usually introduced to Emerson. No doubt there has been trouble enough over the years to explain away just the rights he enumerates. In "Politics" he says you have the right to be employed, trusted, loved, and revered—a brave amendment to anybody's Constitution. But the right to a planetary perspective must have been beyond notice, if not beyond human politics. Could the man really have meant what he really says in "Experience," that the whole universe holds you dear?

Propositions like that were once dismissed as transcendentalism. But given the way you and I have been treating the universe, I think this one deserves a second look. I think it's worth looking back to a time in Emerson's life before he was ever labeled a transcendentalist, a time when he was still, at twenty-nine, the Unitarian minister of Second Church in Boston. He had been reading the astronomer John Herschel along with a popular translation of Laplace, had decided they "elevate and astonish" more than *Paradise Lost*, and in his sermon of May 27, 1832, was ready to reveal to his congregation what he had found out. Together, they were "journeying in a comparatively small opaque planet around a single star and quite too inconsiderable to be noticed among the millions of burning suns." He even told them, models of society though they were, that to suppose they were the model for all the species that populate other planets was a fantasy too improbable to be entertained.

No wonder the word in Boston was that the young minister of Second Church had gone mad. It took two days to go from Boston to New York, five weeks to cross the Atlantic, and Waldo Emerson stood in his pulpit to describe from the mind's transparent lens what you and I have had the privilege of seeing in a photograph, our native planet spinning alone in space.

What's humbling is, he never blinked. Yet the issue was plain then as now. Having seen where I actually live, on that globe of blue, brown, and white surprise, how can I assent to confines as specifically invented as Christianity, capitalism, or the Commonwealth of Massachusetts? Emerson, embarked on his new career as public lecturer, would not offer the easiest advice. "It seems the one lesson which this miraculous world has to teach us," he told his listeners in 1839, "to be sacred, to stand aloof, and suffer no man and no custom, no mode of thinking to intrude upon us and bereave us of our infinitude." In other words, one photograph is not enough. I have a right to an unobstructed view, but it's a right I'd better be ready to defend.

Of course, it would be nothing new to hear that perceptual liberty is threatened, except Emerson was sounding the alarm in the world's first talk-show democracy ("this our talking America," he called it). Somehow he had come to believe—had sensed as if in personal danger—that threats to perception, while less likely in a democracy to arrive on horseback, were the more to be expected from custom and modes of thinking, from all the rhetorics of profession and privilege that we have learned to identify as "discourse" and Emerson identified in his *Essays* as "usage." In his introductory essay, "History," he even diagnosed all history, that sum of usage and discourse, as a village tale. The passage is not easy to miss—not, as I've finally discovered, if you start the book at the beginning—because it is a stunning outburst.

> Hear the rats in the wall, see the lizard on the fence, the fungus under-foot, the lichen on the log. What do I know sympathetically, morally, of either of these worlds of life? As old as the Caucasian man,—perhaps older,—these creatures have kept their counsel beside him, and there is no record of any word or sign that has passed from one to the other.

Today, though, won't the reader shiver at that word "Caucasian"? This one did, and wished it could be edited away until I had read far enough to see it was meant even then to embarrass, the reader meant even then to shrink from the viewpoint of a race that rats and lizards have never addressed.

I am ashamed to see what a shallow village tale our so-called History is. How many times we must say Rome, and Paris, and Constantinople! What does Rome know of rat and lizard? What are Olympiads and Consulates to these neighbouring systems of being? Nay, what food or experience or succour have they for the Esquimaux seal-hunter, for the Kanàka in his canoe, for the fisherman, the stevedore, the porter?

Rome is just village gossip, out to bereave me of my infinitude by being partial to one race, a deficiency we now call racist; partial to one species, a deficiency I may as well call specist; even—

What connection do the books show between the fifty or sixty chemical elements, and the historical eras?

partial to one kind of matter.

Emerson really is that dramatic. But if his diagnosis is as persuasive, as radical next to contemporary formulations of our bereavement as it sounds, it's because it is also practical. It admits a solution. "Broader and deeper we must write our annals," is what he will propose there at the close of his introductory essay. We must expand our history beyond specist, human terms. The irony, I know, is that he proposes to do this by human means: writing. But the irony only demonstrates that for Emerson the way out of the problem was by adding to the problem. The solution was to write not just from History but from *natural* history, to broaden the annals of Love, Manners, Character. Intellect, which he would write, as he discloses in his essay of that name, as the "natural history of the intellect." Prudence, "the Natural History of the soul." The Over-Soul, "natural history of man." It is unexpected, perhaps, because rarely remarked upon, but Emerson's own introductory essay describes what his *Essays* will be about. At first sight, however, and especially for Americans, the essays have a charm independent of their subjects: you have known, have owned them all your life. *A foolish consistency. The less government we have.* The famous epigrams all but connect you physically to the page, though when I first saw them the effect was conveniently heightened. It was a secondhand copy and they were already marked.

I still have that book. Its initial owner is identified on the flyleaf as a senior in the class of 1902 at Galesburg High School in Illinois. And to judge from the pages she has marked, the high school seniors of those days must have read every one of the twenty essays. There, located by her pencil, is the Emerson in our bones, the one who warned that imitation is suicide—

But do your thing, and I shall know you.

Yes, do your *thing*. That is exactly what he wrote in "Self-Reliance" as it appeared in the original, 1841 edition of the first series of twelve essays. A second series, consisting of eight new essays plus the lecture "New England Reformers," appeared in 1844. Three years later a combined edition was issued. By then Emerson had revised his words from "do your thing" to "do your work" (which is the formulation as you see it today in the Library of America's edition). No matter, it was still the same advice. And his original words went somehow free on their own—in reprints or in pirated editions; perhaps in certain editions they were restored—because there they are in my secondhand copy, unaltered, and carefully marked by that high school senior in Illinois. So who is this Emerson she hasn't marked?

The individual is always mistaken.

Do your thing, the individual is always mistaken? What random noise is that? Whatever else, it is not the signal that conjured up rugged self-interest.

All along, I see, the secret has been that the *Essays* are a single book. Editors have devised selections instead, because some of their favorite Emerson wouldn't otherwise be included (the essay "Fate," in particular, or two of my own favorites, "The Method of Nature" and "The Fugitive Slave Law Address"). And readers, being told that Emerson relied on his journals for material, have assumed the essays were cut-and-paste anyway, so rearranging them won't hurt. But composition does leave its clues. That word "light" in the first paragraph of "Self-Reliance" follows directly from the word "light" in the last sentence of "History," though when the essays aren't presented in order how could anyone know? Just as "History" introduces the problem, so "Self-Reliance" is the first step in a course of re-perception that aims at art and poetry (the essays "Art" and "The Poet"), then returns along the arc of experience and behavior to meet in the final essay the issues raised back at the outset by "History." It is the kind of design only passion can sustain. And the object of the passion is so forthright and ambitious I might have passed it by as transcendentalism. Nothing less, insists Emerson, than the "creation of man and nature" is at stake.

The trouble, of course, is nature. Whenever a nineteenth-century American starts in about nature I begin to feel left out. To tell the truth, I feel betrayed. What am I supposed to do with wisdom from a writer who could always wander out alone in the woods to recompose his infinitude? At *Whim*, too, because Ralph Waldo Emerson owned that woods. Any woods I could have entered at whim is long since sold or given away, and everybody knows we are thoroughly implicated in the fate of the rest, that every stick is hostage to industries unaccountable to law or reason, let alone love. Maybe it's time to admit that Emerson is hopelessly quaint for having believed otherwise, for not having known as we know that there isn't any uncorrupt text in nature, no there out there by which to renew our suspiciously human discourse. Except, surprise of his *Essays*, Emerson knew that, too.

> We fancy that we are strangers, and not so intimately domesticated in the planet as the wild man, and the wild beast and bird. But the exclusion reaches them also. . . . Fox and woodchuck, hawk and snipe, and bittern, when nearly seen, have no more root in the deep world than man, and are just such superficial tenants of the globe. Then the new molecular philosophy shows astronomical interspaces betwixt atom and atom, shows that the world is all outside: it has no inside.

Someone who knew the world had no inside would be only mildly shocked, possibly not as shocked as Einstein was, by quantum duplicity.

You would think, however, he might have been depressed. The idea had been to use nature to correct history and now nature, too, was shown to be historical. But Emerson was an Emersonian, and this must be the sort of resolution that made him one: instead of taking nature's state as a cause for despair he would have us seize it as a means. If hawk and snipe, fern and asteroid, are likewise caught in human observations, then the way forward for everybody is still to press on all sides against those observations. Even the universe began (really, these are his words) in a *mere push*. Emerson's insight, probably his necessary insight as a writer, was that he could hitch the wagon of his essays to the Mere Push, seize it as the principle to organize the plenum in his journals. You can see this most clearly in an essay that turns against itself and shoves off from a single well-placed *but*, the way "Nature" does. (In fact, the essay "Nature" turns—tropes—against romanticized nature and Emerson's earlier book *Nature* as well.) But every essay makes in structure this same Emersonian point: it is natural to push back to get ahead.

It is natural in language, too, and with the *Essays* in hand nobody has to go to the journals or biography to prove that Emerson thought a writer works in resistance to language. Language, he says in "The Poet," is a "tomb of the muses"—and we thought we were stern to call it just a prison house. "Every thought is also a prison," he said next, beating us to that one, too. A grim assessment, perhaps, but if you were the first Emersonian it was grim only on one side. The other side was liberation, the joyful rush of freedom ("as if we grew to worlds," he observed in "Fate") which draws the human mind out after it whenever the walls are shivered by a new definition or breached by a trope.

There were critics in the early twentieth century who were anxious to bury Emerson's reputation in a category they called, derisively, "the genteel tradition." They got that phrase from a hostile Santayana. But it could hardly be genteel in Emerson's lifetime—it would be suspect in pious circles even now—to open your remarks on love with the confession that each of its joys ripens into a new want; to identify the supreme Being as "the supreme Critic"; to acknowledge that friendship, like the immortality of the soul, is too good to be believed; or to proclaim in ecstasies of redefinition that our creeds are "a disease of the intellect," our educational system "a system of despair," society "a hospital of incurables," and the poet the only doctor, the "only teller of news."

How could you keep such ecstasies to yourself? By canal boat, steamer, stagecoach, railroad, sleigh, the former minister arrived to deliver his news in towns and cities throughout the Northeast and Middle West. *Emerson lectures tonight. Go to Babcock's Hall*, said the sign at the Rock Island skating rink. *There will be no skating.* Three times he crossed the frozen Mississippi on foot. At Galena, his hosts arranged a sleigh ride on the frozen river to show him the lead mines; the temperature was 22 below zero and that night at the lecture he could barely speak. He survived a hotel fire at Niagara and a boiler explosion on Lake Erie. He gave seventy-seven lectures in 1865 and eighty in 1867, by which time he was sixty-four years old.

In the later twentieth century there were also critics who, in order to lift the stigma of the "genteel tradition" and portray Emerson as an uncompromising theorist, minimized his intention to instruct and inspire. But who could seriously doubt, given his grueling itineraries, that he meant to infuse the public with his discoveries, that the lessons he applied to language he also applied to life? The natural measure of character, he announced to a country that thought anything but, is resistance. "Acquiescence in the establishment," in case they still weren't getting it, is a sign of "infirm faith" instead.

Those exact words are in his essay "Character," but the good news was proclaimed throughout the *Essays*, sometimes in ways we no longer recognize. I always tried to ignore his *thees* and *thous*, for instance, especially the ones in "The Poet" and "Experience." But when Emerson was a minister he rarely used those terms, and an audience alert to the Quaker example would have appreciated the allusion when he chose to use them now, whether in lectures or on the page. The familiar *thee* and *thou* had been historically appropriate to use with intimates—friends, family, servants—but never with one's social superiors, who were always to be addressed as *you*. The forms *thee* and *thou* were thus adopted by the early Quakers to demonstrate that there *were* no social superiors: everyone equal, everyone a thee or thou. In England, Quakers were sent to prison when they refused to say *you* to the magistrates. So when Emerson addresses you as a poet or a scholar—

the universe holds thee dear

he isn't indulging in pulpit unction or poesy. He is insisting on the profoundest democracy, insisting, further, that even in a democracy you should be free.

Good news like that might explain all by itself why Emerson electrified generations of Americans, not only my high school senior in Galesburg, Illinois, but Whitman before her. Yet it takes more than news to explain why the *Essays* themselves were so widely loved, why young readers as unalike as Robert Frost and Gertrude Stein were alike in forming a lasting regard for the very words. The something more, of course, is style. "Emerson really had passion; he wrote it," said Stein. "Emerson had the noblest least egotistical of styles," said Frost. And knowing I agree, agree with both, warns me against trying to characterize that style in anything so partial as a sentence. Try as we can and, still, we are painting the lightning with charcoal.

Emerson made this mistake himself. In a letter to Carlyle he characterized his own style as lapidary—no, what he actually wrote was that he had a "formidable tendency to the lapidary style." I think you can almost hear his mordant Yankee tongue. But the editors of his early lectures refer without irony now to Emerson's "lapidary style," and William Gass, too, has repeated in a highly regarded essay that

Emerson has a "lapidary style" that is "intolerant of qualification, reservation, convolution." No wonder writers learn to guard tongue and letter on the subject of their styles. Because all I need to do with Emerson is turn the page, turn for example to the last sentence of the last essay, "Nominalist and Realist," to see a sentence qualified and convoluted enough to enact its own reservedly insolent (what an ending) ending.

Here is that sentence as you would find it if you had the essays conveniently at hand. Emerson has just summarized his argument with the two philosophers, the nominalist and the realist, of the essay's title. "Could they but once understand," he concludes, "that I loved to know they existed, and heartily wished them Godspeed, yet, out of my poverty of life and thought, had no word or welcome for them when they came to see me, and could well consent to their living in Oregon, for any claim I felt on them, it would be a great satisfaction."

It's a sentence worthy of Gass himself. So did Gass ever read the essay, or read it to the end? Because earlier in the same essay, I admit, you can indeed find the lapidary tendency he had in mind.

> All things show us, that on every side we are very near to the best. It
> seems not worth while to execute with too much pains some one intel-
> lectual, or aesthetical, or civil feat, when presently the dream will
> scatter, and we shall burst into universal power. The reason of idleness
> and of crime is the deferring of our hopes.

The sentences don't even touch. The one in the middle isn't really complicated and the two on either side want to be epigrams. So we could call them lapidary and express our condescending regret. Or we could change the analogy and call them "quantized" instead, for isn't it true that reality deep down is not continuous but discrete? That things happen not *in* quanta but *between*—in transition, interaction, event? Call the style quantized and at once it is Emerson's genius that he doesn't bully his way into the space between his sentences as some writers would. He leaves that space open to event, open to you until, reading, *you* are the transition, you the italics between.

> All things show us, that on every side we are very near to the best. *Thus* it seems not worth while to execute with too much pains some one intellectual, or aesthetical, or civil feat, when presently the dream will scatter, and we shall burst into universal power. *And yet* the reason of idleness and of crime is the deferring of our hopes.

Nobody is going to believe Emerson had figured out quantum mechanics. It is not so hard to believe, however, that the writer who pictured the planet in space, who was determined to write a more natural history, had decided along the way to suffer no man, no custom, and no single sentence, either, to bereave you of your infinitude. "The most interesting writing," he once remarked, "is that which does not quite satisfy the reader." Put that deference into practice and the effect is to make the individual reader all the more necessary—an otherwise unlikely experience that suggests to me how Emerson's *Essays* might indeed provide generations of readers with alternative hope, almost a salvation, from the bereavement he himself feared from already settled discourse.

It also suggests why the isolated epigram won't yield a true feeling of what it's like to read Emerson. "People wish to be settled," he acknowledged. "Only as far as they are unsettled is there any hope for them." You are not sufficiently unsettled in a single sentence. It takes a combination of sentences, a paragraph from "Self-Reliance" or "Compensation"—*any* paragraph from "Circles" or "Experience"—to feel widely unsettled and, to the extent you have yet to settle things, hopeful, before you know you've been up to anything as embarrassing as hope.

I have heard people say, as if to account for not reading him, that no one in America writes prose like Emerson anymore. They are missing the point of what his *Essays* are. Emerson wanted to be a poet; he is always telling us that. But what he was bound to discover as he tried to write a broader, more natural text, was that poetry has its physics, too; that a change in scale requires a change in form. In writing, your style will depend on your frame of composition, and Emerson's frame would be—not the line made up of metrical feet, not even the sentence made up of words. It was the paragraph made up of sentence sounds. To me, it makes perfect sense that it was Frost, born in 1874, who discovered "sentence sounds" and Stein, born in 1874, who discovered that "a sentence is not emotional a paragraph is." Unalike as they were, they were alike from a country that grew up reading Emerson. And different as their examples are, the one's stanzaic sentences and the other's sentency stanzas are testimony to the same sun: after Emerson, the emotional paragraph of sentence sounds would frame the argument of the most oddly American poetry. *Emerson*: "though I would make it kind, I would make it true." *Whitman*: "Make it plain." *Pound*: "Make it new." *Ashbery*: "Make it sweet again!" In this way there is no book, not even *Leaves of Grass*, that is closer to the source of our poetry than Emerson's *Essays*. For American poetry, this prose is home.

The question is, so what? It's an old trick when somebody tells you that *x* work of genius has such style you can overlook its ideas and just love it for the poetry, as if we all had to like Pope or Pound. The question

154

always is, so what? To his credit, I think Emerson forced the issue himself, or why else did he append the lecture "New England Reformers" forever to the end of the *Essays*? Suspecting that organized reform would prove to be only another usage, he had opted out of the communal experiment at Brook Farm. But his reluctance to get involved, the refusal to relinquish his infinitude—wasn't it all just self-delusion on a grand scale? A rejection of adult responsibility?

Not if you are Emerson. In the long run, though I'm glad to know he welcomed John Brown to his home in Concord, sent money for the defense of Kansas, and even campaigned for a Free-Soil candidate for Congress, it is exactly his stubbornness about infinitude that gives his *Essays* their persistent moral proximity. After all, in the years since *Apollo* 8 brought back its famous photograph we have suffered the most fantastic discourse and usage to reassert themselves with no more embarrassment than if the world had been at last proved flat. Yet still it waxes, wanes, above the horizon of the moon. And once you have truly pictured it, how London spins no less than Concord does, then if you are Emerson you will have no use for usage that would pauper the life of perception anywhere on its curved surface. "The Jerseys," he said (he meant New Jersey, of course), "were handsome ground enough for Washington to tread." As Emerson, you would want your readers to be released from the colonial melancholy of those who are forced to value what exists only elsewhere: in London or Paris; in paradise or on other planets; in movies, public opinion, or on TV. "A popular novel, a theatre, or a ball-room," he wrote, "makes us feel that we are paupers in the alms-house of this world, without dignity, without skill, or industry."

Two centuries after the Revolution, and the man's anticolonialist integrity is still astonishing—especially to the Americans. But then, nothing seems less certain in a talk-show culture than independent perception.

> The individual is always mistaken.

Yet what looks like a recipe for despair can be turned, following Emerson, to a prescription for courage. If the individual were not mistaken, the universe would hardly have need of you, or me, or the millions. One would have been enough. In an article for the *Dial* he made it explicit: "A new perception, the smallest new activity given to the perceptive power, is a victory won to the living universe from chaos and old night." And we who have seen how discourse alters nature itself, seen the evidence thick in our bays and rivers and flesh, can easily wonder if this founding father of American literature was not just transcendentalist, but right. For the sake of nature alone, discourse and usage too must admit ecology, be open to evolutionary mistake. Then the universe does hold you dear: dear because you're expensive—it took twelve billion years of murder and evolution simply to get you here—and because your mistaken perceptions are precious among its means.

> Thou art sick, but shalt not be worse, and the universe, which holds thee dear, shall be the better.

Nothing less, I remember, than the creation of man and nature was at stake.

People, especially literary people, frequently like to say we live in a late time, though we are the ones who see more of creation and more of its problems than any generation before. If we make it into space, the sheer organization of it is bound to compromise the free movement and perception of the individuals who go; and if we get to stay on Earth the sheer pollution of it is bound to compromise the movement and perception of the individuals who remain. Would Emerson still contend, as he did in his first great address, "The American Scholar," that it is mischief to believe the world was finished a long time ago, that we who can perceive in more wavelengths than any men and women in history are only latecomers? "Suffice it for the joy of the universe," is what he does say in his *Essays*, "that we have not arrived at a wall, but at interminable oceans."

It's true they have taken our forests and prairies, and I hardly have the sky anymore. Except here in Emerson's essays I do. Here is the nature they cannot take away. Here we arrive at no wall, our infinitude ready as a matter of right at whim, and—could he mean what he really just said?—the happiness of the universe depends on us.

INTRODUCTION TO EMERSON'S

ESSAYS: FIRST AND SECOND SERIES,

VINTAGE / LIBRARY OF AMERICA, 1990

THE PROPHETIC ASHBERY

REMARKS ON ASHBERY

In 1960, during the ten years John Ashbery was living in France, there appeared in the United States a thirty-five-cent French thriller called *Murder in Montmartre*. The translator, having been paid by Dell Publishing Company to add some racy passages for the American market, signed himself Jonas Berry. But if you take a moment to pronounce the name John Ashbery as it might sound in French, you'll have a reasonable clue as to who got the paycheck.

Actually, "Jonas Berry" was not the only translator. Before its publication, his version of the thriller had to be overhauled by one Lawrence G. Blochman. The reason, Mr. Blochman has explained since, was simple. While some translators have trouble with the original French, this Jonas Berry "just couldn't write English."

Mr. Blochman wasn't the first, and he isn't going to be the last to be mystified by John Ashbery's version of the English language. Ashbery's is our language and yet it is not our language—or, more appropriately, it is analogous to our language. For the style of a great poet, according to the great poet Wallace Stevens with whom Ashbery is often linked, is "analogous to the speech common to his time and place and yet not that common speech." Poetry, wrote Stevens, is almost incredibly one of the effects of such an analogy. Mr. Blochman may have been mystified, but the Ashbery mystery has somehow goaded and enlightened its readers and imitators ever since. When its creator returned briefly to the United States in 1963 he returned to an audience already won over in his absence.

I can provide something closer to a "You Are There" re-creation of the moment if I rely on the words of someone who *was* there for that homecoming and later grew up to be an English professor. "I first heard Ashbery read his poetry," writes Professor Fred Moramarco, "in the Summer of 1963 at Julian Beck's and Judith Malina's Living Theatre on Twelfth Street in Manhattan, and it seemed to me at the time that almost every young poet in New York was crammed into the small space of the theater to see and hear this man who had radically altered the nature of their craft with the several strokes of a single book—*The Tennis Court Oath*." That book, which has become known as its author's attempt to take the language apart piece by piece, was Ashbery's second major book. His first, *Some Trees*, was selected by W. H. Auden as the winner of the Yale Series of Younger Poets contest in 1955. His latest, *Self-Portrait in a Convex Mirror*, earned in 1976 a configuration of honors usually reserved for racehorses—a kind of literary Triple Crown made up of the National Book Critics Circle Award, the National Book Award, and the Pulitzer Prize.

If *The Tennis Court Oath* took the language apart, the books that followed have been putting it back together in a style so personal it is recognizable at once, no matter where you break into it. It is called simply "Ashbery," the way when you turn on the radio in the middle of a sonata you say, "Oh, Brahms," or "Oh, Ives."

How did this much-honored style come about? It is a favorite project of critics to rush back and forth tracking down a poet's sources, a literary version of what Alex Haley did in *Roots*. So we could look for Ashbery's sources by retracing his steps in France, before his permanent return to the United States. Or we could look for them by sorting through his career as an art critic. His book *The Double Dream of Spring* shares its title with a painting by de Chirico, an artist Ashbery much admires.

But a style's sources are only footnotes to its most important function: its effect. I remember, for example, my surprise when I learned the genealogy of the sonnet, and its familiar rhythm, as in Shakespeare's "Shall I compare thee to a summer's day?" Rather than springing indigenous from English soil, the sonnet had to be imported. Wyatt imported it from Italy, and Surrey added the English polish. What sounds to us so English, in retrospect, sounded curious to Surrey's contemporaries; or, as Stevens would put it, analogous to their speech and yet not that speech. Whatever its ingredients—and some of them are unquestionably imported—the Ashbery version of our own speech has come to sound as American to many ears as "Shall I compare thee to a summer's day?" sounds English.

Ashbery's is a complicated style, full of logical sideswipes, and organized according to an individual perception swamped by the cultural richness of our time. On the one hand, then, the style is a self-portrait. On the other, it's a measure of our time. Because an accurate self-portrait, as the poem "Self-Portrait in a Convex Mirror" finally tells us, can be realized only on the supporting easel of its society.

For John Ashbery, the first supporting easel stood right here. The self-portrait began when he was born, July 28, 1927, in Rochester General Hospital and brought home shortly thereafter to his grandparents' house at number 69 Dartmouth Street—when that street still had its elms. As a boy, his time was divided between the elm-shaded street in town and the family farm near Sodus. A trip out the Lake Road toward

Sodus Point, and a right turn at Maple Avenue, will bring you to the white clapboard farmhouse. A sign in front still says "Ashbery Farm."

In an interview the poet has remarked, "I go back to my earliest impressions a great deal when writing poetry." Considering where he grew up, it's not much of a surprise to discover that one of those earliest impressions was snow. "This poem," he wrote in a much-quoted work, "is in the form of falling snow."

The boy's upstate easel, however, provided more than the relentless winters from which to fashion a self-portrait. On Barrington Street is Public School No. 23, where he went to kindergarten and first grade. On Monroe Avenue is a branch of, yes, the Rochester Public Library, where he went to read. On University Avenue is the Memorial Art Gallery where he first decided to be, not a poet but a painter. And on East Main Street is Sibley's, where the judges of the first annual Scholastic Art contest awarded honorable mention to a painting by John Lawrence Ashbery, age fifteen. The easel that supports the mature poet's style has enlarged a great deal since then. But the "earliest impressions" are there at the center.

In the long run, to paraphrase a line from Ashbery's first book, a great style is its own defense. A great style brings with it an attitude toward life. And if the style is somehow appropriate to its times, then the attitude it brings can enrich the rest of us. The critic I. A. Richards must have had such an effect in mind as he wrote the following. "When the required attitude has been long needed, where its coming is unforeseen and the manner in which it is brought about complicated and inexplicable, where we know no more than that formerly we were unready and that now we are ready for life in some particular phase, the feeling which results may be intense."

Unforeseen and inexplicable the Ashbery style is. But it is a style that honors its society and this community, honors the easel on which it is held. Because it honors us, it is fitting that we in return honor the man who made it.

DELIVERED AT THE PRESENTATION TO JOHN
ASHBERY OF THE 21ST ANNUAL LITERARY AWARD,
FRIENDS OF THE ROCHESTER PUBLIC LIBRARY,
ROCHESTER, NEW YORK, APRIL 22, 1977

THE PROPHETIC ASHBERY

We are used to hearing of poets so private they speak for all of us. We are not used to hearing that John Ashbery is among them. Anyone who has ever been baffled by Ashbery's work will understand the temptation to conclude that here is a poet so private he is truly private, so difficult he is truly inaccessible. But to arrive at that dead end is exasperating, if only because the reputation leads you to expect much more. Why shouldn't people expect access to a poetry so widely honored for what it is doing with their language? Why shouldn't they expect a poet, as Emerson promised, to apprise us "not of his wealth, but of the commonwealth"? Those are not retrograde or feeble expectations, and because I think they are powerfully met in the work of John Ashbery I would champion him not as our most private poet, but our most public one. The difficulty is that his poetry is *so* public, so accurately a picture of the world we live in, that it scarcely resembles anything we've ever known. Just so, the present is indeed a world none of us has ever known, because the words to describe it can be put together only after the fact. When the poet does put them together the combination comes as a shock. One may at first regard the combination as hermetically private. Only gradually do we realize that it describes the public world we were living in just moments ago, that some prophet has arrived with news of the commonwealth.

I suppose *prophet* sounds as though I'm claiming a generous role for the poet when anyone ought to know the audience for poetry is limited first in size and second in its willingness to suspend, not disbelief but irony. I suppose also that readers of poetry are even more disaffected than most when it comes to the commonwealth. They are not an audience to whom a poet as savvy as John Ashbery would innocently address Emersonian prophecies. True enough, but let me offer a proposition that shouldn't be surprising: the audience that reads the poetry is not always the one for which the poet writes. The events that produce a poet are many and various, but one of them is probably not his first contact with an English professor or first reading at the local poetry project. The audience he would love to reach is more likely "the fair-sheaved many" who don't give a hoot for poetry. It will include the father he could never please, the mother bewildered by her strange offspring, the younger brother who died at the age of nine. It is made up, in other words, of all the unreachable people, the ones who appear in Ashbery's "Melodic Trains" as figures on the station platform while the poet watches them from the standing train. Though he identifies them as "my brothers," it is precisely their remoteness that accounts for the plaintive tone in which he continues.

> If I were to get down now to stretch, take a few steps
>
> In the wearying and world-weary clouds of steam like great
> White apples, might I just through proximity and aping
> Of postures and attitudes communicate this concern of mine
> To them? That their jagged attitudes correspond to mine,
>
> That their beefing strikes answering silver bells within
> My own chest . . . ?

No, he could not communicate his concern, at least not in poetry. If they are reading at all, his brothers are probably occupied with the latest manual on how to get more out of life, and poetry will be far down the list of recommended exercises. One knows this, but it doesn't lessen the insistent wish to reach them. Instead, one dresses the wish in any number of disguises—ironic or even slapstick. In this way you can prophesy to your brothers all you want without fear of looking foolish before the worldly audience that comes to your readings. You release a little horse that "trots up with a letter in its mouth" or in Hollywood fashion direct a butler to enter "with a letter on a tray / Whose message is to change everything." The poetry audience laughs at the joke, but the regularity with which Ashbery returns to the device makes me believe, though he too is laughing, that he is hopefully serious about the prophecy's having arrived.

Arrival is not the same as being understood, however, and we are told that the former Quiz Kid was at first hurt by the baffled response to his work. By now he may enjoy being a mystery, having confirmed his suspicion that it's the mystery part of truth that makes it marketable. But why does he remain mysterious? There are two reasons, and the first is his style. By itself his style is so beguiling or outrageous, depending on your point of view, that the transfixed reader is powerless to get beyond it. The beguiled explain their condition by saying that Ashbery does not "work" or "mean" like other poetry. The outraged assert that it isn't poetry at all, or if it is then its essential ingredient must be obscurity. But no prophet sets out to be permanently obscure; where's the immortality in that? And no master stylist is after a result that fails to "work" its magic. With some effort, and some willingness too, I think we ought to be able to find his style out.

The second reason Ashbery remains mysterious is his choice of subjects, or, it would be better to say, his context. We are accustomed to pinched poetry, the kind whose context is one Incan rock, and we know how to deal with that. In Ashbery we encounter a poet who, as his friend Frank O'Hara wrote, "is always marrying the whole world." Readers who prefer their Incan rock may agree with the reviewer who complained of Ashbery that "you can't possibly quote anything 'out of context' since there is never a context." But every poet marks out his subject matter and it is not possible for him to write independent of that context. It is simply that the Ashbery context is so wide it takes a great deal of reading before you can visit its boundaries. Until then you may understandably feel that the signs along the way point in all directions and nowhere in particular.

Style and context do not occur separately in a poem, and the one is ultimately meaningful only as it is enfolded in the other. Much fool-ishness can be produced by trying to consider them as things apart. But this essay is not a poem and there's no alternative. I must try to untangle them, doing as little violence to their connections as possible, so when they are reunited we may have some idea of how they came to make a coherent whole in the first place. I am going to begin with context—the context of a poet who married the world.

Ashbery announced his engagement in the opening line of his first book: "We see us as we truly behave." The strictness and the generosity are in that "truly." The strictness is that we will not see us as we might have behaved or ought to behave. The generosity is that we are going on a tour of the world as it might look on "a day of general honesty," knowing there is nothing larger or more extraordinary. It will be a vast excursion, and we can expect the itinerary to be recalcitrant even as we follow it: "As laughing cadets say, 'In the evening / Everything has a schedule, if you can find out what it is.'"

One way to learn the schedule is to go along with it; in retrospect, it is easier to see what it was. If this sounds too spineless, think of it as a version of Keats's negative capability. It takes a strong constitution to live into the present so ruthlessly available to whatever is waiting there. And I don't think it exaggerates to say that Ashbery, of the poets I know, is most ruthlessly available to the present. In our time that present is largely to be found in the curricula of the city and its sophisticated outposts. Arguably, it could have been found there longer than this; yet we have grown up with a literature that would look energetically in almost any other direction—to the frontier, the sea, Walden, or to a room in Amherst—in order, as it claims, to front the essential facts of life. Though he started life on a farm in upstate New York, Ashbery has done his "fronting" in the great metropolis—New York, Paris, their suburbs—and a list of his cultural entanglements and cultured acquaintances would be staggering, many times longer than the lists of names he in fact included in the pages of *The Vermont Notebook*. Larry Rivers, Frank O'Hara, Willem de Kooning, Fairfield Porter, James Schuyler, Jane Freilicher, Kenneth Koch—just a few of those names are enough to stand for the enormous and timely experiences that were there to enlarge this poet's life. Nor are we star-struck if we insist on the importance of such a constellation. We are not star-struck to note that Mannerist painters Pontormo, Rosso, and Parmigianino, say, were all in Rome before the Sack of 1527, and that Rosso and Parmigianino worked there, side by side, for four years. It is important that they worked together, one with the other or one against the other, toward a timely style which, unclear as it may have been to them, is now timelessly clearer to us. In making my case I don't mean to suggest that the Hamptons today equals Rome before the Sack. But I would not insist on the differences either. So much as Ashbery moved in a timely world, just so much was he able to make that world available to us.

Just so much, as long as we remember that negative capability was to be our guide. "The mind / Is so hospitable, taking in everything / Like boarders," says the title poem from *Houseboat Days*. Wallace Stevens reports that his mind was similarly commodious, yet he was perhaps choosier than Ashbery when it came to which boarders to take in. Stevens, one remembers, proposed to "live in the world but outside of existing conceptions of it." Ashbery lives not only in the world, he seems to live by all conceptions of it simultaneously, regardless of how contradictory the lot may be. How else would it be possible to bring over into language the ripe complexity of us as we truly behave in this almost "terminally sophisticated" society? When you put his capacity for taking in boarders together with the timely milieus in which the man has moved the result is a brilliant, thus dense, mingling of attitudes and their languages. In the same way that all colors together appear to be no color so what looked to the reviewer like no context is instead many contexts. Or, to use another illustration, it is many contexts tangled into one like parts of a score, interesting in themselves perhaps, but best all at once.

> The conductor, a glass of water, permits all kinds
> Of wacky analogies to glance off him, and, circling outward,
> To bring in the night. Nothing is too "unimportant"
> Or too important, for that matter. The newspaper and the garbage
> Wrapped in it, the over, the under.

I hope I am not taken to mean that negative capability makes Ashbery timely, and headed for timelessness, because it prints out a rebus only for the painters, poets, and culturati who have been his friends. No, in the city one sees a great many real people, most of them strangers. They come and go as types; one sees their faces and hears their news, and "Nothing is too 'unimportant' / Or too important, for that matter." The papers are on the stands, the radio is plugged in, films arrive at the movie theater, and all are filled with suggestive abstractions. To the extent that the city includes the past it is alive with all the suggestions of our culture: "Rome where Francesco / Was at work during the Sack . . . / Vienna where the painting is today . . . / New York, where I am now, which is a logarithm / Of other cities." With your Keatsian apparatus, you can be as big as the city you live in. But, unless we think this must be a painless way to gain an empire, you can also be as small, as passion-strewn, as constantly slapped up or yanked down—in other words, at civil war. "Is not a man better than a town?" asked Emerson, implying that the two were different. The question could hardly occur to Ashbery: "Whatever the villagers / Are celebrating with less conviction is / The less you."

A good deal is said about the impenetrable solipsism of this poet who is so private he is truly private. It is said in exasperation and as an excuse to quit reading, and its best authority is the poet himself, who will tell us, as he does in *Three Poems*, that his "elaborate view" really comes from "looking inside." If he is so solipsistic how can he mean anything? But grant that Keats was right, that there is such a thing as negative capability, and you have begun to answer the question yourself. For if Keats was right then the elaborate landscape of the city and of the poet's timely entanglements in it may indeed be found, in their contrariness, by looking inside. At one time or another the mind will believe every squabbling part of itself, the poem mean everything it says. And thus the trick is turned. How can it be solipsism if he means everything?

> Everything is landscape:
> Perspectives of cliffs beaten by innumerable waves.
> More wheatfields than you can count, forests
> With disappearing paths, stone towers
> And finally and above all the great urban centers, with
> Their office buildings and populations, at the center of which
> We live our lives, made up of a great quantity of isolated instants
> So as to be lost at the heart of a multitude of things.

It has become a cliché to note that the quantity of information in the world has exploded while space has collapsed, and the cliché does not make it the less real. But to say we have turned into a global village is inaccurate. Global is a nod in the right direction but village is a bow to nostalgia. Our culture is nothing so simple or settled as a village. It is more of a stellar explosion caught in an earthly jar, a revolving explosion of needs and demands and diversions, and in the midst of this tumult we take our chances on daily life. *This* is the context of John Ashbery, because only in this reality can we see us as we "truly" behave. While he was living in Paris, Ashbery wrote in praise of Raymond Roussel a line that might have been written prospectively of himself: "It is no longer the imaginary world but the real one, and it is exploding around us like a fireworks factory in one last dazzling orgy of light and sound." To be aware of this context is an immense help to knowing the poems. For example, if a fireworks of attitudes competes for the same pen (or typewriter in this case) won't they comment on one another? Yes, they will, sometimes in the poem itself and sometimes from off-stage. So to have missed the context is also to miss this commentary—a commentary that provides some of the best moments, playful and rueful, that Ashbery can offer.

There are good precedents for such serious play, though probably more in English poetry than our own. I am thinking especially of the influence who peeps at us over two Ashbery titles ("The Picture of Little J. A. in a Prospect of Flowers" and "As One Put Drunk into the Packet-Boat"), and that is Andrew Marvell. Like Ashbery, Marvell saw a lot of the timely world and like Ashbery he seemed to find a single point of view impossible, not even desirable. The masterly example is "The Garden," and a masterly reading of it is the one by Joseph Summers in his book *The Heirs of Donne and Johnson*. What Summers says of the poem's extravagant first stanza strikes me as exactly right: "The outrageous suavity and the calculated rationality of the lines invite us to smile and warn us of extravagances to come. The poem is going to claim *everything* for a life of infinite leisure in the garden; but the ways in which it makes its claim reveal the urbanity of the poet who created this fictional voice, his recognition of values beyond those which he pretends to dismiss and those which he pretends exhaust all the pleasant and virtuous possibilities of human life." Of course I've quoted this remark at length because it applies so perfectly to Ashbery's poems as well. Consider the opening of "Definition of Blue," which has caused its share of trouble.

> The rise of capitalism parallels the advance of romanticism
> And the individual is dominant until the close of the nineteenth
>   century.

> In our own time, mass practices have sought to submerge the
>   personality
> By ignoring it, which has caused it instead to branch out in all
>   directions
> Far from the permanent tug that used to be its notion of "home."

Robert Pinsky writes in *The Situation of Poetry* that this opening is too funny for us "to take any subsequent idea quite seriously." If I read him right, he is disappointed because the poem therefore "fails to convince" us of the value that will be advanced in its lovely last lines. But we do not ask to be convinced of the argument in "The Garden." On the contrary, the outrageous suavity and calculated rationality of the lines invite us to smile and warn us of the extravagances to come. Like Marvell, Ashbery is eating his cake and having it too, being serious and having fun. To know the urbane context in which this is possible is to be let in on the seriousness, and the fun, ourselves.

If we have decided, then, to give up our *gravitas* and go along with the play, we will find it necessary to break free of the confines of a single poem. One attitude heckles another from poem to poem, or forgives it from collection to collection. You can trace this intermural effect in the recurrent appearance of the American garden suburb, whose beauty and boredom make for one of Ashbery's dearest subjects, much as the English pleasure garden was one of Marvell's. *A Nest of Ninnies*, the novel written in collaboration with James Schuyler, is about some nice people who live on Long Island, read Proust, go out for drinks at a Howard Johnson's, and escort their European guests on a tour of the Walt Whitman Shopping Plaza. Then there is "Farm Implements and Rutabagas in a Landscape," where the very form—the troubador's sestina—implies a satire on account of its content. The envoy ends roughly: "Popeye chuckled and scratched / His balls: it sure was pleasant to spend a day in the country." But the boorishness is smoothed out in the same collection by the graceful "Evening in the Country," though we can hear Mr. Offstage Attitude still sniping away in the wings. One has to read twice the last phrase in these lines: "things eventually take care of themselves / With rest and fresh air and a good view of things."

In "Pyrography" the theme hangs on. "At Bolinas / The houses doze and seem to wonder why . . . / Why be hanging on here?" Yet it is both more fun and more poignant if we can recognize in the dozing houses their allusive echo of "The One Thing That Can Save America." That earlier poem began by being fed up with the "overgrown suburbs, / Places of known civic pride, of civil obscurity," yet closed with an elegiac and mixed affirmation brought by another of those prophetic messages, this one telling of danger . . .

> and the mostly limited
> Steps that can be taken against danger
> Now and in the future, in cool yards,
> In quiet small houses in the country,
> Our country, in fenced areas, in cool shady streets.

Nostalgia, realism, goofiness, and even a shred of the American Dream —in Ashbery's suburbia they are all available at once.

There are more complicated examples of serious play in Ashbery than his approach-avoidance bout with the suburbs. Yet that gentle contest will serve as a manageable illustration of how one mixes the wit and the sadness, the transport and debunking, because the world is so contradictory there is no single attitude clean enough for living life straight through. It is not easy to keep many outlooks in the air at once, but it has been done. "I contain multitudes," said the Whitman who seems to have divided his time in Manhattan equally among going to the opera, drinking at Pfaff's, and stalking the trolleys. (It is not one's first impression of him, but in the context of the real city where he lived Whitman's statement suggests a certain savoir faire.) To repeat, the world is very much bigger now, in terms of all the information blazing into one man-sized neocortex. To contain multitudes—the fireworks of experience, language, and belief—must now require an even greater, more elastic savoir faire.

> Something strange is creeping across me.
> La Celestina has only to warble the first few bars
> Of "I Thought about You" or something mellow from
> *Amadigi di Gaula* for everything—a mint-condition can
> Of Rumford's Baking Powder, a celluloid earring, Speedy
> Gonzales, the latest from Helen Topping Miller's fertile
> Escritoire, a sheaf of suggestive pix on greige, deckle-edged
> Stock—to come clattering through the rainbow trellis
> Where Pistachio Avenue rams the 2300 block of Highland
> Fling Terrace.

That is only the beginning of Ashbery's "Daffy Duck in Hollywood," which contains more multitudes to come: the Fudds' garage, the Gadsden Purchase, the Princesse de Clèves and the Wallets; bocages, tanneries, and water meadows; London and St. Petersburg. We cannot reduce this to the still privilege we once expected from poetry. This is the exploded culture in which we truly behave, and it is no help to cry "No context!" because we can't find one small enough to suit us.

Here is no Incan rock but an avalanche, no still point in a turning world but the turning world itself, and it is exploding all around us like a fireworks factory in one last dazzling orgy of light and sound.

⌐¬

To fit the context of the turning world he lives in, Ashbery made the style we call "Ashbery." In fact, our having named it "Ashbery" has apparently released some readers from the worry of whether it is also English. In one fundamental way, of course, it isn't English at all—it is American. It represents our language in the sense Stevens meant when he said a poet's dialect was analogous to common speech and yet not that speech. A poet's dialect is our language gone a little screwy, and it is the screwy part that returns to us the odd things we ordinarily say and do, only they come back a little odder. That is why screwiness may signify "Prophet Speaking." On the other hand it may also signify a fake.

People in this country are notoriously leery of fakes, regardless of their being regularly taken in by them. And those of us who read poetry are no exception to the national virtue. One test many Americans use to identify fakery in a poet these days is the test of diction. If the suspect moves haltingly from word to word, if those words are tight little Anglo-Saxon islands, each one surfacing after obvious struggle in the depths, then the speaker is ipso facto cleared, his authenticity and our integrity proved. But if his words flow like the sea itself, if they alternately recede in demotic eddies and advance in Latinate swells, then we turn away from him, secure in knowing we met temptation and were not weak. For poetry this makes a curious test. Yet it was current long before its current proponents took it up. I haven't read Bronson Alcott's *Psyche* (not poems though surely meant to be poetic). Still, I can sympathize with the abashed Alcott who sent his manuscript to Emerson and received in return the following shalts and shalt nots, via the U.S. mail. "To the prophetic tone belongs simplicity," chided Emerson, "not variety, not taste, not criticism. As a book of practical holiness, this seems to me not effective. This is fanciful, playful, ambitious, has a periphrastic style & masquerades in the language of scripture.... The prophet should speak a clear discourse straight home to the conscience in the language of earnest conversation." Fanciful, playful, ambitious, periphrastic—what an indictment. And not one count on which we could acquit John Ashbery.

Even his titles are playful, periphrastic, a masquerade (taking "As One Put Drunk in the Packet-Boat" from an index of first lines is hardly straight home to the conscience), and they deserve their fraction of credit for whatever confusion the Ashbery style stirs up. His titles are like the hand that looms forward in Parmigianino's self-portrait, each "thrust at the viewer / And swerving easily away, as though to protect / What it advertises." The title "Self-Portrait in a Convex Mirror" is a good example in itself, because it is frequently read as if Emerson's commandment held, as if it had been written straight home to the conscience. Here is the painter's self-portrait, here is the poet looking at the self-portrait, and here as a result must be the poet's self-portrait. The whole poem is frequently referred to now as "Self-Portrait," revealing our bias toward the private. Unquestionably, that is one way to read it. What troubles me is that we should fasten doggedly on the seeming straightforwardness of a single title and poem in the midst of a canon we know is everywhere else artful and foxy. We can hardly fail to recognize the hint, there in the first four lines, that things are being both protected and advertised. Yet we are content to swerve away with the hand thrust toward us—"Self-Portrait"—while leaving the protected remainder of the title very much alone. What does it signify, "in a Convex Mirror?"

Since there is no answer that is not manifold and suspect, I may as well brave it and offer an answer of my own. On the poem's evidence I take the convex mirror to stand for at least three things beyond the physical object it actually is. One is the imagination, the convex brain, the thing called negative capability: "And the vase is always full / Because there's only just so much room / And it accommodates everything." Two is the city, especially New York, which provides the imagination with its raw material: "We have seen the city; it is the gibbous / Mirrored eye of an insect. All things happen / On its balcony and are resumed within." And three, the aspect I want to focus on now, is the poet's style—for how else does an artist make himself an example if not in his style? And what better way for Ashbery to describe his own style than by reference to this Mannerist painter whose work provides in many ways a tantalizing parallel to his own?

> The consonance of the High Renaissance
> Is present, though distorted by the mirror.
> What is novel is the extreme care in rendering
> The velleities of the rounded reflecting surface
> (It is the first mirror portrait),
> So that you could be fooled for a moment
> Before you realize the reflection
> Isn't yours.

Mannerism is almost a synonym for virtuosity, and, timid to the point of priggishness, we are apt to shun it as vulgar and inauthentic. But the idea of *maniera* in early art criticism implied almost the opposite. It was borrowed from the literature of manners where it was something to boast about. If you had *maniera* you had style. You had grace, sophistication, and savoir faire. So when it was applied to the work of Parmigianino, say, it originally meant much the same thing. Here was grace, here was elegance, here was the stylish style. So stylish was his style that Parmigianino eventually became a verb, *imparmiginare*, "to submerge expression of the subject in elegance and delicacy." I can't make a verb equally sonorous from "Ashbery," but the meaning of *imparmiginare* suggests the parallels being dangled before us. To submerge the subject in an elegance that knows just where and how far it is breaking the rules—this is not the mannerism we speak of when we want to say someone is affected. This is Mannerism given its due capital, the style of the savoir faire.

Getting back to poetry, there is a pleasing symmetry to be enjoyed from learning that the same times that produced Mannerism in painting would also produce it in poetry: the same times, if for English we allow a cultural lag sufficient to include the author of "To His Coy Mistress." In his book on Renaissance style Wylie Sypher makes a nice case for such a lag and for the similarities at either end of it. Of the "Coy Mistress," he writes, "Marvell's sharp but unsustained attack— brilliant, sensitive, private—is like the loose and surprising adjustment and counter-adjustment of figure to figure in Parmigianino's paintings, with their evidence of subjective stress." Once again, we can replace the name Marvell with the name Ashbery and the critic's sentence will still make perfect sense. So it is all the more satisfying to reflect that the prize-winning *Self-Portrait in a Convex Mirror* opens with just this Marvell peeping over its first title ("As One Put Drunk . . .") and just this Parmigianino reflected in its last. The idea of guilt by association is something of an outrage (though less outrageous, one sees, in criticism), and it would be a tenacious conspiracy that could span centuries to include Ashbery, Marvell, and Parmigianino. But the choice of titles was Ashbery's, not ours, and one has as evidence against him his own remark about the titles of Tanguy's paintings: "Yet the fact that most of them are titled implies that a choice has been made, and the purpose of this choice is to extend the range of the picture's meaning by slanting it in a certain direction."

In poetry there are a number of rhetorical figures that might be stretched and exaggerated to make a cognate of the Mannerist's stylish style. Not surprisingly, they are the figures described by Longinus in his treatise on the sublime. Not surprising, because only so far as these figures are reckless with the sublime will they display a subjective stress analogous to the self-consciousness of Mannerism—much as Mannerism betrayed its own stress by recklessness with the High Renaissance. Longinus named these figures with some big words, and because it is more convenient in discourse to name a thing than to describe it over and over I am going to introduce them by their names and perpetuate the error, in a way.

1. First is *periphrasis*, who himself likes to name things. But periphrasis is never able to land on a name outright. Instead, he goes at it around Robin Hood's barn, and arriving at one haystack of the thing he names *that*. Therefore, periphrasis is especially good at naming unnameable things, like attitudes.

a kind of fence-sitting
Raised to the level of an esthetic ideal.

2. Periphrasis has a cousin, *apophasis*, who names things by unnaming them. Apophasis is like Peter being interrogated, his denials prove a great deal.

the soul is not a soul

3. Third is that rogue, *paranomasia*, who likes to make fun of the things he names. We know him most often as pun but he is agile in a variety of circumstances.

You walk five feet along the shore, and you duck
As a common heresy sweeps over.

4. Another prankster is *polyptoton*. He likes to keep us in the dark as to their pronouns, so you cannot be sure if she will be doing the talking let alone what tense I might have been in.

But I was trying to tell you about a strange thing
That happened to me, but this is no way to tell about it . . .
And one is left sitting in the yard . . .
As though it would always happen in some way
And meanwhile since we are all advancing
It is sure to come about in spite of everything
On a Sunday, where you are left sitting
In the shade.

5. *Hyperbole* is a show-off. He more than names, he swaggers, and therefore he sometimes gets mixed up. Longinus thought the better hyperboles would conceal themselves but what fun is it getting all dressed up if you can't go to town?

> you my friend
> Who saved me from the mill pond of chill doubt
> As to my own viability, and from the proud village
> Of bourgeois comfort and despair, the mirrored spectacles of grief.

6. But the real virtuouso is *hyperbaton*, mad for taking chances—the most reckless of them all. Hyperbaton will mix words that should never be mixed, like someone who invites rival lovers to the same party just to watch the sparks fly. Even more exhilarating, he will climb a great slide of words and let go, sure as gravity that chance will bring him out to truth at the bottom.

> They all came, some wore sentiments
> Emblazoned on T-shirts, proclaiming the lateness
> Of the hour, and indeed the sun slanted its rays
> Through branches of Norfolk Island pine as though
> Politely clearing its throat, and all ideas settled
> In a fuzz of dust under the trees when it's drizzling:
> The endless games of Scrabble, the boosters,
> The celebrated omelette au Cantal, and through it
> The roar of time plunging unchecked through the sluices
> Of the days, dragging every sexual moment of it
> Past the lenses: the end of something.

His recklessness makes hyperbaton a public danger. Longinus says, "He carries his audience with him to share in the dangers of his long inversions." But like other public dangers he is powerfully convincing, since his conclusions seem not thought up but passionately wrung from him, almost against his will.

In addition to these six, there are other figures that lack such elegant and accurate names. Longinus dealt with one of them, *diction*, but the chapters in which he discussed it are largely lost so we will have to continue on our own.

7. *Diction* can be a dandy or a thug, a matron or an ingenue, depending on how it's dressed. Diction is adept with clichés and can arrange them to put out a stinging accuracy.

> We hold these truths to be self-evident:
> That ostracism, both political and moral, has
> Its place in the twentieth-century scheme of things.

8. *Irony* is getting to be a brat. She may be forthright as satire or burlesque, but since she is often timid in the nature of brats, she also likes to sow her discord on the sly. One of her amusements is to spoof the critics, including perhaps Harold Bloom (as in "The Other Tradition") or even Horace ("And *Ut Pictura Poesis* Is Her Name"). Nor is irony above biting the hand that writes her, as when she prompts Daffy Duck in Hollywood to despair of his own avian self-portrait in a convex mirror.

> I scarce dare approach me mug's attenuated
> Reflection in yon hubcap.

9. *Surrealism* is an ingenious decorator, forever rearranging the furniture. She is also fed up with being thought French. She knows her Emerson ("Bare lists of words are found suggestive, to an imaginative and excited mind") and can squeeze an analogy out of the barest list. She had a field day in *The Vermont Notebook* but often gets stuck in the house where she understandably insists on the sad variety of woe.

> And a sigh heaves from all the small things on earth,
> The books, the papers, the old garters and union-suit buttons
> Kept in a white cardboard box somewhere.

Last will come *prophecy*, but before we can consider him or her without interruption we need to take time out so those two laggards, *parergon* and *paralipomenon*, can make their appearance.

10. *Parergon* likes to enter from offstage, or even speak offstage, when you least expect it—as if to imply that it's by no means settled who are the principals and who the walk-ons in the play. Being odd or ornamental enough to attract attention, parergon also likes to turn up in unlikely locations so you will question where the real action is taking place.

> A few black smudges
> On the outer boulevards, like squashed midges
> And the truth becomes a hole, something one has always known,
> A heaviness in the trees, and no one can say
> Where it comes from, or how long it will stay—

11. *Paralipomenon* has never been easy to keep track of, either, and is continually being neglected or overlooked. When recovered as a supplement, however, paralipomenon gets its revenge, because the

whole rest of the text is now characterized as much by what is left out as by what is included. Paralipomenon may come at the beginning, middle, or end, but the revenge is sweetest when it comes as an afterthought.

> My wife
> Thinks I'm in Oslo—Oslo, France, that is.

12. Now on to *prophecy*, who enters sometimes as parergon or paralipomenon, but also appears in so many other shapes that we will have to extend her gender, Tiresias fashion. She and he are almost a summary of the other figures, but a summary never quite in the picture, and they are therefore sad with yearning. No matter how deeply she may yearn to influence the action, he knows they must remain forever outside that action, enigmatic only, like the prophetic figures who appear in the backgrounds of *The Marriage of St. Catherine* and the *Madonna of the Long Neck*—both by Parmigianino.

> Wait by this
> Mistletoe bush and you will get the feeling of really
> Being out of the world and with it.

So, while prophecy never gives up the attempt, his or her voice arrives oddly anomalous to its source or object, like those letters on trays or fools shouting into the night.

> words like disjointed beaches
> Brown under the advancing signs of the air.

By introducing these dozen figures in such an offhand manner, I don't mean to imply that we should take them lightly. When they are brought into play it is usually because there is serious work for them to do. The elegance of combining many refined figures, and of stretching each in a way that would shiver the woodlots in Concord, is that it makes possible in poetry a world very much like the one in which the poet lives—a world where no attitude can hide from another but all are revealed and commented on at once. It is largely the abundance of these dozen figures that makes the Ashbery style exasperating to some readers and makes them fear they are being taken in. But when the playful figures are deployed for serious work, and when an abundance of them appear in a single poem, then that may be a serious poem indeed. One would not like to see this indulgence extended to poets across the board. But when we turn to a book like *Houseboat Days* we see how high is the high seriousness of which the stylish style is capable.

We should not leave the matter of Ashbery's style without some mention of his unabashed borrowings from all over the place. These do not seem to annoy the critics much; no one expects honor among thieves. On the contrary, people who are otherwise baffled may pick out the borrowings with pleasure. They are like the people you see in a museum who have just come into the gallery, spied a famous picture whose reproduction they have seen many times, and are now congratulating each other on its presence, saying, "It's here! It's here!" This is good fun; we have all enjoyed it and we can extend it to poetry. Take "Melodic Trains," where we have been waiting in the station and are suddenly asked by the poet, "How do they decide how much / Time to spend in each?" Now, that question is a nugget of naive wonder, and nuggets of that kind have been polished to such perfection by James Schuyler that it's hard to resist pocketing them for oneself. If this nugget was borrowed from Schuyler it is only one example of how the New York School is quarried for Ashbery's poetry, though Ashbery would not find such a comment very meaningful. Nor should we, in terms of the long-range appeal that makes us want to keep reading him. But his New York School friendships and collaborations with Schuyler, Koch, and O'Hara are factual and momentous. Had you collected Pontormo and Parmigianino around a table in 1525 and informed them of their Mannerist fellowship they probably would have responded, "Not very meaningful." They would have been right and so would you.

Ashbery's affinities for certain European writers, writers in the big lump known as Surrealism, are also fact. His "Into the Dusk-Charged Air," with its Rousselian list of every river in the encyclopedia, was published in the same summer as his translation of the first chapter from Roussel's *Impressions of Africa*. He has also translated from another favorite, Giorgio de Chirico, the painter who can make sentences that sound remarkably Ashberian. It was from de Chirico that Ashbery borrowed the title *The Double Dream of Spring*. But we could go on like this at length, citing Hesiod, the Book of Common Prayer, "An Ordinary Evening in New Haven," even the books for which he once wrote jacket copy at Oxford University Press—among them Henry Steele Commager's *Freedom, Loyalty, Dissent*, and an edition of Schumpeter's *History of Economic Analysis*. After all, if there is a disposition called negative capability which will take in a host of attitudes then it will take in a host of other writers, too. In an interview Ashbery was asked: "What types of diction are you aware of incorporating into your poetry?" The answer was, "As many kinds as I can think of."

One gets the exasperation in that answer. One also gets its truth. A poet cannot make a style so canny, to express a world so wide, and remain totally unaware of how he is doing it. In evidence we have his identification with Wyatt and Surrey in his poem "Grand Galop." Wyatt is famous for importing the sonnet to England and Surrey for domesticating it. Famous now, but we are told that people who were reciting English poetry in those days found the sonnet curious, its iambic pentameter baffling. To some of them, perhaps, it didn't even sound like English. The parallels must have been tantalizing to the poet who wrote "Grand Galop," who likewise imported a good deal into the American language and knows what it feels like to be thought curious. In fact the parallels must be sweetly tantalizing to Ashbery, for everyone knows that the odd little sonnet turned into a monument of English form.

> But if one may pick it up,
> Carry it over there, set it down,
> Then the work is redeemed at the end
> Under the smiling expanse of the sky
> That plays no favorites but in the same way
> Is honor only to those who have sought it.

We have interrupted the poet making a style and his eyes are wide open. It is the first test of the savoir-faire that you know how far you have come. Harder to know is where you are going. The Mannerists perhaps thought they were taking the High Renaissance higher. Like Ashbery, they knew how to make a style but couldn't know the sense of its effect. That is for the rest of us to say.

Now that I have put style and context asunder, I would like to get them back together where they belong. You can entertain them separately according to your interests but what makes poetry ultimately meaningful is that style and context come together as a whole. To believe this, of course, is to believe meaning resides in poetry at all, a belief we have shriveled a great deal. We may let people find their meaning in movies, but not in poetry, and the wonder is we don't realize we do this at our own expense. Instead, we are dogged by revelations like the one Mallarmé visited on Degas. The painter, in search of advice, has confessed to having some ideas for poems, only to be notified by Mallarmé that poems are *words* not ideas. One waits in anticipation: will Degas take this remark seriously, or will he perhaps reflect that his friend's pronouncement is also made of words? No, the remark and others like it have been taken so trimly to heart, for both painting and poetry, that one still hears sensitive people praise a picture by saying, "The importance of the painting is the paint." Or one hears them praise a poem, saying, "The poem's sole meaning is to be." It is all right for painters and poets to protect themselves by saying such things. The rest of us really ought to be less timid. In the paint and the words is conveyed something more: the artist's sense of the world.

It is a sense of the world for which we remember Emerson, Moore, or Stevens (from whom, of course, I borrowed the phrase). And it's a sense of the world that can make the poet a prophet of the commonwealth, someone, as Stevens wrote longingly, who is "the axis of his time."

> What is the radial aspect of this place,
> This present colony of a colony
> Of colonies, a sense in the changing sense

Of things? A figure like Ecclesiast,

Rugged and luminous, chants in the dark,

A text that is an answer, although obscure.

That was Stevens, in canto XIX of "An Ordinary Evening in New Haven," but the question and its project fixed on Ashbery at the start and have stayed itching at him ever since. If no other poet lives so ruthlessly into the present, I think it is also true that no other is so relentlessly in pursuit of the up-to-date, the radial aspect of right now. In poem after poem we are returned to the timeliness (and thus datedness) of fashion—of pyrography, of Mannerism, of names like Linda, Pat, and Sheila. In poem after poem we are returned to the problem of defining the present: "Is anything central?" "What time of day is it?" The anxiety is catching and, like the figure of hyperbaton which is often used to express it, takes the reader along for the ride. I suspect this anxiety, unidentified as it first is to many readers, is another of the mysteries that make Ashbery initially uncomfortable to read.

In restrospect the itch is easy enough to identify. It was there to make *Three Poems* a torment and a transport, and if one remembers that those three were written at the end of the restive 1960s one can catch Ashbery itching for the present in their very titles: "The New Spirit," "The System," "The Recital." We are talking here about a poet who writes with the stereo on. "The New Spirit" was written to Elliott Carter's *Concerto for Orchestra*, premiered in 1969, which owed its own origin in part to the poem *Winds* by St.-John Perse. Carter says his concerto was inspired by that poem's prophetic descriptions of a United States swept by transforming and obliterating winds, winds like the "self-propagating" ones that now blow through "The New Spirit"—winds "fresh and full, with leaves and other things flying."

Something *is* happening. The new casualness had been introducing itself, casually, of course, but suddenly its credentials lay everywhere. . . .
It wasn't the lily-pad stage yet, but there was buzzing everywhere as
though the news had already broken out and was flooding the whole
city and the whole country.

Is it unreasonable to suggest that a poet so preoccupied with the
buzzing news might aim to be the Ecclesiast of whom Stevens spoke?
Granted, you are not likely in a sophisticated society to announce the
embarrassing ambition to be the axis of your time. But you might reveal it anyway in a playful manner which, like the hand in Parmigianino's self-portrait, both protects and advertises: "Little by little / You
were the mascot of that time." Or you might state it outright by pretending its parody.

> How to explain to these girls, if indeed that's what they are,
> These Ruths, Lindas, Pats and Sheilas
> About the vast change that's taken place
> In the fabric of our society, altering the texture
> Of all things in it?

How to explain? You adjust a style to the context of your life and chant
a text that is an answer, though obscure: your sense of the world.

I am not pretending an Ashbery who argues a programmatic poetry.
There are different sorts of prophets. We might speak of the visionary
prophet who does have a program, however vague, and nothing would
please him more than to fix it on the future, or at least on his readers.
But we can also speak of the vatic prophet whose enterprise is to recognize the world as it is and give notice to the rest of us. The visionary
looks to another world and in proportion may be optimistic and inex-

act. The vatic looks to the world around and within him and in proportion may be accurate to despair. His predicament is by virtue of his negative capability the predicament of others; to use Ashbery's own word, he exemplifies.

> It is the lumps and trials
> That tell us whether we shall be known
> And whether our fate can be exemplary, like a star.

It would be a mistake to expect programs from a poet busy with the lumps and trials. But if it's an example we're after, then we can read it in his fate or—which is the same thing for a poet—his sense of the world. If by means of his context he has given accurate notice of our predicament then how he extricates himself from that predicament through style will be an example, as it is put so touchingly, like a "star."

I have already characterized this poet's context as an apposite analogue for the tumultuous context of real lives as they truly behave. And whoever has been even momentarily bewildered in their own life by the blandishments of this bit of lifestyle or that may be willing to agree. Certainly the cultural tumult as experienced in Hollywood by Daffy Duck is little stranger than the tumult experienced by others, in evidence of which we've had the recent testimony of Jerry Rubin. "In five years," reports Rubin, "from 1971 to 1975, I directly experienced est, gestalt therapy, bioenergetics, rolfing, massage, jogging, health foods, tai chi, Esalen, hypnotism, modern dance, meditation, Silva Mind Control, Arica, acupuncture, sex therapy, Reichian therapy, and More House—a smorgasbord course in New Consciousness." Now there is a course equally as confused as the duck's. One could even lift a few lines from Ashbery's "Fragment" in order to say that if this is a culture it is one of "incomplete, good-natured pictures that / Flatter us even when forgotten with dwarf speculations / About the insane, invigorating whole they don't represent."

The problem is that the American self is hardly content to understand either self or world as an incomplete picture. The Emerson who could discern from particulars the perfect whole has long since carried the day. This may be our cartoon idea of Emerson. But it was Emerson who first identified our new consciousness and said he could state it with precision: *the individual is the world*. The burden of the equation, of course, is that when your self is the world it behooves you to find it as fast as possible. More than an ordinary burden, the search becomes a duty as enormous as salvation once was. Unfortunately, however, the individual who is bent on redeeming his transcendent self from today's particulars will confront an embarrassment à la Rubin or Duck. There are too many particulars.

> Like a rainstorm, he said, the braided colors
> Wash over me and are no help. Or like one
> At a feast who eats not, for he cannot choose
> From among the smoking dishes.

Yet the individual who is the *world* has no recourse. He must go on discovering himself via each and all ad infinitum. As a result his inner life must come eventually to mirror the chaos of the culture around him, while his connections to reality—which he had thought to strengthen—fail of direction and atrophy. He is Daffy Duck at the corner of Pistachio Avenue and Highland Fling Terrace and he finds everything choked "to the point of silence."

He might also be Parmigianino, lost in alchemy—because it would not be implausible for us to compare the embarrassment of riches that confronts the individual today to the similar cultural chaos that threatened him in the wake of the High Renaissance. Arguably, this is a comparison Ashbery was making for us in "Self-Portrait in a Convex Mirror." One should remember that the poet is also an art critic. He was critic for the Paris *Herald Tribune* for five years and executive editor of *Art News* for nine. By the time he was named art critic for *New York* magazine, in 1978, his byline had appeared on more than five hundred reviews, articles, and catalogue notes. He was surely familiar with many self-portraits—baroque, academic, surreal, pop— and could have picked any of them to stare at, but he chose the one in the convex mirror. "Our time gets to be veiled, compromised / By the portrait's will to endure," he wrote. "It hints at / Our own which we were hoping to keep hidden."

In order to make something of that hint, to lift that veil, shouldn't we consult art history? If we do we will find in Arnold Hauser, for example, the suggestive description of Mannerism as "the new spirit" that sought to redeem itself from cultural anarchy. We will discover that Hauser locates the birth of the modern artist in this new spirit. And, still following Hauser, we would learn that this new spirit engenders among artists a proportion of cranks, eccentrics, and psychopaths which increases thereafter day by day. Given this view it is not surprising that the very figures in Parmigianino's pictures suggest a progression toward private idiosyncrasy. In both *The Marriage of St. Catherine* and the *Madonna of the Long Neck* you can see the several figures gaze in as many separate directions, apparently intent as individuals on their separate psychological moments and with no center to socialize their attentions. Before his life is out, Parmigianino (his real name was Francesco Mazzola) will lapse into melancholy, entirely neglect his appearance, and devote his energies to alchemy. One can imagine him like Daffy Duck, a character for whom everything is getting choked to the point of silence.

Taken by himself such a character would appear to be a candidate for psychotherapy. In fact the chaotic and borderless personality frequently on view in Ashbery's poems has a near look-alike in the personality now being described in the professional literature on pathological narcissism. For the sake of convenience, and to the horror no doubt of the trained clinician, I am going to introduce that personality by reducing it to two parts. On the one hand we see an all-inclusive —what psychoanalyst Otto Kernberg calls a grandiose—conception of the self. But on the other we see an experience of reality as fragmented, chaotic, and inauthentic. Obviously the dilemma is built right in, and leads the grandiose self almost as a matter of course to a sense of formlessness coupled with the perception that his feelings or her feelings are no longer associated in any accurate way with real-world action. This is the distress we hear sounded in Ashbery's "Fantasia on 'The Nut-Brown Maid'" by each of those characters, *He* and *She*, who never quite manage a dialogue. And it is likewise the distress of that ruminant sensibility in "The System" who laments at length his insufficient presence in a world of plenary indifference.

It could be . . . that there is no such thing as a void, only endless lists of things that may or may not be aware of one another, the "sad variety of woe." And this pointless diversity plunges you into a numbing despair and blankness. The whole world seems dyed the same melancholy hue. Nothing in it can arouse your feelings.

In that voice we have the paradigmatic complaint of the narcissist on the couch. He cannot feel. She is a blank. There is no other of sufficient salience to rouse either of them from the self.

I did not trot out this complaint from *Three Poems* in order to prove Ashbery the prophet of the clinically disordered. It is true the journals for some time have carried reports of an increased incidence of narcissistic analysands. It is also true that some of these reports have concluded that narcissism has become the dominant symptomatology of the late twentieth century, as hysteria was of the nineteenth. But what makes this shift in symptomatology of interest to social commentators—among them Christopher Lasch, Richard Sennett, and now Hans Morgenthau—is the extent to which it is promoted or exacerbated by the cultural and social context. If clinical narcissism is truly encouraged by some general cultural event that has overtaken our society then that event will affect the rest of us in the same direction, if not to the same degree. We won't all require the couch, but might better understand ourselves in the confines of a common cultural aspect. The poet who shows us the dimensions of those confines has indeed brought notice of the commonwealth and its predicament.

One has to admit, however, that it's not exactly fun to be returned to a predicament—which may explain why there are those who feel trapped in an Ashbery poem. Fun would be to participate in escape instead. So here is where we bring style back into the picture, for how does a poet engineer his escape except through style? Let me make the case in sequence, starting with the proposition that a logical way to escape a predicament is to examine your assumptions and attitudes, for these may be all that hold you there. But—and the poet knows this instinctively—people are not persuaded from their attitudes by logic. They are seduced from them by style. That is why the poet gets to be, as described by Stevens, "the appreciatory creator of values and beliefs." It's not that you invent the alternative attitudes, it's that you make them stylish enough to make them desirable. It is as though poetry were an emotional enabling legislation you could enact single-handedly for the public benefit. If true, this would make you an exalted laureate indeed, and as you might expect from Ashbery he is the first to say it isn't so.

> There was no life you could live out to its end
> And no attitude which, in the end, would save you.

It seems the poet is not accepting our nomination for prophet, for the Ecclesiast invoked by his precursor Stevens. But only at first, because the demurrer I just quoted pops up in a poem titled, of all things, "The Ecclesiast." We have noted before that one line comments on another, one poem on the next, and now we see a title encroaching on the poem beneath it. We have seen that we cannot take Ashbery at his word; we must take him at all his words. Taking him that way here, one might read the poem to say something like this: *There are no life-saving attitudes and those are the ones I sing*. Truly poetry cannot help itself. For to say beautifully that there are no attitudes is still to create an attitude. And to call the poem in which you do so "The Ecclesiast" is to let ambition's cat ever so slyly out of the bag.

Having found his ambition out, we can observe Ecclesiast turn his style to the problem at hand: how to get loose from the predicament of which the narcissist seems at once product and avatar. Given the Ashbery view of our culture, there is not much to be done about the individual's experience of reality as fragmented and inauthentic—reality *is* fragmentary. Even a poet cannot synthesize the storm of information that besieges the Daffy Ducks or Jerry Rubins. To pretend otherwise, to opt for a poetry that polishes one Incan rock, would be to renege altogether on the vatic enterprise. But when it comes to the other side of the narcissist dilemma, the grandiose, or, as some critics like to call it, the Emersonian self, we are indisputably back in the realm of a poet's competence. Whatever self one harbors by the grace of Emerson is harbored, after all, by the grace of poetry. And what poetry has done it can also alter. What if, for instance, Emerson overrated the self? What if it is not the world? Then the world must lie elsewhere, and at the moment there is an elsewhere there is a way to wriggle free.

> Each person
> Has one big theory to explain the universe
> But it doesn't tell the whole story
> And in the end it is what is outside him
> That matters, to him and especially to us
> Who have been given no help whatever
> In decoding our own man-size quotient and must rely
> On second-hand knowledge.

Put them side by side with Emerson and the preceding lines from "Self-Portrait in a Convex Mirror" seem to read as an outright rebuttal. I remember, however, that I promised us seduction and not an argument. So let us play those Ashbery lines again, keeping in mind this time that seduction is almost by definition successful in gestures that go at first unnoticed. And let us stop when we get to one of those gestures, "man-size quotient." Right there, in one stylish subversion, is the grandiose self undone. Long after one has forgotten exactly where the lines occurred, or exactly what it was they said, one will be able to recall the tone and seductive attitude imparted to them by that phrase man-size quotient. Long after one has forgotten the phrase itself one will remember the skill by which our friend paranomasia shifted attention to his pun, *man-size*—which in the language of commercial packaging promises "more," but in the context of a transcendent self can only suggest a diminished amount. Emerson, still teaching the infinitude of the private man has been upstaged, not by argument but by style. He has been upstaged by a gesture that simply subverts the subject by expressing it, but expressing it (to bring back the verb *imparmiginare*) with such savoir-faire that its premises have begun to slip.

Having seen what paranomasia can accomplish one will be ready to keep an eye on the other stylish figures we meet in Ashbery as well. For it turns out they can all be pressed into service to the same end, seducing the American self from its dual burden of infinitude and unique integrity. We have seen how apophasis can reduce that burden with a single coy negative: the soul is not a soul. We may not have noticed, however, that polyptoton was up to the same result, blurring persons in a way to suggest that identity, far from being unique, is likewise blurred.

> How many people came and stayed a certain time,
> Uttered light or dark speech that became part of you
>   . . . until no part
> Remains that is surely you.

Equally important to the grandiose self has been an analogue for its greatness. Emerson settled on nothing less than Nature, declaring that the universe was the "externization" of the soul. In doing so he set himself up for hyperbole, who now finds the sport irresistible. We hear from Ashbery of "*angst*-colored skies," "pain in the cistern," even a "jock-itch sand trap." After such externizations as these, one becomes conditioned to accept the following.

> Yes, friends, these clouds pulled along on invisible ropes
> Are, as you have guessed, merely stage machinery.

A self analogous to the universe would also have to be unbounded, and, sure enough, Emerson was true to his analogy: "There is no outside, no inclosing wall, no circumference to us." But where do parergon and paralipomenon come from, for example, if not from outside some circumference? Each time they appear they teach us their revisionist lesson.

> the soul is a captive, treated humanely, kept
> In suspension, unable to advance much farther
> Than your look as it intercepts the picture.

Since it knows no bounds a grandiose self must also dwell in an arena of unlimited possibility. Said the unforgiving Emerson: "Men cease to interest us when we find their limitations. The only sin is limitation." Against the enormity of this judgment the Ecclesiast must marshal a host of figures: surrealism to collapse the arena in which potential might flourish; periphrasis to warn that what is possible is nonetheless unnamed and unknowable; irony, pop diction, and paranomasia to persuade us that potential has gone already stale and there is nothing to be discovered new. Instead, writes Ashbery, we are only "free to come and go within a limited area, a sort of house-arrest of the free agent intentionally cut off from the forces of renewal."

Finally, a self wrought on the universal scale must also be a self that is always in control, responsible by its own order for keeping the world intact. "There is no chance and no anarchy in the universe," was Emerson's statement on the matter. And to pull the rug out from under this assertion who could do better than hyperbaton, whose very presence insists on chance?

> Hasn't the sky? Returned from moving the other
> Authority recently dropped, wrested as much of
> That severe sunshine as you need now on the way
> You go.

Once you have watched those stylish figures as they perform in concert, it may seem ironic that the poetry of John Ashbery could ever be dismissed as private, as a hermetic celebration of the self. For to see the performance as a whole is to witness the poet at work on an attitude that in fact diminishes the burden of the American self. How to get loose from our data-clogged predicament? Why, one need only style the self as the exiguous facture it truly is. At that moment the universe must cease to be the externization of the soul. At that moment it is possible to regard the exploded context of our culture not as the self's convex mirror, but as a public theater for action. And at the moment the world is a theater one is free. Our cultural clutter, so threatening to the grandiose self, becomes for man-size persons the mulch for their serious business, play.

This mulch for
Play keeps them interested and busy while the big,
Vaguer stuff can decide what it wants—what maps, what
Model cities, how much waste space. Life, our
Life anyway, is between.

In those lines, as elsewhere, one senses how Ashbery too must have paid his Emersonian dues. Didn't he, too, struggle to match the "big, vaguer stuff" and come out on top, struggle to beat the dire sin of limitation? Didn't he, like others, discover that the big, vaguer stuff was getting the better of it, that whoever would match the stuff without invites a commensurate vagueness within? Yes, he must have done so. But what makes the poet an example like a star is the way he has won through these lumps and trials to the stylish, seductive expression of an alternative attitude. Let the big stuff decide what it wants. A right life, kept to proportion, may be artfully lived "between." Agree with it or not, here is an attitude at last fitted to the exploded context Americans live in now. If the poetry that delivers it has caused a commotion that is because its arrival is not a private, but a public event.

*BEYOND AMAZEMENT: NEW ESSAYS
ON JOHN ASHBERY, 1980*

JUSTIFIED TIMES

Although John Ashbery's poetry is securely eminent today, there was a time when it reduced his critics to sputtering. It did no good in those days to placate them with the funny story of the translator who complained that his colleague "Jonas Berry" just couldn't write English. Since the source for that story was David Kermani's annotated bibliography of Ashbery's work, one was safe to assume it was reliable and revealed in good humor. But the critics couldn't get the humor if they were missing the point: this poet who wasn't writing English was doing it with such authority you had to admit what he really *was* writing—an American so roomy and sure that its appearance among us amounted to a national gift. "I guess I was trying to 'democratize' language," is the way Ashbery explained it, referring in an interview to the prose-poem meditations that make up his magnificent *Three Poems*. Then, in his eleventh major collection, *A Wave*, he placed the vast prose vistas of *Three Poems* within the lyric measures he had realized most explicitly in *Houseboat Days*. In retrospect it seems an inevitable triumph, and the trio of *Three Poems*, *Houseboat Days*, and *A Wave* may someday be seen by his devoted audience as the gravitational core of this poet's style.

Not everyone is a member of that audience. But anyone approaching Ashbery's work for the first time, even the exasperated second time, will be generously greeted by the poems in *A Wave*. They are as lovingly addressed to the reader as any in our poetry since Walt Whitman offered to stop somewhere waiting for you. Still, is it enough to explain a poet's influence by saying he is affectionate toward the reader, or has tried to democratize language? The diction in a poem like "Just Walking Around" is pure enough for a hymn in common measure. But when the poet writes elsewhere of gonzo or chroniqueurs, when he chooses at a critical juncture to describe a moment as cimmerian, then he is not exactly writing "plain American which cats and dogs can read"— to judge by Marianne Moore's prescription.

A more complete explanation would have to recognize how this poet writes not just in American, but in an ionized version that looses the poem from attachment to anyone, or anywhere, in particular. Ashbery is insouciant about place; he is prodigal with pronouns, profligate with tenses, and extravagant with hyperbole. Who, what, where, why, and when—they are spun off like freed electrons. The result is a poem that really is "ionized," a poem seeking to combine. At the conclusion of "Just Walking Around," the poet asks the reader to "grant that we may see each other." The poem likewise seeks to be completed in that meeting. The Ashbery reader must be not so much reader as communicant.

Ashbery's work is available today in many languages besides English, or that is to say, American. Readers in those other languages are not likely to lust after a precise rendering of the American vernacular, even if it could survive translation. More likely, they too are attracted by the translatable ionization of syntax and grammar which turns them into communicants. From *A Wave*, an example certain to find its translators is the beautiful if foreboding "Rain Moving In," a poem that is destined to be widely known and quoted in full.

> The blackboard is erased in the attic
> And the wind turns up the light of the stars,

Sinewy now. Someone will find out, someone will know,
And if somewhere on this great planet
The truth is discovered, a patch of it, dried, glazed by the sun,
It will just hang on, in its own infamy, humility. No one
Will be better for it, but things can't get any worse.
Just keep playing, mastering as you do the step
Into disorder this one meant. Don't you see
It's all we can do? Meanwhile, great fires
Arise, as of haystacks aflame. The dial has been set
And that's ominous, but all your graciousness in living
Conspires with it, now that this is our home:
A place to be from, and have people ask about.

It is remarkable that a poem so periphrastic and evasive can be so frankly chilling at the same time. *The blackboard is erased in the attic*—the mind of Ronald Reagan? Or perhaps that we all, as a civilization, are without memory. *Great fires / Arise*—is it nuclear attack? *The dial has been set.* It is long since programmed and there is nothing we can do. Nothing, except bask in the bargain we've made with the very danger that is upon us, nuclear peril or the price of the dollar, the approach of mortality, or the ominous weather. Hard to believe on this evidence that Ashbery was ever accused of writing frivolous verse. A poem that says we have made our danger our home would be recognized, on a threatened planet, as engaged and political.

Or one could at least read it that way. As the poem's communicant, you can find in it what you please. "I contain multitudes," enthused Whitman. "So much variation / In what is essentially a one-horse town," writes Ashbery, and it doesn't sound like he is complaining, either. At a reading in 1984, Ashbery told the audience that an idea for his poem "At North Farm" had come from the Finnish folk epic, the *Kalevala*. Helen Vendler later identified the traces of Keats in that same Ashbery poem. Our culture is thick with literary luxuries. But the poet, though he once acknowledged "the luck of speaking out / A little too late," seems pleasantly surprised by his luck. How nice to have awakened among all the treasures that are yours to rearrange when you live at the apex, spatially and temporally, of empire.

Described that way, Ashbery's prospects sound a lot like postmodernism, and if you ever felt strongly about the postmodernist ethos you've probably felt likewise about this poet's work. The critic Fredric Jameson, having done much to define postmodernism, went on to lament it as a failure of the new, a sad admission that the consumer economy had rendered us "incapable of achieving aesthetic representations of our own current experience," our times. Instead, we were left to combine off-the-shelf allusions (Keats and the *Kalevala* are good examples) in a pastiche of culture that equals no culture, as all colors together equal none. But, before giving way to a verdict of despair in the case of Ashbery, we ought to remember we are dealing with a poet here, and remember what a poet really does. His off-the-shelf allusions are not the pertinent evidence if, as Samuel Johnson informs us in his dictionary, a poet is "one who writes in measure." Period.

It sounds so old-fashioned, measure. What can it have to do with a poem like "Rain Moving In," the poem three paragraphs back with the flaming haystacks? No *abba* rhyme scheme, no iambic pentameter. But look, there are fourteen lines, and at lines eight and nine even a "step / Into disorder" to turn us into the sestet. The poem is a sonnet. Maybe it's in free verse but it's a sonnet nonetheless. There are likewise two double sonnets, a tailed sonnet, and a heroic sonnet, all in the same Ashbery book. Given their sometimes teasing titles, I suppose you could say these sonnets are more proof of pastiche. The sonnet is rich pelf, for sure, and its display at the end of the twentieth century is arguably proof positive of the failure of the new, a sign of conspicuous cultural consumption and no more. But only if you flaunt it. In "Rain Moving In," Ashbery reclaimed the form so thoroughly that it took me much sleuthing to be confident the form was truly present. A lot of readers will never know it's there.

And who knows, maybe Ashbery doesn't know it's there. All the better, because he is demonstrating in his poems how to choose the sonnet, say, as if you were actually innocent of its cultural price tag. Not so innocently chosen, perhaps, are his pantoums. But he is radiantly fresh with the ballade, the Japanese haibun, and the three-part ode—one of which, "But What Is the Reader To Make of This?," could be read as a sketch, or crib sheet, for the project of his whole career.

> and the general life
> Is still many sizes too big, yet
> Has style, woven of things that never happened
> With those that did, so that a mood survives
> Where life and death never could. Make it sweet again!

Sonnet, ode, or the general life, the way a poet makes it sweet again is by writing in measure, just as Johnson's dictionary says. In *Houseboat Days* and *A Wave*, Ashbery's measure shows itself in the longish, lenient lines that are his special contribution to American poetry and a powerful influence on the work of younger poets. With their prosy cadence and many unaccented syllables, with their strong and frequently medial caesura (the pause within the line), his lines can evoke the French alexandrine—itself brought close to free verse in the works of Verlaine and Rimbaud. If Ashbery's is truly a free verse that beats to a distant alexandrine, then what the critics have been missing is a new American measure. Lax and roomy, it would be just the thing to accommodate a poet's need to write in measure with Emerson's stern admonition that it's the meter-making argument, and not the meter, that makes the poem. Make a sonnet from such a measure and you've engaged not in pastiche, but rejuvenation.

There are 802 of Ashbery's rejuvenating lines in the title poem from *A Wave*, the same number as in his previous ballad for two voices, "Fantasia on 'The Nut-Brown Maid.'" So the invitation to treat both poems as ballads is hard to resist. A traditional ballad is fueled by the unifying tension that propels it and its characters toward the inevitable climax and catastrophe. In "A Wave," that climax is already over when the poem begins; it is summarized in the first three lines as an accomplished fact. We are left with the poet to consider our emergence on the "invisible terrain"—the long anticlimax of the present—which stretches for another 799 lines ahead. Is the traditional ballad dramatic and objective? Then "A Wave" will be the opposite: an iterative, inconclusive analysis of private motivation and attainment. In fact, it is nothing less than a postmodern dialogue of self and soul, what the poem itself will call the "subjective-versus-objective" approach. Ashbery once admitted to removing subtitles in order to make his work more mysterious. It was a generous clue, because he is not the only writer whose work makes more sense if you furnish it with subtitles of your own. Try labeling the alternate stanzas of "A Wave" as *A* and *B*, and you will discover that the poem blossoms without losing its mystery or going to seed. "Were we / Making sense?" asks *B*. And in the following stanza *A* offers not so much a considered response as an alternative perplexity. "Isn't this 'sense'— / This little of my life that I can see . . . ?"

The sense at issue between *A* and *B* is very much the one that troubled the landscape of postmodernism. How were individuals to make sense of the "invisible terrain" of their own times? How do you image the world? In our culture, with grace and good works equally suspect, this has become the issue of salvation itself. It's been the issue at least since Emerson reported to his journal, on October 25, 1840, the dream in which an angel presented him with the world—and he ate it. Of course, if you digested the world in 1840 you might treat yourself to a pretty grand salvation. All human incursions were "so insignificant," wrote Emerson in *Nature*, amounting to no more than "a little chipping, baking, patching, and washing, that in an impression so grand as that of the world on the human mind, they do not vary the result."

Well. Tell that to a reader approaching the twenty-first century, who, if he or she eats the world, will have incorporated a resource-limited, environmentally compromised, politically bewitched little ball that can be made to go poof in an instant by one culturally arrested septuagenarian. Can it be good for your health to digest an image like that? In "A Wave," there is disagreement. *B* proposes that you "come up with something to say, / Anything," because the love that ensues will be "richly satisfying, / Like rain on the desert." *A* isn't convinced, beset by the opposing view that once you put things in your own words you will be locked in the tiny cell of the self, *"frei aber einsam."* Free but lonesome. Yet *A* and *B* aren't really arguing the point. They are arguing past it, which is how an Ashbery poem performs its trick. It is so busy settling nothing that it keeps you occupied until long after you've started to image the invisible terrain of the present according to the poem's new style.

The brave hearts in every generation must need to feel their times are new and worth imaging in their selves and souls. How much those feelings depend on the assurance that the planet has prospects beyond one's own lifetime is a matter on which we can only speculate. Certainly there are millions in both hemispheres who believe they have been dispossessed of that assurance, and long to have it back. They do not all, nor even most of them, read John Ashbery. But their longing helps to explain how his work has become an international event, at least in poetry. In the face of our factual dispossession he has created a language that restores newness as you read, a language that is always cresting with potential like a wave. This isn't parody or pastiche, but an affirmation of the individual refashioned in such a way that it can be put back into poetry without embarrassment. No wonder his readers return his affection. If you let him, he will restore you to a world we thought was lost, where the times are justified in the spirit of the individual—you.

THE NATION, 1984

THE NEW YORK
SCHOOL REVISITED

UNLIKELY ANGEL

Our continuing romance with the poets of the New York School derives in large part from their own romance with the artists of their time, notably the painters of the Tibor de Nagy Gallery. With the gallery as a venue, the poets and painters fashioned a ferment of affairs, rivalries, and collaborations that seems to exemplify our bravest bohemian dream of youth. One may suspect it's a youth that never was. But the suspicion passes and we are left dreaming anyway of the poet-and-painter pairings: the plays, parties, poem-paintings, and legendary poet-and-painter pamphlets—the Tibor de Nagy Editions—which constituted in each case the poet's first book.

When we try to enter those dreams, however, whether to follow or reject them, the romance the New York School most closely resembles is the primal, read-only kind whose origins were obscured by one's own birth. Looking back, we are encouraged not to look too far. We get creation stories instead, and they are all to a degree metaphysical. In the version advanced by the gallery director John Myers, the original moment occurred when the gallery was proposed to him by none other than Jackson Pollock: a miraculous ordination, to be sure. But in the more popular, random-walk version, Myers was just one among many, who collaborate as casually as if they meant to leave on a picnic until someone suggests they open a gallery—which, with no other preparation, they do.

In a physical world, events have causes and foregrounds. So it only makes sense if the evidence reveals our New York School romance to have a longer foreground than the creation stories allow. The surprise may be that the discovery is liberating, though it always is when an official spell dissolves, the curtains part, and one sees the machinery behind the metaphysics. In the case of the Tibor de Nagy Gallery we can see the money, connections, advice—for the printing of the early poet-and-painter pamphlets, even the personal favors—and they can all be traced. They reveal a pattern of cause and effect that has reached us directly from the hopes and disappointments of a preceding generation in another country.

I'm not sure we would have ordered a foreground like that. I, for one, am the throwback type that likes to believe that the New York School—however much they crowed of their French influence, however much O'Hara's heart was in his pocket with poems by Pierre Reverdy—was indigenous, as its name implies, to our own civilization. It was America waiting to happen, released by the end of war and the convergence in a great city of the republic's best energies. Nothing prepared me for the discovery that such an America might wait on the financial indulgence of a London-born, Oxford-educated sophisticate with the elevated name of Harry Dwight Dillon Ripley.

Ripley's story was unusual and complex; it's hard to imagine a less likely angel for the New York School. Although born an American citizen (his expatriate father was an heir to the Union Pacific Railroad fortune), he didn't want to be an American. He and his partner, Rupert Barneby, sharing a lifelong devotion to botany, were attracted to the United States by its rare desert plants. In Nevada they found a new species, a kind of desert parsley they named after Ripley, *Cymopterus ripleyi*. Even then they expected to return to England. They ended up in Dutchess County, New York, instead, which is where they were when much of Nevada was turned into a nuclear test site and an atom bomb detonated directly above *C. ripleyi*. The species has since been rediscovered, but Ripley was never to know it had survived. Understandably depressed, he almost gave up botany. He redirected his attention, and lucky for us his checkbook, to the fortunes of the Tibor de Nagy Gallery.

Given the drama of these events (they add up, arguably, to the Big Bang theory of the New York School), it seems odd they went unremarked while more prosaic stories took their place. It's true that Ripley was the "silent backer" as he is called in a biography of his friend Clement Greenberg. But associates of the gallery understood, all the same, where the money was from. The poet Harold Norse remembered it simply as "Dwight Ripley's gallery." He had reason to know; he was Ripley's infatuation during the year the gallery was founded. Myers recalled that Ripley promised a subsidy of four times the gallery's rent (it was five times, at least in the first year). He also insinuated that Ripley was drunk when the promise was made, as if to deny him the merit of intent. One senses in this tale a mix of gratitude and resentment, which isn't exactly resolved by the condescension on display. The irony is that Ripley was no longer rich. His fortune could not be extracted from England intact, and for the rest of his life he was chronically short of funds. Yet the damage of first impressions was done. He was "millionaire dillittante Dwight Ripley" as Judith Malina spelled it in her diary.

All accounts agree that Ripley did drink too much and had many talents. The gallery's codirector and namesake, Tibor de Nagy, described him as an alcoholic and a genius. Friends said he was fluent in fifteen languages, which seems a lot, although we have as evidence the poems he wrote in Catalan for his *Poems* of 1931, and in Polish for the American newspaper *Gwiazda Polarna* during World War II. On the strength of these poems in Polish he was visited after the war by Czesław Miłosz, who was then a diplomat from communist Poland.

They met at the Plaza Hotel and again in Dutchess County. Ripley reported by letter to a friend that Miłosz had a "thick neck." But not one of Ripley's talents—not poetry, botany, art, or alcohol—seems enough by itself to explain what we see in an exhibition of his drawings. The talents added up, it appears, to more than their sum as parts.

Ripley's custom was to work in series, so his surviving drawings come sometimes with serial titles. *The Bomb No. 1* is from a show called *The Bomb*, held in 1955 at Tibor de Nagy. An earlier drawing, untitled but since called *Evolution with Mushrooms, Bud, and Pineapple,* was likewise one of a series. When exhibited in 1946 at Peggy Guggenheim's gallery, Art of This Century, this drawing and its companions were described in the *New York Times* as "evoking ideas of the biological world." According to his diary, Ripley had just purchased *Genetics and the Origin of Species*, the landmark work by Theodosius Dobzhansky that synthesized genetics with natural selection and opened the way to modern evolutionary science. The Dobzhansky, the description in the *Times*, the surviving drawing itself—these taken together illuminate all of Ripley's work and unfasten his reputation as a "dillittante." They free us to speculate that his multiple interests in botany, etymology, and art were not fractured enthusiasms, but elements of a coherent worldview that was focused by the logic of evolution. The diversification of words, as in etymology, or of styles as in art, would emerge in this view as a wealth of speciation like that in a great botanical genus such as *Astragalus*, which he and Barneby had studied and collected in the deserts of the American West.

Larry Rivers observed once in *Art News* that Ripley's drawings were as witty as Steinberg's, which may be true, though I would have added that they are more affectionate. The drawings of his Birds, Fish, and Cages series take gentle liberties, for instance, with the botanical and zoological illustrations that he loved in childhood. Equally tender were the responses visible in his *Evolution* drawing. He began that drawing with a stylized send-up of Surrealism, particularly the variant known as Biomorphism, which was so popular at Guggenheim's gallery. Then, with a sassy application of collage, he forced his biomorph forms to fruit, i.e., to reproduce—granting them, at least on paper, a future in which to evolve and fend for themselves. This must have been a joyful alternative (consider it from their point of view) to their being trapped permanently in a surreal departure from the ideal order, whatever it was, whose loss the Surrealists seemed secretly to regret. Ripley's drawings, in other words, were free of self-pity. They hint at a mind shaped in England, and a familiarity with the English brand of Surrealism that the New York School poets would later regard as "pale" in contrast to the flashier, continental kind.

No one is going to conclude from his drawings that Ripley had a major aesthetic influence on the painters and poets at Tibor de Nagy. Schuyler described how the poets were affected by floods of paint, while Ripley worked in colored pencil. We can't say he had no influence, however, because there is always the quantum possibility that some product of his interests, relayed by Myers and de Nagy, or sensed by a younger artist who happened on his drawings at the gallery, got mixed into the artistic inheritance that has devolved through generations since. It's intriguing to discover drawings from his Birds, Fish and Cages period that represent, for example, the first poem-paintings to be seen at de Nagy. The difference, allowing for the colored pencil, is that Ripley's were *self*-collaborations, the work of someone who was the poet and artist both. There was also the example of wit. Reflecting on Ripley's show of January 1954, critic Stuart Preston wrote approvingly in the *New York Times* that it was "high time the 'School of New

York'—today's abstract expressionists—found an artist to buffoon it." To place that appraisal in its suggestive context, one needs only remember that four years had yet to elapse before the appearance of "homespun Dada" (as it would be labeled by the same critic) in the first solo show of Jasper Johns.

Ripley's financial influence requires, however, no suggestion. In the gallery's first twelve months he contributed $5,155, which was not only five times the gallery's rent but 18 percent of his income. One might even claim, based on the money trail, that we would have no New York School of poets without him. Thus we could exchange one creation story for another. We might as usefully say we'd have no New York School without the farsighted owner of the San Remo bar, or the farsighted admissions officer at Harvard Graduate School who declined to accept Ashbery, bumping him on to Columbia University in New York. With or without Ripley, each of our poets would be present in the anthologies today. But could the manner of their convergence have been the same? There was to be no Tibor de Nagy Gallery without Ripley, no advice to that gallery from his friend Greenberg, no guaranteed cast of painters and collateral poets. And the poets would not have entered the purview of Myers—an alternative history some might have looked on wistfully, as it was Myers who invented the label "poets of the New York School," reviled immediately as inaccurate and confining, though it turned out to be a conveyance, surely, to the stars.

Having seen the sociability in Ripley's drawings we might logically wonder why the painters and poets never told us about their artist angel. But there was no conspiracy; they barely knew him. Myers explained that Ripley refused to interfere at the gallery and was modest concerning his own art. His modesty is credible, too, because it wasn't thoroughgoing; privately, he sulked when his drawings were ignored. At the same time, he exulted in the success of "his" artists, collected their work, and even wrote a play in verse to celebrate their arrival on the scene. This was "Beach at Amagansett," a parody of the poets' plays that Myers was producing for the gallery's adjunct Artists' Theatre. The Ripley play was never produced; perhaps it was never submitted. It featured two camp angels, modeled on Barneby and himself, who eventually leave the stage to the artists, remarking as they go that it's been a privilege to witness the birth of a school, not the "New York" school but the *scuola* Myers.

Label-free, meanwhile, and seized with the anxious business of being young, the poets and painters would scarcely have leisure or latitude to lift their patron into a future they themselves were unsure of making. Today, with the riches they created securely around us, we can afford what they could not. We can afford to consider the hopes that preceded them and continued out of view beside them for twenty-three years. Ripley died in 1973. The drawings of his last decade, the most productive of his career, are the more remarkable because he was no longer connected to the gallery and had no prospect of an audience. He must have relied, instead, on the habits that served him in his new country, contributing to its culture and pursuing his interests, while he staked his artistic survival on the proposition that these were subjects as fit for colored pencil as they were for paint or poetry.

CHECKLIST ESSAY, *UNLIKELY ANGEL: DWIGHT RIPLEY AND THE NEW YORK SCHOOL*, POETS HOUSE, NEW YORK, FEBRUARY 9–MARCH 18, 2006

A HIDDEN HISTORY

OF THE AVANT-GARDE

In the annals of a pivotal institution like the Tibor de Nagy Gallery
there are always anecdotes or images that become famous and seem
to stand for their entire moment. They are convenient, irresistibly repeated, and they weigh on the hearts and minds of those who come
after them with the authority of art itself. One such anecdote was born
in April 1953 when Frank O'Hara, working that day at the front desk
in the lobby of the Museum of Modern Art, telephoned his friend
Grace Hartigan with the news that the museum director Alfred Barr
and curator Dorothy Miller had just alighted from a cab and were
struggling to get through the revolving door with her painting *The Persian Jacket* held between them. It was the final day of Hartigan's third
solo exhibition at Tibor de Nagy—the discouraging final day, because
she had not sold one item from the show. In fact, she had sold only a
single painting in the two and one-half years since she joined the gallery at its inception in November 1950. Suddenly, although Barr and
Miller were at last forced to give up their struggle and take the painting
through a side door, she was about to realize an artist's dream. Her
work was entering the museum.

THE FORBIDDEN FUTURE

Today, we would have to recapture the supposed innocence of an earlier age to judge how stunning was the triumph of this thirty-one-year-

old painter and her gallery. It was not totally unprecedented. In March the Museum of Modern Art had purchased de Kooning's already notorious *Woman I* direct from its showing at the Sidney Janis Gallery. But Hartigan, though she was still signing her work "George" instead of Grace, was not an ambiguous figure like the image in *Woman I*. As reported by writer Roland Pease, the devoted ally of the de Nagy gallery since its second year, she had "the breeziness and good looks of a young Ingrid Bergman with the brain of an articulate feminist." In the pugilistic context that attached to Abstract Expressionism, such were not the expected attributes of a painter. Hartigan was a woman; and, yes, the news of her sale direct from the show to the museum was received as unprecedented.

The sale was transformational, too, in a way that made the young painter not unusual but representative among her fellow artists at Tibor de Nagy. It marked the emergence of a future that had been forbidden, a future that could retain abstraction while it also embraced the return of figuration to the canvas. Like her colleagues Larry Rivers, Alfred Leslie, and others, Hartigan was selected for the gallery's initial roster by Clement Greenberg, the critic who—as everyone has heard by now—banished the figure from modern painting. Greenberg's vision, inflected by the political emergencies that people of his generation could not escape, seemed sometimes to reveal a grand analogy: as the state should wither away in politics, so should the figure wither away in art. And by this analogy, your figurative painting was not just provincial, it barred the way to a better world.

One of the first to disagree, or perhaps she simply ignored the imperative, was Jane Freilicher, who excited both admiration and competition among her friends when she completed the descriptively titled *After Watteau's* Le Mezzetin—a painting in which the famous image of a lute player burst through the mandatory push-and-pull of paint rather like a vexed dolphin that has surfaced through an oil spill, to sing in spite of it all. This breakthrough led her to still-life works, including the much-loved *Painting Table*, which were even more independent in style. Meanwhile, her infatuated friend Larry Rivers followed up on Freilicher's example with an unexpected tableau, *The Burial*, thus gathering the momentum that would result in his epic painting *Washington Crossing the Delaware*. There were critics, seeing that epic for the first time, who thought it was a send-up; but their perspective eludes me. Barr was certainly right to decide, after some deliberation, that *Washington Crossing the Delaware* belonged, too, at the Museum of Modern Art. The painting is a masterpiece of forlorn collectivity, and it grows timelier, more affecting, and more irredeemably accurate every day.

Excitement among artists does not make regiments, however. The ultimate prize was freedom, not figuration, and that prize could be sought against the odds in abstraction, too. By the time of the Hartigan sale, the de Nagy gallery had already exhibited Helen Frankenthaler's immediately consequential *Mountains and Sea*. Stained directly on unprimed canvas, this was the work that revealed how a refinement in technique might retain the action-painter drama while avoiding its sometimes rebarbative physicality. Likewise popular had been the exhibition of Leslie's vertically striped paintings, oil over newspaper collage, which were influential because of their vigorous surface luxury. I am not the first to imagine how one of these, such as the red-and-white-striped *Survivor*, could be rotated ninety degrees to form an incipient flag in the unconscious mind of Jasper Johns.

O'Hara observed first-hand this ferment among his artist friends;

no one on the planet Poetry needs to be told he also participated in it. He set out to codify the shared excitement by composing an essay, "Nature and New Painting," which appeared in 1954 in the loose-leaf magazine *Folder*, an intimate compendium of new literature and the arts. "Painting exists in time as precariously as a voyage or a ballet," he wrote memorably in that essay, "and it is dangerous not to respond—more dangerous to respond to rumors." The suggestive nod to ballet signaled the influence of his friend, the poet and ballet critic Edwin Denby. To illustrate his essay O'Hara discussed seven painters, four of them—Hartigan, Freilicher, Rivers, and Elaine de Kooning—friends who would show their work at Tibor de Nagy. (The other three were Wolf Kahn, Robert de Niro, Sr., and Felix Pasilis.) The art world, needless to say, was smaller then. But even at the time his contemporaries must have suspected that O'Hara's naming of personal friends—Rivers even a sometime lover—was as much programmatic as it was coincidental.

More subtly programmatic was the way O'Hara's essay began to legitimize, so subliminally we would notice it only in retrospect, a nascent tradition in poetry that he saw anticipated in the work of Denby. He might be surprised, however, to discover his tradition now firmly established and identified, despite the protests of its practitioners, as the poetry of the New York School. The defining poets of this uneasy amalgam are generally held to be O'Hara and yet another four of his friends: John Ashbery, Kenneth Koch, Barbara Guest, and James Schuyler. It is no coincidence that the first books of all five were published as limited-edition chapbooks by the Tibor de Nagy Gallery.

By the time O'Hara published "Nature and New Painting," his, Ashbery's, and Koch's chapbooks—with drawings by Rivers, Freilicher, and Nell Blaine respectively—were each in print. The glamour of those fragile publications has cast such a spell backward over their era that it can be difficult sometimes to remember who came first at the gallery, the poets or the painters. The spell hasn't been broken, either, by the advent of memoirs, biographies, letters, and diaries, all suggesting that a communal case of *ut pictura poesis* must have escaped from the paintings and poems into the affairs, rivalries, and mutual defenses of a very charmed circle indeed. At the center of this circle one consistently encounters O'Hara ("he was everybody's catalyst," in Denby's words), a remarkably durable achievement that he accomplished in the span of fifteen years. Ashbery, recalling the confluence of ambition, talent, and youthful high spirits which brought the rest of them together before O'Hara's arrival in New York, observed once that the sole ingredient then lacking in their circle was O'Hara himself, whose indispensable skill was "to kind of cobble everything together" and tell his friends what they, and the less favored others, were doing.

For anyone that has aspired to life in the metropolis, the picture thus painted must be broadly allusive. In my mind, for instance, the iconic anecdote of *The Persian Jacket*'s appearance at the door of the Museum of Modern Art has become permanently conflated, thanks in large part to the charm of Ashbery's observation, with the equally iconic photograph taken of O'Hara in 1960 as he exited the museum onto Fifty-Third Street through that same revolving door. There is the poet in his prime, confident, a little arrogant, and certainly capable of doing his cobbling. His program is working, his nucleus of painters and poets is launched, the future is within their grasp. More than that, the image is forceful enough to project its claim over futures it could scarcely contemplate.

And yet there is something that troubles this well-known picture, something that makes one hesitate. Perhaps the hesitation is prompted by our having witnessed, if only dimly and at a distance, the transformations in the disciplines of history and other liberal arts which have caused scholars to question whether a focus on intellectual trends and iconic figures isn't hiding something, whether truly constituent transactions aren't being reduced to ephemera. History, in this suspicion, is like a photograph that elides the information beyond and prior to the frame. The question to be asked is whether our image of the poet at the revolving door is hiding something. Or, to put it another way, Who provided the door?

The question is not impertinent, though it does mean to emphasize the obvious. The undeniable presence of a museum in our picture implies a kind of intellectual infrastructure—the museum itself; the networks of collectors, critics, and viewers; the rival bohemias; not least the Tibor de Nagy Gallery—already in place and functional when O'Hara arrived. The history of the museum is well known, and helps us to locate the poet's contributions and those of his friends on a continuum of modern art and poetry. But the story of the gallery, which can trace its own origin to the historical avant-garde, has been known to only a few. In fact, the details were apparently kept secret in deference to its founding financial backer, Dwight Ripley ("a Gidean character," whispered Judith Malina of the Living Theatre to her diary).

Scholarly works have begun to appear in which the de Nagy gallery seems to rank alongside the Hamptons, the Club, and *Art News* as one of the critical venues in a model of avant-garde coterie. These studies make it all the more important to consider the gallery's history and its relation to ourselves. We have the advantage of recently published memoirs, letters, diaries, and biographies. We also have access to archives that are now, or soon to become, available. These include the obvious sources, such as the Rivers archive, and less expected ones such as the papers of James Merrill, the poet whose generosity to certain artists and activities of the gallery may come as a surprise even to its longtime friends. Merrill made the down payment on Rivers's house in Southampton, subsidized the gallery's adjunct Artists' Theatre, and donated works by gallery artists to important museums. The Rivers at the Brooklyn Museum, *July*, was a gift from the poet, while the one at the Lyman Allyn Museum in New London—the beautiful *Watermill Prospect* cited by O'Hara in "Nature and New Painting"— was displayed at Merrill's home in Stonington until the end of his life.

Even as we welcome the additional resources we must expect them to arrive, however, with a certain attendant disability. There is the distinct possibility that exaggerations and errors, already resident in the archives or inserted in the memoirs, will be adopted as credible and find their way by repetition into history. The unavoidable case in point is *Tracking the Marvelous*, a memoir written by the gallery's original artistic director, John Myers, and arguably intended to erase the memory of his business partner and gallery namesake, Tibor de Nagy. Reading it myself, I finally had to conclude that accuracy was not Myers's concern as I stumbled over the address he provides for the gallery during its first five years. He puts it at 219 when instead it was 206 East Fifty-Third Street, just east of Third Avenue on the downtown side of the street. Myers's slip is not negligible (an odd-numbered address is on the uptown side of the street, he was there five years, he could check the stationery) but a warning sign. Nonetheless, it has been adopted and disseminated by authoritative sources, including at the time of this writing the website of the Archives of American Art.

Myers habitually made himself an easy target, and it appears from the record that everybody enjoyed taking aim. "There is a lot of information on him, not all of it self-promoting," remarked Pease wryly. But Myers was not the only figure attached to the gallery to confuse autobiography with history painting. As a result, anyone trying to relate the story of the gallery has been forced to proceed by a kind of social triangulation, hoping not to offend or omit, and thereby assembling a version that begins when Myers and de Nagy first formed their marionette company to stage artful plays for children. Artists admired the plays, as did the *New Yorker*; but the audience dwindled when a polio scare caused parents to keep their children home from public events. The company failed to profit, and the normally taciturn Jackson Pollock prevailed on the puppeteers to form a gallery. Oh, but not to suggest a divide, so did de Kooning. The result is like a famous photograph. However winsome and true, it turns out to be a thin slice of the more revealing story to which everyone with affection for the Tibor de Nagy Gallery—artists, collectors, associates, poets—automatically belongs.

A SECRET ORIGIN

If a single incident can qualify as the moment of conception in the life of the new gallery it occurred in December 1949 near Wappingers Falls, New York, at the barely renovated farmhouse shared by Ripley and his partner, botanist Rupert Barneby. The dealer Betty Parsons was downstairs in the living room with Ripley's friend Marie Menken, the underground filmmaker and painter whose works had been exhibited the previous month at the Parsons gallery. The two women were staying the weekend. Their host, who had gone upstairs to bed, was a botanist like his partner but hadn't made it a career as Barneby had. He was also a poet, and in casual accounts you may read he was a painter—though that should be taken metaphorically. Against the tide of Abstract Expressionism he worked consistently in ink and colored pencil.

Although colored pencil was regarded in some circles as a hobbyist's medium, Ripley was serious about his preference. Drawings were intimate and portable: he sometimes sent them in place of letters through the mail. Peggy Guggenheim included six of his drawings in a group show at her gallery, Art of This Century, in 1946; they were "expert," said the *New York Times*, and four were sold. But she closed her gallery the following year and moved back to Europe. Apparently she thought Parsons would take each of her artists, not just Pollock, and apparently Ripley thought so, too. It turned out he was wrong. In a letter to Menken, written after the weekend visit was over, he confessed that he was wondering how his drawings would look on the Parsons gallery wall when he heard Parsons mention his name downstairs. "After Miss Bushmaster's voice had dropped a trifle," he continued sarcastically, "I only caught an occasional word—one of which I *thought* was 'drawings', on an unpleasant note (as Ivy would say)." The whole letter—he also calls her Lady Moccasin and Madam Sidewinder—is a gem of wounded artist's pride and a glimmer of the gallery to be.

No one reading his letters could be surprised to learn that Ripley had a campy Oxford accent. It was not an affectation. Born in London, the son of a wealthy American father and a London actress, he was raised on an estate in Sussex, met Barneby at Harrow when they were schoolboys, and entered Oxford a year behind Auden and one ahead of Stephen Spender. In his second year at the university another student, Edouard Roditi, published in the *Oxford Outlook* the first Surrealist manifesto written in English. Proclaiming that the anglophone muse, too, had "learned to dream like Lautréamont," it thus invoked the author whose example of a sewing machine and umbrella on a dissecting table was celebrated as the kind of unlikely conjunction that defined the new reality. Ripley made his response evident on return visits to Sussex: he buried a boat in the garden, installed a gilded tree in the drawing room, and kept a favorite Surrealist totem, an anteater—though his was conveniently stuffed.

In 1931, the year he left Oxford, Ripley was introduced to someone who was to alter his life and affect the lives of everyone ever touched by the Tibor de Nagy Gallery. Her name was Jean Connolly. She was born Jean Bakewell in Pittsburgh but couldn't wait to get to Paris, which she accomplished by the age of seventeen. There she met and later married the young literary lion Cyril Connolly, who would be editor of the English journal *Horizon* during the war and early postwar years. In London she paid for their flat in Chelsea, their parties, and in a classic pattern put her own ambitions on hold. She had gone to Paris to become a painter. "I don't think that she will ever paint really well," wrote Connolly to a friend, "but she is good at rather amusing drawings."

After the collapse of France the Connollys decided Jean should return to the United States. She meant to proceed to Los Angeles where Ripley and Barneby, Isherwood, and other friends had already settled. At her husband's request, however, she stopped first in New York to locate the author of "Avant-Garde and Kitsch," which had appeared the previous year in *Partisan Review*. This, of course, was Clement Greenberg. Connolly wanted Jean to persuade the critic to write for *Horizon*, but her success outran the plan. "I believe I was seduced," wrote Greenberg to a friend, beginning a three-year affair with Jean that seemed to consist for him of equal parts sex, society, subsidy, and finishing school. The new couple toured the museums and galleries, where Greenberg discovered that Jean's taste was "inevitable, especially in pictures"—a heart-stopping observation in light of her early ambitions, as well as a hint that makes one wonder who was explaining the pictures they saw to whom. She introduced him to Auden, Isherwood, and in January 1942 at a restaurant on Park Avenue, to Ripley and Barneby, who were considering a move from Los Angeles to New York. "They are both botanists and English. Something new," reported Greenberg.

When Ripley and his botanist partner moved the following summer to the farmhouse near Wappingers Falls, they found their friends in turmoil. Greenberg had been drafted, responded with horror to basic training, and was about to be granted an early discharge. Jean was writing his column in the *Nation* so he wouldn't lose the position while he was in the service. She had also become involved with the Surrealist artist Laurence Vail, former husband of Peggy Guggenheim. Greenberg, who discovered the situation on his return, seems to be fighting back panic when he writes to a friend: "Strange to say, I don't miss her but I do miss her milieu."

It was natural that Jean would introduce Ripley to Guggenheim, whose gallery was then the flagship of the avant-garde. Like many Americans, Guggenheim surrendered willingly to an English accent, and Ripley's was unimpeachable. She encouraged his drawing, prompted him to buy paintings, asked for his help in hanging shows. "Jean Connolly, Dwight Ripley, Matta, Duchamp were around a great deal," remembered Lee Krasner. "They were at all the parties." Guggenheim did not mention Ripley in her once scandalous memoir, *Out of This Century*, but there's a reason for that. He was helping her write it. They were also having an affair. Ten years her junior, he was not yet puffy from booze. Nell Blaine, whose early painting *Blue Pieces* was featured in a group show at Art of This Century, recalled that Guggenheim looked at the time "like a sexy witch."

The affair ended, of course, but it did not destroy the friendship; Ripley continued to share in projects at the gallery. After buying a new Pollock (*Composition with Pouring II*, now at the Hirshhorn), he described it in a letter to a friend and related his excitement not from his own perspective but in terms of the gallery's success and the artist's career. Sophisticated, cynical, perhaps he assumed nonetheless that the excitement would last forever. But Jean divorced Connolly, married Vail, and returned to France. Breton went back; Masson returned. Finally, Guggenheim too departed for Europe. There will always be disagreement about the Surrealist influence in New York. Thomas Hess, editor of *Art News*, called it "a petty debt." Barbara Guest had a more generous estimate. "We were saved by those artists," she said in an interview. "We were taught so many things. All this wisdom that came over." With the wisdom departing and Art of This Century closed down, it must have seemed to Ripley that the air was going out of the balloon. Then Parsons popped it.

THE CONTINUITY OF THE AVANT-GARDE

If you were among the three million visitors who passed through the Museum of Modern Art in a single recent year, or if you've attempted an opening-night tour of a neighborhood overwhelmed by galleries, then the notion of a shortage in art venues will seem too quaint to be entertained. But the postwar complaint that New York counted only a handful of galleries was justified. And none, as eavesdropper Ripley discovered, was as ready to provide a home for avant-garde experiment as Guggenheim had been.

Most accounts observe politely that Guggenheim owed her success in large part to her advisers, notably Duchamp. Thanks to his long friendship with Jean Connolly, Ripley could turn to an adviser of his own—Greenberg—for the critical insight to form a gallery. But who would be the dealer and do what Parsons wouldn't? It's easy for us, looking back, to identify Myers and de Nagy. After Ripley's death, when de Nagy felt free to be forthright, he described to an interviewer some events that led to the gallery's formation. "And then all of a sudden John Myers got hold of Dwight Ripley who was very much involved with Peggy Guggenheim," he said. "Otherwise we wouldn't have had a gallery." Set aside for a moment the question of who proposed a gallery to whom—an order of priority that de Nagy likely took on faith from Myers—and you are still left with a mystery. How did this "all of a sudden" come about?

Prominent among Jean's entourage in prewar London and Paris was the wealthy patron Peter Watson, who financed *Horizon* and once subsidized a book of poems by the American poet Charles Henri Ford. Visiting New York shortly after the war, Watson called on Ford at the offices of *View*—the Surrealist arts magazine, founded by Ford, which had become one of the vanguard cultural forces in America. There he met the managing editor, Myers, and was invited home to dinner. Myers, through this connection, was to learn all he needed to know about Jean's friend Ripley. He arranged to attend a party where Ripley was present, and the contact was made.

Having met Myers myself I can testify that he sounded, even late in life, exactly like the posturing "John Myers" portrayed by O'Hara and Rivers in their mock drama *Kenneth Koch: A Tragedy*. Too eager, it seems, to make an impression, he only invited the recoil that led friends and enemies alike to discount his genuine cultural achievement, much of it realized in his tenure at *View*. Beginning as a native of Buffalo, where he published a small literary magazine that featured nationally known writers, he was approached on the strength of that magazine and offered a job as managing editor of *View* if he would relocate to New York. He never looked back.

Myers's arrival in 1944 coincided with the appearance of the magazine's autumn issue, featuring a cover by Léger and a translation of de Chirico's *Hebdomeros*, identified since by Ashbery as "the finest" of the Surrealist novels. The next issue carried the first major essay on Lautréamont to be published in America. Within a year Myers was involved in producing the lavish number that *View* devoted to Duchamp; it was the first monograph published anywhere on Duchamp's life and work. As managing editor, he met many of the contributors to the magazine. He recalled asking Duchamp why he had never held a job and receiving the kindly reply that lazy people cause the least trouble. He remembered his meeting with Surrealist master André Breton as "a religious experience," because he understood every word even though the great man refused on principle to speak in English.

A brave autodidact, Myers was a precarious balance of insight and gaucherie. Merrill, who shared his interest in puppetry and met him not long after his arrival in New York, recalled Myers as "an ageless, hulking Irishman with the self-image of a pixie." Rivers remembered that "his eyes were green and changed size with every idea that crossed behind them." This is all good fun—and because Myers in his dealings with the artists and poets was often spiteful and vindictive, there's plenty more of it. But after reading his letters and considering his legacy, I've had to grudgingly modify my opinion and am willing to believe that the point about those green eyes is, indeed, there was something crossing behind them. Myers, the autodidact, had achieved at *View* as he would at Tibor de Nagy a position in the cultural vanguard that young graduates with Oxford or Harvard diplomas might envy today.

If Myers the editor can serve as an individualized example of the infrastructure elided by our image of O'Hara at the revolving door, then *View* stands for the institutional examples also hidden from attention. Because Ripley saved his copies of the magazine, I once paged through them and was surprised to discover that much of their content was as timely as enthusiasms I'd heard of only yesterday. In addition to Lautréamont, *Hebdomeros*, and Duchamp, there were reviews of jazz and John Cage, a poem by Ford about Billie Holiday, an essay on Florine Stettheimer, reproductions of work by de Chirico, Hélion, Léger, and Cornell, translations of Henri Michaux and Raymond Roussel—if you are a poet that table of contents begins to read like a mimetic soup from which the New York School will fashion its DNA. Since *View* had a circulation that never topped three thousand, I suppose we might regard it as ephemera swept from the streets before the New York School poets and their artist friends arrived on the scene. The strength of cultural evolution, however, is that it leaves its imprint not on the street but on the human mind.

In 1951, shortly after O'Hara began working at the admissions desk of the Museum of Modern Art, his new friend James Schuyler dropped by to say hello. Schuyler found O'Hara selling tickets with one hand and effectively writing a poem with the other, an anecdote frequently repeated to illustrate O'Hara's genius for composing a poem under conditions that might seem less than ideal. The rest of the anecdote is usually suppressed. Near his poem O'Hara had placed a copy of Breton's *Young Cherry Trees Secured Against Hares*, translated by Ripley's old Oxford colleague Roditi and published by *View* under its View Editions imprint in 1946. Likewise telling is the case of Kenneth Koch, who was reading *View* in Cincinnati at the age of eighteen and was allowed to keep his subscription when drafted into the army. In service from 1943 through 1945, he became, as he put it, "probably the only soldier in the Philippines with a subscription to *View.*" If he looked into every issue then Koch first saw Roussel's novel *Impressions of Africa*—translated by Roditi and published in three installments in *View* in 1943 and 1944—while he was a rifleman overseas. The novel greatly influenced Koch, and the possibility that it reached him in a distant theater of global war suggests for that work an element of *gloire* that even Roussel, its fame-deluded author, might not have envisioned.

Although Roussel may seem too esoteric an example to prove anything, many will have come under his influence without suspecting it on their visits to the Tibor de Nagy Gallery. His work constitutes what the *Encyclopedia of the New York School Poets* has called a "secret meeting ground" for the poets of that school. The novel *Locus Solus*, considered by many to be his masterpiece, lent its title to a journal of the same name edited by Ashbery, Koch, Schuyler, and Harry Mathews. I will admit, however, that this secret meeting ground is one

I've never had nerve enough to enter, perhaps for fear of disturbing the power it exercised on my life through the work of those same poets and their younger friend, the poetical painter Trevor Winkfield. At the age of twenty-three, Winkfield thought he had abandoned art, only to return to it eight years later. In the meantime, he translated a posthumously published work by Roussel called *How I Wrote Certain of My Books*. That book is not the practical guide its title suggests, but translating it prompted Winkfield to realize, as he later explained, that "there were many other ways to put together a painting than the simple ones I already knew."

The result for Winkfield was a succession of unexpected works, chief among them the unforgettable *Cottage Industries*, which was exhibited in 1980 and quickly became for poets of his and a younger generation what *Washington Crossing the Delaware* must have been to their predecessors. It all but demanded a change in attitude. I recall a lecture the poet Tim Dlugos delivered at Cooper Union the year after we had all seen the painting. The lecture was brilliant, as Dlugos was, and I can still hear him proclaim with an authority that would have done credit to O'Hara himself: "They wanted a de Kooning in the room. *We* want a Winkfield." Tim was staking a claim; but I didn't have a clue it could be associated, by any contingency whatsoever, with attitudes on offer decades earlier in an avant-garde magazine called *View*.

After *View* ceased publication in 1947, Myers tried his hand at publishing chapbooks of poetry. He also thought of the marionette company. The familiar story from *Tracking the Marvelous* is that he met the perfect investor, de Nagy, at the New York City Ballet. But that was more posturing. According to de Nagy, their meeting was not so theatrical. De Nagy had become acquainted with a playwright, Waldemar Hansen, who was Myers's roommate. The playwright mentioned Myers's need for an investor, and de Nagy, thinking of some family jewelry he had brought with him to the United States, agreed to be introduced.

De Nagy first arrived in New York in December 1947, so near the new year that the date is frequently given as 1948. An officer of the National Bank of Hungary who was under surveillance by the occupying Russian authorities, he was on a diplomatic mission in Prague when he was approached by allied agents, offered a visa, escorted to a British plane, and found himself suddenly free in London. From there he continued to New York. Except for the jewelry—two rings that had belonged to his mother—he was penniless. He was certainly not used to that condition. He had been born into a landowning family, but after his father's death grew up in Budapest. His first stepfather, a judge and patron of the arts, died when de Nagy was seventeen; his second was a retired army officer. A relative was director of the National Bank. His wife's family owned sugar refineries with business connections throughout Europe.

At the time of his marriage, de Nagy built a baroque villa on the Buda side of the river and filled it, not with avant-garde but seventeenth- and eighteenth-century Flemish and Italian art. He was hosting a dinner party when the Germans entered Budapest in March 1944. He was seized one month later and loaded onto a cattle car bound for a camp in Poland. The train was forced back by the advancing Russian army, and after six months of harrowing relocations he escaped, only to be arrested and imprisoned by the Russians as a spy. Released, he became for a while the de facto director of the reorganizing National Bank in Hungary; but because of his contacts with banks outside the country he was imprisoned again by the Russians, who, it seems, planned to force him into financial espionage. It was shortly after this last imprisonment that he obtained the visa in Prague. Meanwhile, he had divorced his wife so she could escape with their daughter to the United States by marrying a Danish friend and traveling on a Danish passport. Pease, who met de Nagy at the Tibor de Nagy Gallery in 1952 and became his lifelong friend, noted that "when someone discovers that Tibor has been a prisoner of the Germans, then of the Russians, a tone of 'Do tell us all' comes over the inquisitor." Pease found this patronizing, which it probably was, but remembered that de Nagy "is usually good-natured and dredges up a few horrors" for polite company.

Even when penniless, de Nagy, who spent two years at Cambridge and graduated with honors from the University of Basel, had the European bearing and sartorial dignity bound to appeal in image-conscious New York. He never mastered, however, or thought to master the provocative veil of indifference that appeared to migrate unchanged from the face of Duchamp to the faces of Leo Castelli and Jasper Johns. Pease pictured de Nagy as "animation personified, eyes twinkling, staccato, hands and arms dancing, humor foremost." The humor could be expressed with a lugubrious panache that must have been baffling to his brash American artists. Hartigan once wrote him in caps "I NEED MONEY" after he sold her painting *Ireland* to Peggy Guggenheim. De Nagy did not reject the request, but he discovered so many expenses to be met before he wrote the check that the artist can scarcely have been satisfied with what she finally received. To mollify her, he described a dinner where Guggenheim praised the painting. "I promised Peggy to visit her in Venezzia," he wrote. "I want to see 'IRELAND' in Venice, before it finds its poetic end in the deep ocean. Titians, Veroneses, Giorgiones and Hartigans will die together." The compliment may not have given the artist much comfort.

Nobody at the time they met would have expected Myers or de Nagy to become an art dealer. The explanation attributed to de Nagy was that a concerted voice arose gradually among their artist friends, urging them to fill the vacuum created by Guggenheim's move to Venice. Myers, on the other hand, claimed the idea as his own, though he feigned modesty by relating that he thought of it as a project for a friend. That way, he didn't have to be surprised at the idea—only at the offer of money—when it was proposed by Ripley at a famous French restaurant of the day. "I shall never know whether he was drunk or sober," wrote Myers, "when, one day at the Chambord, Dwight suggested I go ahead with my plan to open a gallery." The sentence is all charm, until you realize it takes advantage of a benefactor's reputation for alcohol to deny him the merit of intent. And there the history might rest if Ripley's drawings, albums, and pocket diaries had not been discovered, twenty-five years after his death, in a loft where they were casually stored. Some of the rescued items were displayed in an exhibition at Poets House, where it was obvious that the diaries were appointment books and their penciled notations few and far between. This made certain entries all the more prominent, such as January 12, 1950, which reads simply "Clem Plaza lounge 6.0."

Ripley, stung by the Parsons incident, had lost no time preparing an alternative to her gallery. Less than two weeks into the year that followed her rejection he met Clement Greenberg, as the diary reveals, at the Plaza Hotel. The timing could not have been better. Robert Motherwell had canceled his spring show at the Sam Kootz Gallery and Greenberg was selecting a group exhibition, *New Talent 1950*, to replace it. In preparation, the critic had compiled a list of favorite young painters—Hartigan, Rivers, Leslie, and Robert Goodnough among them—who, like Ripley, had no immediate prospect of a gallery to advance their careers.

It was three days after meeting Greenberg at the Plaza that Ripley took Myers to lunch at the Chambord. He promised a subsidy of four times the gallery's rent (this was 18 percent of his income and more than he could afford; he would have to sell his art collection to pay his own bills). Finally, at six-thirty the Monday evening of January 23, he escorted Myers to Greenberg's apartment at 90 Bank Street in Greenwich Village for an interview. Ripley and Myers, wrote Greenberg's biographer, "came to Clem's apartment to consult with him about a noncommercial gallery that Ripley would finance as a silent backer and Myers would run. Clem gave him the *Talent 1950* list."

You can almost picture it. The long arc of his association with the historical avant-garde passed from Ripley into the prospects of artists whose names were offered in that instant to the aspiring director of their new gallery. The first chapbooks of the New York School poets were contingent on the same event. There ought to be a plaque on that Bank Street door.

AN AFFAIR OF ART

The romance of art is linked so profoundly to its creation that it's only natural to measure the success of the new gallery by the careers of painters and poets who have made it famous. In each case we impose a frame that is like the iconic photograph. We know that outside the frame is an infrastructure of friends, family, viewers, and readers without which the successful careers can scarcely be imagined. This is not a truism that should remain abstract.

In fact, there is no better correction to our customary focus than a real-life incident that ought to be as well-known in the history of the Tibor de Nagy Gallery as *The Persian Jacket*'s entering the museum, or the overheard conversation at the farmhouse. This occurred shortly after the gallery's first anniversary when the thirty-year-old Roland Pease stepped out of his midtown sublet onto the sidewalk, determined to pound the pavements one more day in search of a job that would permit him to make a new life for himself and his children by relocating to New York. Near the end of the block, not far from the gloom (or, depending on your brand of nostalgia, the *noir* glamour) of the Third Avenue El, he saw something peculiar. Even today, there is enough chance and wonder left in the city that you can recognize immediately the kind of surprise encounter that Pease would record in a memoir years after the event.

> What is that? I asked myself one day directly after Christmas in 1951 as I hurried along New York's East 53rd Street between Third and Second Avenue. My eyes had been caught by an object inside a first floor window. It looked unfamiliar. I couldn't imagine what it was. I thought it was a mistake. The tenement building was a shabby affair, one of those walk-up rooming houses. I stopped briefly to peer in at the object I could not identify. Perhaps this was a shop but then I saw a name: Tibor de Nagy Gallery. What kind of a name was Tibor de Nagy? I had

never heard of such a thing. This was an art gallery, I assumed, although it certainly did not look very promising. No one seemed to be in it that I could see. Was an art gallery open to the public; free? I was in a hurry and rushed on.

It would be satisfying to know what was in the window that day. Frankenthaler, not on Greenberg's original list, had since joined the gallery and her first exhibition was mounted as the final show of the season. There are photographs of the artist supervising her installation. In some of these you can see an object at the window which indeed looks unfamiliar: a combination fish bowl and birdcage placed there as part of a preceding exhibition of drawings by Ripley. Perhaps the cage had remained in the window. But whatever the object, we know in advance its impact was sufficient to bring the gallery's unexpected friend back for a lengthier visit.

Pease was in New York because he felt he had no choice. It was not the first time he looked for a new life in the city. Ten years earlier, while Myers was still in Buffalo and de Nagy in a bank office in Budapest, Pease was a student at Columbia. He had spent two years at Dartmouth before he realized instinctively that he was in the wrong place. Returning suddenly home to Boston, he told his surprised parents he needed to move to New York. Sensibly, they asked what he planned to do there. "I hadn't thought of that," he recalled, but quickly proposed a solution, which was Columbia University. An urban romance soon followed: a few days after the attack on Pearl Harbor he met nineteen-year-old Polly Saltonstall, who was likewise in the city on a pilgrimage from Boston. They were married the next June and two weeks later he was inducted into the army air force. When the war was over he resumed his studies and rented a cottage for his young family in Connecticut, where, one evening in 1946 after dinner, Polly—described by Pease as "blond and breezy and crisp"—went into the kitchen, collapsed, and died instantly of an inexplicable heart attack.

Devastated, no doubt panicked, Pease returned with his two children to Massachusetts, found a job as a reporter and theater critic for a paper in Wellesley, and set about creating the ideal postwar life of the right house, right clothes, right people, and appropriate cocktail. Finally, his instinct resurfaced as it had at Dartmouth and he resolved to find a way back to New York. "Outsiders drone on," he wrote in a paean that will warm the heart of every urban chauvinist, "about how New York is a good place to visit but not to live, but they are wrong. It is the only place in America to live if your sensibilities are easily ruffled. In New York *the mind* is one's home, even for sensualists." It was for the sake of home, then, that he came to be living in a sublet on Fifty-Third Street while he looked for work and a suitable apartment. He discovered, predictably enough, that there were plenty of theater critics in town already; he found a job as a financial reporter for the United Press instead. Although he meant the job to be temporary, it was to last five years. He was in the throes of learning to talk finance when he returned to the gallery with the unusual name, walked in, and it's no exaggeration to say that what he saw there ratified the new direction he had chosen for his life.

Six feet four inches tall but so properly self-effacing he was unobtrusive even in portraits and photographs, Pease was a scion of New England Puritans (his and his wife's families belonged to that vanished Boston, as satirized in the toast, where the Lowells spoke only to

Cabots and the Cabots only to God). He might have remained securely in a world that was several blocks, if not strata, from the gallery in a tenement building. Of course, he could no more stay away than he could avoid moving to New York. Passing by on the sidewalk, he was bound to notice when the gallery opened its new season with a show by Goodnough and followed with Leslie's exhibition the next month. Schuyler, who saw the Leslie show, was to remember it for its "glopped-together" collages and "saggy bedsheet picture"—and given the strength of Pease's reaction it's tempting to believe the bedsheet was among the works he encountered the first time he entered the gallery. "One day I poked my head in the door of the Tibor de Nagy Gallery," he wrote, "and abstract expressionism hit me full in the face. I recognized my subterranean horrors instantly spelled out on the canvases; here they were on parade, the artists my soulmates. I began meeting them all."

Eventually, Pease would own paintings by most of the gallery's early artists, but primary among his new soulmates was Hartigan. "Grace the idealist," he called her, referring to the abstract but incandescently erotic *Venus and Adonis* which he purchased shortly after she finished painting it in 1952. It was her first major sale—her only major sale before Barr and Miller carted off *The Persian Jacket*—and it would be hard to overestimate its importance in the fabric of confidence a young artist needed to weave around her work. "Perhaps never in my life will there be more than a handful of people," she wrote that December in her journal, listing Pease in the handful. When Pease surveyed his collection many years later, the Hartigan was prominently displayed. "I like to sit in the dark and see what I can make of the art reflected on my walls," he wrote. Also on his walls were a Rivers, a Freilicher, a

Porter, a Frankenthaler that had been a present from de Nagy, and more (the collection is intact today at the Frances Lehman Loeb Art Center at Vassar). "These are my loves," he admitted, "dearer than words can tell."

The encounter—we should probably call it the love affair— between Pease and the de Nagy gallery is more than anecdotally appealing. It is a challenge to piety, as well. One of our current pieties, after all, is the belief that an artwork is completed by its audience. You don't have to wait long to hear that the poet permits us to assemble the poem or the artist seeks our dialogue in the creative act. No one hearing this ever seems to feel patronized. But Pease didn't fall in love with the paintings because he participated in painting them. He didn't love them because he could describe them, either; those "subterraneous horrors" he recognized may not be what the painters thought they were creating. He fell in love with the paintings for something he could not describe. Their attitude must have seemed to him on the cusp— where what he could sense, but didn't know how to appreciate, met what he knew how to appreciate but could no longer bear. It's no surprise if people can't describe this cusp fluently in words. If they could, what would be the point of art? In the presence of the right poem or painting, the question will answer itself.

A VANGUARD OF FRIENDS

We can justly envy Pease his chance to witness the reciprocal enthusiasms and durable networking of the painters and poets whose careers began with the new gallery. Last avant-garde or not, these artist friends of his defined a special moment in our cultural history. Some of it was due to postwar timing (Rivers, O'Hara, and Koch each benefited from the G.I. Bill) but a great deal had to be improvised along the way. One originating instance took place in 1945 when the twenty-two-year-old Rivers, playing saxophone in a jazz band, hired a new pianist to accompany the band on its tour to Old Orchard Beach in Maine. The pianist happened to be Freilicher's first husband. Freilicher, who went along for the performance, spent her free time painting—a devotion that captured Rivers's attention and sparked his own ambition. On their return to New York the two aspiring painters were introduced to Nell Blaine, whose *Blue Pieces* had just been exhibited at Art of This Century. "She lived in a white painted loft on 21st Street," remembered Freilicher, "the first I'd ever seen, and her life as an artist seemed glamorous, courageous and attractive." No doubt the glamour added to the strength of Blaine's advice, soon accepted, that her new friends study painting with Hans Hofmann.

The fortunate events that brought Freilicher and Rivers together with Blaine in her loft at 128 West Twenty-First Street did not occur, needless to say, in cyberspace. This would be too trite to mention, but the extraordinary example of that single city block does make you wonder if artistic communities initiated by physical proximity can ever reoccur. Blaine had rented her loft without knowing that photographer Rudy Burckhardt was a few doors east, and Denby across the street at number 145. Nor could Denby and Burckhardt know when they first arrived that they would be sharing a fire escape with de Kooning, whose studio was then next door. Fairfield Porter, too, maintained a studio on that block. When Freilicher met Koch, Ashbery, and O'Hara after their successive graduations from Harvard, she was able to include them in a circle that might have been radiating right from Nell Blaine's loft. "In a way everything is through Nell," as Rivers remarked. But in a way everything is through West Twenty-First Street, between Sixth and Seventh avenues. Considering its history, I wouldn't be surprised to see people walking on that block suddenly lose their balance as they pass through the coordinates where art and poetry once assembled to make an aesthetic reality that hasn't yet been surpassed.

In total, of course, it is undeniably correct to observe that the early careers of the painters and poets, their first masterpieces and chapbooks, could not have transpired as they did without the de Nagy gallery as a channel of introductions, theater of events, and generator of the ambient scene. The opening night parties, crammed frequently into the small apartment rented by Myers, made an important part of that scene. Merrill remembered the parties in Myers's apartment as the best he attended in New York, and observed that "A bomb falling on one of these gatherings would have set the arts in America back six weeks." Merrill made this remark in a more innocent time, and of course he was teasing. The celebration after the first Rivers opening provided the occasion for Schuyler to meet Ashbery and O'Hara both, and that was indeed a momentous event in American arts. It was an event we can trace to Ripley and the historical avant-garde, as well; a gallery ledger reveals that the rent for Myers's apartment and the expenses for his parties were paid from the subsidy he received from Wappingers Falls. Soon Pease would host gallery parties, too, including one made memorable by an ebullient Koch seated at the piano shouting "Tee-Boar, Tee-Boar, Tee-Boar de *What*?" Koch's performance was greeted, recalled Pease, by much laughter and hilarity—

which can only indicate, as do many such stories, that you had to be there to appreciate it.

At the gallery itself there was likewise a defining ambience. Freilicher once called it "a kind of salon," while Koch referred to a "certain ambience" that consisted of "seeing each other all the time and being envious of each other or emulous of each other and inspiring each other and collaborating." Koch was thinking of the New York School nucleus, but it is morally appropriate to remember that the gallery also attracted the indispensable, though generally elided people who give an avant-garde its heft and stamina. Some openings had all the ambience of duds. Others were electric. Hartigan reported to her journal that the opening of Blaine's show in 1953 was the most crowded she had ever seen. The opening of her own *Persian Jacket* show, better known today for its exhibition of the paintings she made to correspond to O'Hara's *Oranges*, was likewise exciting. Myers mimeographed the poems as a hand-out and persuaded her to paint covers for the two dozen copies he would sell at the opening for a dollar each. "So the day before the opening I sat down on my studio floor and did twenty-four individual paintings on the covers and we sold about four of them," she recalled. "I remember we sold two to the de Koonings. John was delighted with this young, enthusiastic painter-poet life we had."

Friends of the gallery are familiar with the explicit collaborations of its artists. Of equal, perhaps more lasting interest were the implicit collaborations that produced work which remains valuable without reference to its extraneous sociability. The aesthetic affinity that arose between Porter and Schuyler made theirs perhaps the greatest instance of painter-poet friendship in the history of American art. Their near competition for the title, as it turns out, was the steadier, more elusive rapport that linked the works of another painter-poet pair associated with the gallery: Freilicher and Ashbery. It's true that the shared concerns of this latter pair may be not so apparent. We are always entitled, however, to look for clues; and a logical place to begin is Ashbery's mirror-like essay "Jane Freilicher." In the casually delivered credo of that essay he praised her work as "tentative," going on to state his belief that most good things are tentative, "or should be if they aren't." The observable paradox may be that the works of both are *steadily* tentative. But the paradox only reveals that Ashbery's idea of the "tentative" must be another way to identify that combination of disinterest and concentration which delivers us in Freilicher's painting, as it does in his poems, from the erosive claims of faction and time.

Since Freilicher and Ashbery are artists whose careers moved in chronological parallel, it's tempting to compare their origins. These suggest that a career, too, may have a hidden history. Origins are sometimes isolated, not because they were false steps, but because they represent power to be kept permanently in reserve. In Freilicher's case we remember the breakthrough of *After Watteau's* Le Mezzetin, an example all the more suggestive as it appears that the painting no longer exists. In a less dramatic way, Ashbery's poems can be measured by their distance from the experiments of his early book *The Tennis Court Oath*. Yet in each case the artist preserved the initial radicalism at the heart of the work. Freilicher seemed to acknowledge that original power when she placed cameo images of *Le Mezzetin* in the context of two sets of work for which she is renowned: the disabused meditations directed toward Mecox Bay, as in her painting *The Lute Player*; and the steeply foregrounded views onto the West Village as in *Serenade*.

Over the long interim represented by the distance between the cameos and the masterworks, Freilicher practiced a deflective citizenship that allowed her to create in conditions as close to freedom as one can probably get. This strategy was made visible in *Self-Portrait in a Mirror*, a mid-career summary that surrendered a view of the artist which was almost shockingly intimate, but protected at the same time by virtue of its being a reflection— even deflection—in a mirror. It was two years later that Ashbery wrote his poem "Self-Portrait in a Convex Mirror," whose now famous opening describes a likewise deflective posture. Scholars naturally analyze the poem in terms of the Parmigianino painting of the same name. Some scholar, someday, will compare it to Freilicher's self-portrait, as well.

It seems an irony of history, or at least of scholarship, that the Tibor de Nagy Gallery is increasingly studied for its extracurricular collaborations when the artists at the time were not always convinced that these were such a good idea. Some of the painters actively resented the attention Myers devoted to his Artists' Theatre, which produced plays by the poets with sets by the painters. The poets, meanwhile, were inclined occasionally to agree with Pease, who noted gently that their plays had not been staged by "the director a playwright might have wished for." From the perspective of poetry, however, there can be no doubt that the publication of the Tibor de Nagy Editions—the chapbooks that ushered the works of the young poets into the world— were the gallery's unique and (why not say it?) *immortal* extracurricular achievement. O'Hara and Ashbery were twenty-six, Koch twenty-eight, when their respective chapbooks appeared. Ashbery remembered his as "probably my greatest publishing experience." There can be no doubt, either, that the warranty of the immortal achievement was the gallery's invention, through Myers, of the New York School tag itself. Although every single New York School poet has at one time criticized it as a misnomer, the label does not discriminate. It has crowned them all with inexhaustible fame.

Readers once associated the label's origin with its appearance as the title of a landmark anthology, *The Poets of the New York School*, edited by Myers and published in 1969. It turns out that the phrase first appeared in an introduction Myers wrote to a selection of New York poets published in *Nomad*, a little magazine based cheekily enough in Los Angeles. But it was undeniably the anthology, with its fashion-photographer portraits of the poets, and black-and-white drawings by some of the painters, which provided the lasting artifact. Prior to its publication, Porter and painter Neil Welliver were invited to inspect a mock-up of the album-sized book in Myers's office at the gallery, by then on West Fifty-Seventh Street. Asked by Myers if the book wasn't marvelous, Porter, well known for being brusque, said simply "No" and went directly to the elevator. On the way down to the street Welliver asked why he had said such a thing; Myers was crushed. Porter responded that a book of poems should fit in your pocket. When Welliver asked, "Why didn't you tell him that?" the answer was "He wouldn't have understood."

I always like to agree with Fairfield Porter (it makes you feel more upright somehow) but this time he was shortsighted and wrong. The awkwardly shaped anthology is autonomous and gravitational: no matter how dog-eared, it will never reproach you like an abandoned pet. Only a moment's focus is enough to see that a planet is on the table. In *The Poets of the New York School*, as much as in *The Persian Jacket* or *Washington Crossing the Delaware*, the gallery transcended any one individual's need. The Tibor de Nagy Gallery became its own masterpiece. In its collaborations, combinations, and collegial genius it created for its artists a future most galleries could never supply—a literary future—because it knew enough to give its history a habitation and a name.

CATALOGUE ESSAY, *TIBOR DE NAGY*
GALLERY PAINTERS & POETS, 2011

THE DRAWINGS OF

DWIGHT RIPLEY

Evolution as Identity

When I first encountered Dwight Ripley's drawings I didn't expect to take them seriously. I had read in the diaries of Judith Malina that he was "fabled Dwight Ripley." But by 1998, twenty-five years after his death, what mostly remained of his reputation was the ambiguous label *polymath*. As early as his first exhibition, in a group show at Art of This Century in 1946, he was identified by the *New York Times* as "linguist, poet, botanist, artist." The description stuck.

You can hardly blame his contemporaries. As a linguist, he not only spoke fifteen languages, he had published a book of poems written in seven of them while still a student at Oxford. And as a botanist he was renowned, in both Britain and America, for the unusual species he discovered in remote habitats and brought home to flower in his gardens and greenhouse. The filmmaker Marie Menken paid homage to that aspect of his reputation in her underground classic, *Glimpse of the Garden*.

My problem, decades later, was that I immediately liked his drawings for themselves. This was initially confusing, as it took some research and reflection to conclude that the reputation had perhaps been missing the point. Imagine if we'd been introduced to John Cage for mycology, or Nabokov, butterflies. The polymathic riches go over our heads. They act as diversions from the secret that unifies and drives them to eventuate in art.

Or maybe it isn't a secret, really. Because a good place to look for the secret of art is on its surface, where an obvious attribute of Ripley's drawings is their unobstructed color.

Color is fugitive in a garden, easy to miss or misapprehend. To you or me, this might register as a passing regret. But to certain artists the inconstancy of color seems to be alternately as rapturous and painful as a heartless lover would be to the rest of us. Ripley was such an artist; his lifelong response to the sweet cheat of color was to monitor it with an attention that can best be described as stalking.

The stalking was epic. It began in England, where the precocious only child designed a "contrary garden" composed of flowers whose colors would be *not* as advertised. And it continued in the United States, where he arrived with his partner, Rupert Barneby, to search for rare species in the American West. In their ongoing pursuit, he and Barneby made seventeen thousand collections at distant sites, sent fifty-three thousand specimens to herbariums at Harvard, the California Academy of Sciences, and the New York Botanical Garden, and discovered seventy-four previously unknown species in the western United States and Mexico.

That's the record to keep in mind the next time you view *Glimpse of the Garden*, a record that illustrates, by the way, why polymath does not mean dilettante.

Some of the species Ripley collected are now classed as threatened. But in his day the isolated regions of the West were laboratories of evolution. He witnessed—essentially he traversed—the drama of natural selection in the field. To a friend in Edinburgh he related the excitement of scaling cliffs to find a rare subalpine phlox, long assumed by botanists to be white or at best pale lavender, which turned out when he finally reached it at the top to be pure scarlet instead. Evolution had painted it.

That anecdote opened my eyes, as the scarlet had his. It revealed the secret of his art sufficiently to let me see that the drama of evolution, with a capital E, appears as insistently as color on the surface of his drawings.

Evolution, after all, is the inherent narrative of the scientific binomials he used to configure the landscapes in his Travel Poster drawings. It's inscribed there in the scenery, in plain sight. It is there in his Language Panels, too, particularly those in which the cartoon *sapiens* he depicted in the drawings can be seen learning to recognize and identify certain plants and animals. Their word balloons give them away. In some cases they display a kind of evolution more attractive to the linguist than to the botanist: the proliferation in the vernacular of confusing common names. These Language Panels are little allegories of evolution *and* etymology.

Ripley was a collector's collector of art, in addition to plants. He owned two of Miró's Constellations and was among the first to purchase works by Jackson Pollock. You don't need to look long to see the Pollock-like dance—or, for that matter, a nostalgic reference to the automatic drawing of the Surrealists—in the underlying écriture of his Travel Posters. The allusions might be parody or homage. But in the light of his evolutional aesthetic they emerge as constituents in a taxonomy of artistic styles.

Larry Rivers's remark that no one was as witty as Steinberg, except for Ripley, was both provocative and alert—as a comment by Rivers almost always is. It didn't do justice, however, to the undisguised affection Ripley extends to his subjects, craft, and audience. There is nothing corrosive about his wit, nothing in drawings like *Evolution with Mushrooms* that stoops to mere ridicule.

Instead, there's a sociability in his drawings which is the more notable when one learns he was all the time dogged by a foreboding of cosmic doom. He had a real stress disorder about the bomb. The first species named for him grew on the site of the first atomic bomb test in Nevada. He complained in despair about the *Vertilgungskrieg* the human race was waging on defenseless plants. Yet even that complaint materialized in his drawings as wistful terror, a tender dread.

The irony of his reputation as a polymath is that Ripley's breadth of attention probably did account for the appealing charity in his work. Led on by color, he had arrived at a custodial empathy for all the endangered species and transitory examples that evolution bestows on a thankless planet. No doubt he identified with them. Parts of his life are now obscure, and some works lost. But we can recover enough to affirm that his anxiety for the precarious and the diverse—a theory of evolution conceived as self-identity—was the inclusive principle that melted his multiple interests into art.

On first sight, Ripley's drawings didn't look like the kind I was accustomed to admire. They looked more like paintings instead. They may have looked that way to Ripley, too, because *painting* was the word he used to describe his work. A few years before he died he wrote to a friend, "I am radiantly happy & painting with all the aplomb, if not the technique, of Tintoretto."

Rest assured, he was not the type to be conventionally happy. It's the "aplomb" we can believe in. Only aplomb can explain how drawings reach across decades, to the surprise of someone who never expected to care for them. But the sympathy wasn't mine to give or withhold. In the presence of these drawings I felt the conviction of a prior intelligence, whose example was to follow pleasure to its sites of peril and rescue it.

CATALOGUE ESSAY, *DWIGHT RIPLEY: TRAVEL POSTERS AND LANGUAGE PANELS*, TIBOR DE NAGY GALLERY, NEW YORK, JANUARY 28–MARCH 10, 2012

THE NEW YORK

SCHOOL REVISITED

Now that you know the name Dwight Ripley you may react as I once did. I didn't need to know it, thank you. I had my facts in place about the New York School, their poems, and even the poets themselves. I knew how Ashbery, Koch, and O'Hara met at Harvard, how the poets and their painter friends centered around the Tibor de Nagy Gallery, how the gallery had been started by John Myers and Tibor de Nagy with the sale of a few pieces of jewelry that Tibor smuggled out of Hungary in his pocket.

So when I learned from the botanist Rupert Barneby that some of this legend was true, but it was his partner Ripley's idea to start the gallery and Ripley who footed the gallery's bills, I resisted the information. Actually, I resented it. It didn't fit my romance of the cultural world we lived in.

I credited the New York School for that world, and still do. This isn't their fault, of course. In college I got as far as Eliot and Stevens, but after that had a pre-law kind of education: history, economics, and poli sci. Certainly I never heard of Lautréamont until I met up with the New York School, had barely heard of Auden, and never could have imagined a world that might contain Ronald Firbank or Raymond Roussel.

As far as I was concerned, the New York School invented these authors just as it must have invented New York itself. I resented this Ripley person as an outlier trying to muscle in. But the more I learned, the more he kept muscling in. And he did it with a kind of innate authority that seemed almost unforgivable.

From David Lehman's book *The Last Avant-Garde* you know, for example, that Ashbery wrote his senior thesis at Harvard on Auden. It was a daring thing to do when the English departments heavily favored Yeats. Auden had won a Pulitzer Prize for *The Age of Anxiety*, but it was still pretty daring. This was 1949.

Now, for the sake of comparison, let me share a letter from Ripley written two years earlier, on August 12, 1947, to his friend Willard Maas, the poet and underground filmmaker. The letter was in response to Auden's *Age of Anxiety* and it represents the sort of evidence I had begun to encounter. Here is what Ripley says to his friend:

> You're right about Wystan, & in the end the effect of the alliterations
> is a bit nauseating (tho not if read in small doses & not all at one gulp).
> Remember it is a 'baroque eclogue' and takes its tone largely from the
> Ronald Firbank quote; at least that's my guess—I took the whole thing
> as a piece of deliberate & colossal camp—

The Firbank, by the way, was from *The Flower Beneath the Foot* and Auden used it as an epigraph to one of his chapters. "'Oh, Heaven help me,' she prayed, 'to be decorative and to do right.'"

Well, the more I explored the more I was caught. I became curious about the rest of Ripley's friends, here and during his youth in England. Among his closest friends was Jean Connolly, the transatlantic muse who figures as "Ruthie" in Isherwood's novel *Down There on a Visit*. I found Jean seated next to Ripley in a photo that also included her husband Cyril Connolly, Stephen Spender, Spender's boyfriend Tony Hyndman, and others at a house party in Sussex in 1935. Jean was an

American, born in Pittsburgh. She went to Paris when she was seventeen and met Connolly there in 1930. In his journal, Connolly lists the three reasons he fell in love with her: her boyish figure, her independent income, and because when he met her she was reading the novels of Ronald Firbank.

Jean was in Paris reading Firbank and John Ashbery was three years old.

You see my dilemma. If you compare the poets of the New York School to the New Criticism, to Robert Penn Warren and Lowell and Allen Tate, they seem like a radical departure. If you compare them to Ripley and Jean Connolly they seem like latecomers to the party.

Ripley even had something to say about Lautréamont, as it turns out. He liked to enclose poems and limericks with the letters he wrote to friends. In another letter to Willard Maas, also in the late forties, he included a poem he called "Miss Potts."

> Eccentric Potts, who wears a parka,
> Prefers Lautréamont to Lorca,
> And thanks the stars each summer night
> She was born bright, but not too bright.

Now you will understand if I feel like trespassing on the title of David's book by posing the question: How avant-garde, really, was the last avant-garde?

It's a question David deals with explicitly in his book. And it's a question Ann Lauterbach deals with more *im*plicitly in her poems and in the essays of *The Night Sky*. There, she considers what it could mean to respond aesthetically to the changed conditions of our own lives today, not the conditions the New York School encountered in their youth.

In approaching my question, I also want to bring up an observation Jed Perl made in his early book *Paris Without End*. New York, he said there, was indeed the center for new art—at least it was when he wrote that book—but Paris still had the important lesson to teach. Paris had what New York didn't, the experience of "keeping a tradition alive."

Jed's more recent book, *New Art City*, seems to be a book-long amendment to his earlier observation. It describes how the Paris experience was happening in parts of New York, after all, right under our avant-garde noses: the experience of keeping a tradition alive.

What I want to do, then, is draw an analogy from New Art City to Poetry City. Because if you use Ripley as a window to open a perspective—a long perspective—on the New York School, it's possible to argue they weren't the last anything. It's possible to see them, instead, as the *first* generation to come along and take advantage of the institutions—the avant-garde infrastructure, if you will, including the Tibor de Nagy Gallery—which were in place and already functioning when they arrived.

But let me leave the gallery aside and return to the intellectual background of our story, the story as we knew it before we encountered Ripley or Jean Connolly. It was pretty well stated by Ashbery in his introduction to the *Collected Poems of Frank O'Hara*; and it basically amounts to saying that poetry presented a closed system to the New York School when they were starting out. There were oddball examples like John Wheelwright, the visionary parts of Hart Crane, or the abandoned side of Dylan Thomas. But there were otherwise no models for the poetic liberation that O'Hara, as Ashbery put it, instinctively needed.

Instead, just as you see when you look in the anthologies, you had only the poets that Kenneth Koch would call the poets *of the baleful influence.*

That was certainly the view I had until Frank and I met Barneby and were introduced to his late partner's library. Here was the library of a sophisticated New Yorker, very much of its time, and there was not one of the baleful-influence poets to be found on its shelves.

I found the modernists, of course: Eliot, some Pound (but no Williams), Marianne Moore, and Auden—who can be explained because Ripley knew Auden from Oxford. Then I found George Barker (a *lot* of George Barker), Dylan Thomas, David Gascoyne, a 1946 Pasternak, and books and manuscripts by Maas, who had once been the rising star of American avant-garde poetry. Except for the Pasternak, the poets in this last group practiced what now seems a similar style.

Ripley's Gascoyne was a limited edition, published in 1944 with weird, strangely congenial illustrations by Graham Sutherland. The poems have an affinity with the "force that through the green fuse drives the flower" style of Dylan Thomas. Barker's style was similar. Maas was influenced by Barker, and for a while those two were close friends. Barker did the voice-over for Maas's pioneer underground film, *Geography of the Body.*

There was also in Ripley's library a little book published in 1942, written by Francis Scarfe about the poets in England at the time. It was instructive to discover from this book that the whole group of MacNeice, Spender, Auden, and Day Lewis (sometimes referred to as the single poet Macspaunday) were already considered passé, along with their communism and their ambitions for political poetry. The new poets according to Scarfe were Gascoyne, Barker, Dylan Thomas, and an interesting writer named Nicholas Moore. These new poets were Freudian and expressionistic, intent on finding an individualist escape from disillusion and the war. Scarfe even called his book *Auden and After: The Liberation of Poetry.*

The liberation wasn't just in style, either. None of these new poets had been to university, all three spent time in America, and all lived on the edge of respectability. Dylan Thomas we know about. Gascoyne was queer and didn't hide it, while Barker had one heterosexual affair after another, resulting in at least fifteen children. Among his lovers was the Canadian poet Elizabeth Smart. She had two of the fifteen children and left a memoir of her affair with Barker, a fictional memoir with the wonderful title *By Grand Central Station I Sat Down and Wept.*

When Dylan Thomas came to the United States in 1950 his visits on campus were described by John Malcolm Brinnin as "a Dionysian experience for the academies." One of those academies was Harvard, where Frank O'Hara heard him read. Apparently, O'Hara was not impressed. We have it on record, thanks to James Schuyler, that what O'Hara actually said was, "I can't stand all that Welsh spit."

So there were indeed models for liberation; they just weren't to everyone's taste. Instead, writes Ashbery, one had to look to France. And by France we usually understand him to mean the freedoms of Surrealist literature.

Ashbery frequently acknowledged, for instance, the influence of the novel *Hebdomeros*, written in French by de Chirico in 1929. He even called it the masterpiece of Surrealist literature and it's easy to understand why: if you read it in translation you may forget you aren't reading Ashbery. He wrote a lovely piece that now serves as the introduction to the American edition of *Hebdomeros*, and he observed there that the masterpiece was unobtainable and all but unknown until 1964 when it was reissued in France.

But it turns out, if you were Ripley, Jean Connolly, or their friends, you didn't have to wait for the novel to be reissued in France. In the art histories of their era—the Peggy Guggenheim era—you will come across mention of a magazine called *View*. This was a Surrealist magazine edited by the poets Charles Henri Ford and Parker Tyler, published from 1942 to 1947. Ashbery once credited this magazine with helping to feed his own Surrealist enthusiasms. He told Mark Ford in their book-length interview that he first saw it at Deerfield Academy sometime after 1943.

Ripley saved his copies of *View*. They were still in his library. The issue I'm holding here, the one with the cover by Léger, is for Fall 1944—the year John was seventeen. So I don't need to tell you I thought I'd opened a time capsule when I turned its pages and discovered the first English translation of *Hebdomeros*, published right here in New York in 1944, and translated by none other than Paul Bowles.

The December issue from that same year has been chewed on by a mouse. It's interesting to remember about this magazine that for three years, from 1944 to 1947, its managing editor was John Myers—the same John Myers who would become director of the Tibor de Nagy Gallery and publish the first chapbooks of Ashbery, O'Hara, and Kenneth Koch. And it's totally fascinating to recall that Koch had a subscription to *View* when he was in the army and read it while serving in the Philippines.

This same December issue carries the second installment of *Hebdomeros*. But that's not all. It has a long article on Lautréamont, an essay on comic books by Paul Goodman, a piece on the jazz fiddle of Stuff Smith, and a longish Surrealist poem by André Breton. If you look at the Breton sympathetically, and maybe squint a little, the lines resemble those of Frank O'Hara's "Oranges," written at Harvard three years later. Those are the "Oranges" that make up the contents of the famous mimeographed chapbook with the twenty-four hand-painted covers by Grace Hartigan.

Of course, the point Ashbery was making is that none of this—not the Surrealism or the Welsh spit—could add up for O'Hara to his beautiful I-do-this-I-do-that poems. For those, he would have to refine Surrealism through the American vernacular, much as the New York School painters themselves had done.

So if we keep that vernacular in mind, and think for a moment of Ashbery and Koch as well as O'Hara, I wonder if we could identify which of them wrote the lines I'm going to read next. I admit it's a professor's trick and I apologize. But if you know their poetry you will hear instantly why I can't resist. Here is the first example, a kind of Surrealist list refined by the vernacular.

> The open-air morgue of the Colorado Desert
> Is searched by the sun of the China Sea
> Through white Cordova hies the Crocodile River

Yes, you made the right association. But no, it is not Ashbery's "Into the Dusk-Charged Air." So let me try another example: Surrealism processed as a kind of vernacular narrative.

The neurasthenic mulatto on the beach
Waits for you to read in an unemotional voice
But instead you turn to the Baron Munchausen
Who offers you a glass of moselle which you refuse
But you do take one of those small cakes from an Irish-Italian bakery
And since it is gummy, put it in your purse....

The trick, of course, is that those lines were published in 1944—witness the dated use of the word mulatto—a year when the poets of the New York School were still teenagers. So, just as the first example was not Ashbery the second was not "You Were Wearing" by Kenneth Koch. In both cases the lines are by Charles Henri Ford and they appeared with *Hebdomeros* in the same December issue of *View*. Two years later, when O'Hara was a freshman on the G.I. Bill at Harvard, Ford even published in *View* a poem about Billie Holiday. "The distress we feel in your presence," he wrote, "is like hearing footsteps that will take us away." It would be another thirteen years before O'Hara wrote his own Billie Holiday poem, ending in a similar diminuendo with the observation that her whispered song along the keyboard caused everyone plus the poet to stop breathing.

We could say, oh, these issues of *View* are just magazines. But isn't that really the point? As magazines, they represent the kind of ephemera that makes up the intellectual climate of their time. Meanwhile, there is an ultimate ephemera that doesn't make it into the anthologies, and that is people. I don't have the patience, or perhaps the skill, to diagram the overlapping relations between Ripley's friends and those of the New York School. But the art world was indeed smaller then and the overlaps were significant, especially at first. The same names are met in both circles—the Living Theatre's Judith Malina and Julian Beck; the filmmakers Maas and his now more famous wife, Marie Menken; John Cage; Paul and Sally Goodman.

Consider just Goodman, for example. In Ripley's satirical poem "Beach at Amagansett," he included Goodman along with Kierkegaard and Henry James as names to be invoked, like Foucault in our own day, for social cachet at parties. It was Goodman who discovered Joe LeSueur in a bar in Los Angeles, inspired his move to New York, and introduced him to O'Hara. And it was Goodman, as Brad Gooch reveals in his biography of O'Hara, who provided the theory for the passionate social networks that O'Hara went on to create.

Goodman's theory made its appearance in an essay he published in the *Kenyon Review* in 1951. The essay was titled "Advance-Guard Writing in America," and it defined the avant-garde writer in terms of the writer's audience—an audience the writer would need to *invent* in a society otherwise characterized by widespread alienation, boredom, and artistic loneliness.

> If the persons are estranged from one another, from themselves, from their artist, he takes the initiative precisely by putting his arms around them and drawing them together. In literary terms this means: to write for them about them *personally*. The advance-guard action is to create such a community, starting where one happens to be.

There you have practically a recipe for being Frank O'Hara. The only part O'Hara didn't follow is the last, because where he happened to be when he read that article was not New York but Ann Arbor, Michigan.

Writing from Ann Arbor to Jane Freilicher, he told her to rush to the newsstand for the Goodman. "It is really lucid about what's bothering us besides sex," he wrote. "Just knowing he is in the same city may give me the power to hurt myself into poetry."

It turns out, once he had arrived, that O'Hara and Goodman didn't exactly hit it off. But this only demonstrates that our wider perspective is real. The people who made up the existing avant-garde—Goodman, Ripley, Jean Connolly—they weren't waiting around to be perfected by the New York School. They were contingencies, necessary if the New York School was ever to happen, but in the meantime they were achieved artists with hopes and disappointments in their own right.

And that brings me to the point where I began, having learned something I didn't want to know. Once I realized that Ripley was more than a conduit to the promised land, I could see that his work and interests had stature of their own. I *liked* his careful attention to botanical species; I *liked* the choices implied by an accurate terminology. I liked the pleasure he drew from intelligence in the face of danger. These seemed to be useful ways to confront one's fears—his anyway, and perhaps ours—whether they were needed or not by the more fortunate New York School that came between.

DELIVERED AT THE PANEL DISCUSSION
"ANOTHER LOOK AT NEW YORK SCHOOL ORIGINS,"
WITH ANN LAUTERBACH, DAVID LEHMAN, AND
JED PERL, POETS HOUSE, NEW YORK, MARCH 2, 2006

THE MENACE AHEAD

POETRY AND THE

MENACE AHEAD

Amy Gerstler's *Bitter Angel* is a book to inspire big thoughts about the courage of poetry in the postmodern condition. People once theorized such a condition, but Gerstler confirms it with a menace we can understand. "I was born without immunity," she writes, "to this din in the air."

Of course, the din will only proliferate—in image, signal, sound— if the economy is not to collapse; and one dream of poetry must be to negotiate the proliferation without lapsing into that dendrite-stunned morality with which we are now depressingly familiar. "The absence of readable feeling" is how this poet describes it. The dream is not for iconoclasm—there are too many images to smash—but a kind of icon-o*crit*icism, where naming the names of beauty remains the root project of a poem. Imagine how knowing those names might vaccinate us against the din-shrouded menace ahead.

So the poems in *Bitter Angel* would blaze beauty through dread by marking the "luminous gunbelt" of an aurora, the "dry lakebed" of doubt, the "deep green justice" of chlorophyll. They would redesign images against which the poet had no immunity (Gerstler specifies Nancy Drew, and Perry Mason's assistant, Della Street) as if these were pathogens she carries to this day. And they would map the potentiating datascape of our culture from the one pole that ought to matter most, as identified in "Often," her ominous, truly postmodern aubade: *Icy joy invaded me: you'd / lived through the night.*

Although Gerstler laments that there is no place for "studied devotion" anymore, she means to make such a place from the written word, and the thrill of her project is identified in a single allusive line: "You, reader, are pardoner." She can't be the only one wishing it true—that even in the approaching din it might be reading that stays the executioner, reading that saves, at the last minute, life.

POETRY PILOT, 1990

DEAD TECH

In 1886, at the railroad station in Redwood, Minnesota, a depot agent named Richard Warren Sears prepared to sell off an unclaimed shipment of watches, discovered so many takers among the local citizens that he experienced sudden insight into his main chance, quit his railroad job to found what would become Sears, Roebuck, and transformed the landscape of North America. In the decades that followed, as Redwoods across the country were colonized by mail-order commerce, the locals saw their Main Street stores turn shabby, their towns shrink to depot, post office, and grain elevator, and their offspring board the trains for someplace where life might live up to the catalogues. It was a complex story, and if you've ever glimpsed its traces in the scenery of small towns, ever looked on a place as commemorative of the way motive and technology can intersect to alter millions of destinies, you have started to "read" the landscape. You have entered the field of landscape studies.

At its best, this field promises a powerful alternative to the ecstatic, media-aggravated amnesia that ordinarily afflicts us where our sense of history ought to be. So it's no surprise that the question of *how* one reads landscape bristles with implications aesthetic and political.

Just how prickly these implications can be is demonstrated by two attractive and programmatic books that focus attention on the ruins left us by aging technologies. *Metropolitan Corridor: Railroads and the American Scene* is an eloquent survey by John R. Stilgoe, who teaches landscape studies at Harvard and seeks here a reappraisal of the environments and attitudes inspired by the railroads during their years of prominence in the United States. His book, my authority for Sears's depot-based insight, is generously illustrated and richly produced by Yale University Press. The other, *Dead Tech: A Guide to the Archeology of Tomorrow*, is a photo dossier, the work of German photographer Manfred Hamm, which means to present a provocative view of military and industrial ruins in both the United States and Europe. Originally published in West Germany, with an introduction by futurist Robert Jungk and text by journalist Rolf Steinberg, the album-sized paperback was translated by Michael Stone and brought to North America courtesy of the Sierra Club.

In an era that seems to consist largely of electronic rumor, both of these books are remarkable for insisting on the existence of real macroscopic things. Among the exhibits in *Dead Tech*, most unexpected is the Military Aircraft and Disposition Center outside Tucson, a forty-square-mile boneyard where the United States Air Force has laid aside some 4,000 has-been aircraft, including two hundred B-52s. In the reduced scale of an aerial photograph, these planes that carpet-bombed Cambodia resemble giant lawn ornaments set out on the sales lot of a suburban garden center. But the authors would not appreciate my frivolity. To them, the B-52 boneyard—along with the disabled nuclear power plants, collapsing piers, dismantled aircraft carriers, crushed automobiles, and derelict fortifications also portrayed in their dossier —is to be read as a harbinger of worse to come. "The corpses of dead technology," writes Jungk in his anti-nuke introduction, are "omens to warn us of the final collapse"—and much of his and Steinberg's text is an even jollier mix of hyperbole, pathetic fallacy, and an eschatology so fervent it is practically camp. Judge this book on its text and you will ask for your money back.

But the photographs are another story. Serene, noiseless, unblinking—forty-seven in color and seventy-four in black-and-white—they are images that might be sent back by an unmanned probe of *this* planet, and, like the industrial landscapes in Hamm's earlier books, *Berlin – Landscapes of a City* and *Berlin – Monuments of an Industrial Landscape*, they reveal something of the shift to postmodernist perceptions. Not too long ago, many would have agreed with Jungk (born 1913) that the ruins surveyed here are "ludicrous and horrifying." I don't know what Hamm (born 1944) thinks, but his camera finds the ruins beautiful; it adores, mutes, and composes them, as it has done for the listing West Side piers of Manhattan, almost as if to protect. And his camera is true to the day: those listing piers are so popular as locations for fashion photography that he was probably lucky to get a clear shot of them. Think of it, the wreckage of technology as a successful selling tool. Far from being "ludicrous and horrifying," such images have achieved exchange value. As conspicuous waste, the ruins they depict are just about the greatest tokens of consumer affluence of all time.

Of course, the authors of *Dead Tech* intend us to be horrified, not seduced. But can the deserted pleasure piers of the English Channel, where generations of ordinary people used to enjoy themselves, really be as horrifying as the vacant casemates at Verdun, where 800,000 mostly conscripted soldiers were slaughtered in 1916? Can an abandoned launch pad from the Apollo moon project, representing one of the epic ventures of the human species, be as truly sinister as the remnants of the Atlantic Wall behind which Hitler planned further to maim European civilization? The attempt to read these landscapes as equally horrific ends by rendering them equally aestheticized instead—beautiful images from which the reckoning of historical cost has disappeared. It is this failure to distinguish, rather than the book's intended message, which makes *Dead Tech* a troubling essay. As long as technology remains a human attribute, we can hardly learn to live with it by exhorting it indiscriminately from our midst.

The humanity, even the humaneness of technology on the landscape seems by contrast to be keenly felt by Stilgoe, whose *Metropolitan Corridor* is billed as an introduction to the railroad-shaped environment "as a visual image." Stilgoe is the author of the widely praised *Common Landscape of America, 1540 to 1845*, which he closed by pleading gently with his fellow citizens to break free of the landscape prejudice that favors pastoral vistas but condemns urban environments to disgrace and decay. Now, in *Metropolitan Corridor*, he confronts this prejudice head-on by initiating a revaluation of trackside aesthetics. Someday, people will perhaps return to the landscape of the metropolitan corridor, and if they do they will surely be looking for the one portrayed in his book. Here it is in the days of the *Twentieth Century* and the *Broadway Limited*, the railroad glory years when goods and people moved across the United States in patterns that Stilgoe clearly regards as more efficient and more civilizing than the contemporary automotive sprawl.

The avatars of that earlier era were the great train stations exemplified by Grand Central Terminal. These were more machines than buildings, writes the author approvingly, where "precise flowing movement spoke of new forces capable of entrancing the human spirit, of the future, of ages of organized human and mechanical energy rising to the height of poetry." What happened to that high poetic future? Stilgoe's nearly explicit answer is like the one offered in poet Robert

Pinsky's *An Explanation of America*: "Somebody might explain a troubled time / By saying 'It's because they killed the railroads.'"

True to his generation's fascination with ruins, Stilgoe (born 1949) would like to bring the railroads back to life. To this end, he proposes a taxonomy of the metropolitan corridor in thirteen parts—terminal, express train, power station, et cetera—and raises as if from the dead the public attitudes that evolved to meet them. Sometimes he speaks for the dead himself (Stilgoe won the 1982 Parkman Prize for history writing), as when he describes the response of earlier Americans to a crack express: "Riding the express meant riding a long, sinuous, racing city, a city of luxury racing into the future." Or, from magazines and trade journals of the day, he digs up testimony that is sometimes pithy (in 1906, engineer A. E. Dixon complained that the average power station looked like "a shoe box crowned with a piece of stove pipe") but is more often swollen in the ecstatic way of corporate flackery ("the tremendous, almost inconceivable magnitude of this giant industrial exposition" reads one description of a steel mill from 1901). He has also resurrected advertisements, illustrations, and photographs. Compared with the cool espionage of Hamm, the passionate chiaroscuro of Alvin Langdon Coburn's photographs of Pittsburgh in 1910 is clearly from another age.

On such evidence, *Metropolitan Corridor* makes its case. From 1880 to 1930, Americans did, in fact, develop a mostly positive aesthetic of the metropolitan corridor—the point being that if they loved it once, they can love it again. This is an agreeable argument, although there is something worrisome about a methodology that has historians like Stilgoe poring over old trade journals, catalogues, and advertisements in search of what people of earlier eras really thought. Throughout the 1920s, reports Stilgoe, journals and popular monthlies sought to develop an industrial-zone aesthetic that would "capture the forms and light of the new built environments" along the railroad rights-of-way. The Pennsylvania Railroad's promotional calendar for 1927 featured an 18 × 24-inch color illustration of the *Broadway Limited* passing the Pittsburgh steel mills at night. Then, along about 1930, such images suddenly disappeared from calendars and magazines. In painting, the companion aesthetic known as Precisionism likewise peaked in the late 1920s and thereafter declined. Charles Demuth's apotheosis of the grain elevator, *My Egypt*, was completed in 1927; Charles Sheeler's spectral Ford plant, *American Landscape*, in 1930. Did something happen to alter the "forms and light" of the factories? No, but the Great Depression erased the motive underlying their popular appreciation. For ambitious Americans after 1929, the railroads and railside factories no longer represented their main chance.

When opportunity did reappear, it turned up in the great automotive economy whose own ruins are easily imagined today. In this new moment of transition, *Dead Tech* and *Metropolitan Corridor* both seek to nudge us toward a less arrogant future, one by an aroused morality, the other by a reawakened aesthetic. Yet the operative distinctions, those that will help us the most, may turn out to be distinctions not of morality or aesthetics, but of cost. Or, to put it sensationally, the French and German high commands could ravage Verdun unceasingly from February all the way into August 1916 because to them the bodies of boys were free. In the United States, Sears could achieve his catalogue empire because the distribution infrastructure was already there, built on the largess of 158 million acres that the railroads got from the federal government for free. If costs such as these had to be encountered by those who seize on technology to alter the land, maybe we wouldn't get a more humane landscape, but at least we'd know ahead of time who stood to gain and who to be passed by.

Already, of course, the main chance has moved again. Those are not Lionel electric trains or toy Studebakers the kids are playing with in the basement, but home computers, the training gear for recruits who will act out their destinies in the new environment of the electronic corridor. Perhaps they can even foresee the shape that their new environment and its attendant aesthetic will take. But if they read in the landscape what motive and technology have accomplished there before, they can also expect a day when the main chance moves again, until—what? Will there be ruins on microchip?

ART & ANTIQUES, 1983

THE ENDURING INFLUENCE

OF A PAINTER'S GARDEN

It feels very special to join you in a discussion on painter and gardener Robert Dash—it's a little painful, as well—though not being a horticulturist or art critic, I did wonder what I could add. Anything I could say about Bob or his garden, Madoo, seemed so obvious it must be common knowledge: that there are ghosts among the plantings and within the walls that make Madoo a place, and Bob a figure, of truly lasting cultural significance.

Then again, what seems obvious frequently goes unsaid, so maybe it isn't common knowledge, after all. I can still see in my mind, for instance, the cover of one of the most important books of poetry in our time. The title is *Three Poems*, although when you open the book it looks like prose. It was published in 1972 and I first read it, stunned, that October. But what could it have to do with our subject today? I wasn't to meet Bob Dash for another year.

You will sometimes read that the photo on the cover of this book, *Three Poems*, depicts the poet—it's John Ashbery—in an upstate New York landscape. That would fit his origins, since he was born in Rochester. But if you kept your eye on the barns in the photograph, and compared them with the barns you'd see from the roof of the summer house at Madoo, you'd discover that they're exactly the same. They are the barns of the Fosters' farm, Bob's neighbors in Sagaponack on the east end of Long Island—the part known as the Hamptons. They're not upstate at all. The *ocean* is just out of sight beyond the horizon.

That view from his summer house roof was one of Bob's favorites, and he made it the subject, in different moods and seasons, of several of his paintings. One of these, *Evening Blow*, is in the permanent collection at the Parrish Museum. Bob painted it in 1971, the year before *Three Poems* was published. Ashbery, who was a frequent visitor at Madoo, would have seen it in progress.

Bob was a great gardener as well as a painter, and the combination made his house and studio unique. The buildings and their interiors shared so thoroughly in the aesthetic of his paintings and his garden that it was impossible to tell where the daily living left off and the art began. I was introduced to the place by Ashbery in the summer of 1973. In those days it was called simply "Bob's" by his friends. Today it is an eminent garden conservancy, known as Madoo. When Bob first acquired it, the building that became his studio was a collapsing eighteenth-century barn surrounded by scattered sheds. He had spotted the barn above the tree tops, some distance from the road. He liked to say it winked at him.

When you came to visit you approached the place from the east, turning off Sagg Main Street just beyond the general store and post office onto a rutted, muddy lane that brought you to an auto court built of pebbles. The pebbles rattled under the car. In the hot sun they were torture on bare feet. The studio occupied most of the ancient barn, while the living quarters were in the sheds. Bob had attached them to the barn, realigned so the whole summer house structure formed a kind of lopsided U that was shorter on its east side to accomodate the auto court. Originally, the garden was almost entirely enclosed inside this lop-sided U, protected from the wind and salt off the ocean.

From the auto court you could walk past the studio into the garden, then go directly up an outdoor stairway to a deck on the roof. Now imagine yourself—you're young, perhaps have secret aspirations to be a poet, and you're on your first visit to Bob's. You climb those stairs to the roof and find yourself suddenly, unexpectedly, standing in the view depicted on the cover of *Three Poems*, looking out on the barns of the Fosters' farm. You are standing right where Ashbery stood for his signature photograph. It could change your life.

Ashbery was not the only poet to be inspired by Madoo. If you kept your eye trained long enough on that view from the roof you might see it morph into the cover image of yet another book, this one by the philosopher-poet John Koethe. The title identifies his book as *The Late Wisconsin Spring*, but of course the barns in its cover image are not in Wisconsin at all. They belong to the Fosters' farm, as seen from the roof deck at Madoo—not a photograph this time, but a silk-screen by Bob.

Two major poets ought to be enough to prove one garden's influence. But Madoo was also the place where I met the poets James Schuyler, Barbara Guest, Kenneth Koch, Anthony Howell, and Peter Schjeldahl, the painters Trevor Winkfield and Darragh Park, the art critic Robert Storr and cellist Rosamund Morley. Later I introduced poets to the place myself, notably Donald Britton, Marjorie Welish, and the English poet John Ash.

Koethe has called Bob's garden "one of the great literary salons of the later twentieth century," which might seem a bit immodest since he was part of it. Yet in terms of this single garden's enduring impact, he must be essentially correct.

Some of the poets I mentioned were more than casual visitors. Also in the Parrish Museum is a painting by Bob that depicts John Ashbery reading at the table in the summer house, located directly beneath the roof deck. Through the window beyond the table you can make out those barns of the Fosters' farm. Bob once shared a studio with his friend Fairfield Porter, a bit of art history which is incorporated in the look of this painting and others like it. This one dates from the time John wrote his poem "Happy Autumn Fields," a reference not just to Tennyson or Keats but to the fields of Sagaponack. If you stood near the Fosters' barns, looking back toward the window where John is seated, you would have been looking over a great field of goldenrod that extended in those days from the edge of the property right up to the window. The first stanza of "Happy Autumn Fields" includes a reference to "the pointed roofs that called to you through the trees," which identifies the location as Madoo. The second stanza pays homage to the goldenrod.

> It's insane how the seasons continue:
> Autumn, September and soon
> The business of winter with a suggestion
> Lifting into February and the dim light of spring.
> How many years? How many does a man have?
> How many can we use? Lots more, certainly,
> But not too many, surely. There are limits.
> Yet this lime sun on frizzled goldenrod—
> Perhaps there simply isn't enough of that.

There was something about being at Bob's that just elicited poems, and I don't think it's sentimental to say the something sprang from the mind of its creator. There's a photo of Bob, taken probably in 1970 when he was forty years old, which shows him seated on a bench in a sea of goldenrod—as if he's considering plans for the lush foliage of the future. In the background is another barn, not the Fosters' this time but a second old barn on Bob's property, which turned out to be a godsend. He converted it into his winter house, because the sheds that had become the U-shaped summer house proved impossible to heat.

The interior of that winter house was sunnier than you'd expect for a former barn. Frank and I first stayed there over Thanksgiving 1974 and again at Christmas that year, when we were joined by Trevor Winkfield, Darragh Park, and most grandly, James Schuyler. In the winter house we actually watched Schuyler—Jimmy, we called him—as he sat silently one afternoon in a high-backed wicker chair while writing one of his best-known poems, "Dec. 28, 1974." I tell this story frequently, because it's so instructive and so encouraging that every poet should know it. Imagine you are James Schuyler, it's that day in December, and you are writing a poem.

> The plants against the light
> which shines in (it's four o'clock)
> right on my chair: I'm in my chair:
> are silhouettes, barely green,
> growing black as my eyes move right,
> right to where the sun is.

I should quote the whole thing; it's such a lesson in heroic observation. But now that you've heard its origin story I'll leave it to you to discover the poem, in its entirety, on your own. It's likely you know it already.

But what, beyond the mind of its creator, were some of the specific things that made Bob's place conducive to poetry? For one thing, there were poems hung on the wall as if they were paintings. *I had never seen that before.*

You could be sitting bleary-eyed at breakfast, look up at the wall and notice that there among the paintings and sketches hung a poem by Jimmy, or John, or a poet you didn't yet know. Bob took the poems written by his friends, trimmed them down to 8 x 10, and framed them in those plastic box frames you could get from the Pottery Barn. In his painting of John at the table you could see there's a framed object on the wall beyond. It's a poem, with the light reflected off the plexiglass. John once said to me, "If you write a poem for Bob, maybe he'll put yours on the wall, too."

Of course you didn't have to write the poem *for* Bob, as John wickedly implied. Nathan Kernan showed Bob a poem he'd titled for an allée of poplars in *Provence*, somebody else's garden altogether. It was seized immediately for the wall, giving Nathan the same validation it gave the rest of us—myself finally included—when a poem made the defining leap from a draft on the table to an artifact on the wall.

The poems weren't hung coyly, either, or as mere decoration. The hanging was dynamic. Next to the potted papyrus there would suddenly appear a poem that wasn't there last time you visited. The poems moved around the house like paintings. And this habit of Bob's, of mingling our efforts with the work of the real artists on the walls, caused you to think of the poems as paintings, which is to say, as objects.

In the guest bedroom there was a work by Joe Brainard—one of his smaller icon-like assemblies—on which Joe had painted in his trademark block letters the motto I USUALLY FIND THAT THERE

IS NOT MUCH YOU CAN DO WITH A PAINTING BUT LOOK AT IT.

This was hung next to the toilet, by the way, and I remember thinking it was the profoundest thing I had ever seen. Because once you regard poems as paintings they become a lot less intimidating. They become subject, like a painting or the plants in the garden, to re-arrangement—culling, even—according to the great creative principle of trial and error.

Because the paintings, books, and poems turned up so frequently in unexpected places, Bob's place seemed "immersive," long before that word gained its present currency. It was immersive outside, too. The house didn't enclose the garden so much as it embraced it. There was a continual commerce between the two, which Bob encouraged. One of my favorite photos of Frank was taken as he was pruning the roses, when I interrupted, as one does at that age, to take pictures of the boyfriend.

Not everyone was entrusted with something so skillful as pruning. I was restricted to use of the riding mower. And Bob never tired of telling his story, surely apocryphal, that Marjorie Welish offered to help him weed, but only if she could wear gloves.

As the garden expanded it maintained its sense of embrace. John Koethe writes that it was on a visit to Bob's that he and his first wife, Susan, decided it was time to have a child. And Gerrit Henry in his poem "Alive in the Hamptons" claims to be quoting me to the effect that it was so beautiful at Bob's you could hardly bear it. "I still find it wonderful," writes Gerrit, "still sigh to live this way."

So the question is, what could make one garden work for such rad-ically different individuals? The answer, of course, was Bob, who effectively painted this immersive scene for the rest of us to occupy. Jimmy Schuyler said it best, and most directly as usual, in one of the eight poems he wrote about Bob and the garden. "I sit and stare . . . and think about / these paintings, this house, / this garden, all as beautiful / as your solitary inner life."

It's true, the beauty around us revealed Bob's solitary inner life. In public he hid that inner life behind a social persona that became the stuff of legend—or gossip, if you prefer. His wit could be deadly. In his poem "Melancholy of the Autumn Garden," John Koethe tells the story of Bob's dealer, Aladar Marberger of the Fischbach Gallery, who arrived in the summer house one day dressed head to toe in leather. With a zipper up the front. And Bob's greeting to his own dealer was, "Aladar, you look just like a purse."

Aladar did not remain as Bob's dealer.

In a poem dedicated to Bob the poet Donald Britton recalled the "gush and pop" of conversations over dinner when Bob was present. It was like skating on thin ice, he wrote. I remember that Bob once read a new poem I'd brought him, put it face down on the table next to his overflowing ashtray and said, a little too emphatically, "No, no, *no*; you're not Jimmy."

The environment where Bob's aesthetic was revealed as a fabric was the garden. There was nowhere but the studio he looked so at ease. Here was the living map of his painting aesthetic, his everyday aesthetic, what he hoped perhaps to encourage in you as your poetry aesthetic. You know that phrase *ut pictura poesis*, as is painting so is poetry? This was *ut pictura hortus*. As is painting so is gardening, as is gardening so is poetry.

Rob Storr remarked once that Bob was an amazing gardener and a pretty good painter, and ultimately the good painter suffered. I wonder if this isn't one of those judgments that sounds wiser than it really is. What Rob kindly didn't say is that Bob drank too much. Drunk, he would lay waste to his friends. But Bob was an organism like the rest of us, and it seems to me you can't divorce what Marjorie might call "the art practice" from the program of the organism as a whole. You can't pull an artist apart and put the pieces back together according to your superior principles. If you could, wouldn't you have a different artist?

Bob implied as much in his book, *Notes from Madoo*. "To my way of thinking," he wrote—and that way of thinking was best exemplified by the garden as it looked in the mid-to-late 1970s—"a garden is not a succession of small rooms or little effects but one large tableau, whose elements are inextricably linked to the accomplishment of the entire garden, just as in painting all passages conduce to the effect of the whole."

So you might learn from Bob in the garden, but the lesson was clearer in conjunction with the paintings he was making at the same time. In the dozen or so years from 1970 to 1984, Bob seemed one of the finer and more singular landscape painters the country has produced. Influenced at first by Porter, he adapted his de Kooning-esque gestures to fast-drying acrylic (Bob was allergic to oils) and the needs of landscape. His painting *Sagg Autumn* was on the cover of *American Artists* in 1974. That painting, with its sweeping foreground of agitated vegetation, recalled the overgrown field between Madoo and Sagg Pond, as you could see it—and as you could walk it—in those days. Bob was crushed by the destruction of this field for the sake of the development that squats there now. In *Notes from Madoo* he quoted a poem by Koethe to the effect that the verdure that came right to his house was the very soul of the place—and indeed it was—"working backwards year by year" until it reached the center.

The aesthetic on view in *Sagg Autumn* was hugely influential to me, and perhaps to others. Composition, said Bob, is like a garden; it's not random at all, but "a precise combination of loose, intuitive shapes."

The place where those intuitive shapes reached the canvas was, of course, the studio. It's simply wrong to say, as I've heard, that Bob didn't paint in the summer when he was gardening. It's possible he didn't paint in front of strangers in the summer, or anyone whose agenda made him uncomfortable. I once asked him to paint for a film crew and he froze. But I certainly saw him paint in the summer and so, from the record of yet another poem, did James Schuyler. "You got up at seven and went / right to work," wrote Jimmy. "How I envy / you your creative energy! / Painting, painting: landscapes / of Sagaponack."

One could admire not only the creative energy, but Bob's practice of it. I was struck by his file of photographs—I should say pile of photographs—and the way he would attach a photo to a sort of ping-pong paddle that he held in one hand as he painted with the other. You can believe I went right home and propped a photograph next to the typewriter on my desk.

Not everyone reacted in the same way to Bob's influence. The most elusive of visitors to Madoo was no doubt Marjorie Welish. Because Marjorie, in addition to being a poet, is a painter herself—one whose practice is radically distinct from Bob's—she was probably inclined by nature as well as principle to resist his example. Or it might be more accurate to say she was beyond his example. And yet her memory of the place clearly endures, because she recently wrote a poem that quotes an exchange with Bob which occurred on her first visit to his garden more than thirty years ago.

The poem is called "Some Foreground" and you can find it in her book titled *A Complex Sentence.* As you read it, listen not for a logic of syntax but a logic of syllables, referents, and repetitions. The first line suggests that Marjorie, too, must have heard Bob's story that he had spotted Madoo above the tree tops, and it winked at him. "Statement unto tree tops aphoristic," begins the poem. Then, in the following lines, you can identify the exchange that was prompted by Bob's impatient question when, the day after Marjorie arrived, he still hadn't received the compliment he was expecting.

"So what

Do you think of the garden?" "It's Abstract Expressionist," adjacent

as a green   the unmowed   and

Realized at or near the condition of roving through the concept

to leave out

Flowers is not to leave out roots, branches, leaves, the garden

reworded.

If Bob were alive, the entire poem would have been destined for the wall.

John Koethe has likewise revisited the garden in a poem written decades after his first visit. Stylistically, John's work is more transparently discursive than Marjorie's, though in its own way equally analytical and at least as skeptical. He divides his garden poem into two strophes, the second of which begins—all too aptly, perhaps—with a quote from Pound's version of Li Po: "And we were drunk for month on month." The poem, "Melancholy of the Autumn Garden," is from his book *The Swimmer* and its second strophe goes like this:

> I remember walking through the garden
> Without any clue beyond its beauty. There was something
> Marjorie wanted me to say, and now I can't remember what it was—
> Maybe something about gardens over time, who knows?
> In spring it's open to the public, but now the view is mine alone,
> Taking in the trees with no leaves left, the enclosure with its stubble,
> Swaths of gray on gray, the simple placard reading Closed.
> It's there for all to see, and yet its meaning lies beneath it or beyond it,
> In the fantasies of its creator, which is to say, nowhere at all.
> I digress, I acquiesce, I conjure what I want to see from nothing—
> That's the way it works. It sounds like fantasies fulfilled,
> And yet it's more a record of the things discarded on the way
> To a mild November morning, watching the skull beneath the skin,
> Or better still, a carapace from which the mortal flesh is gone.
> The beauty is what's left. It doesn't make any sense, but there it is.

Koethe remarked once that if it were not for Bob and the garden, he might not have continued when he did in writing poems. He was exaggerating, I know, and yet I can testify to a degree likewise. I needed the thrill of *Three Poems* to get started, followed by the surroundings depicted on its cover to continue. We were all so lucky to find this place where art, garden, friendship, buildings, and interiors came together to demonstrate how beauty is an object—an object that both elicits and requires, in those memorable words of Elizabeth Bishop, a "self-forgetful, perfectly useless concentration."

So perhaps I'd be more the pragmatist than either John or Marjorie, and try to define the garden not for what it means but for what it does. I have in mind a dramatic painting of the terrace at Madoo, called simply *The Terrace*, which is also in the collection at the Parrish Museum. I spent memorable hours on that terrace, read Emerson there, worked on manuscripts, and was writing a long poem at the very time, early summer, when Bob was making the painting. Clearly he wasn't gardening all the time.

He was gardening some of the time, however, because this painting originally featured an ordinary garden hose. The hose was coiled at lower left, and extended across the foreground of the terrace toward a hedge on the right—behind which Bob's other neighbor, Kurt Vonnegut, had his swimming pool. The hose was twisted, the way hoses always are, and gave the painting a look of busy, everyday reality. I admired that painting as it emerged into view, but was a lot less sure of my poem, one part of which wasn't working. The next weekend Frank and I came out from the city for another look at how the painting had progressed.

But if you've seen the painting at the museum then you're already ahead of me, because you know that in the completed version the hose is gone. The painting that weekend had become just as you see it now, with an empty terrace more mysterious and alive for whatever action has left, or is about to come onstage. As a lesson in trial-and-error artistic courage this experience of Bob's intuition was profound. I had the poem with me. I took it to the table in the summer house, applied a pencil to the troublesome part—a part twisted like the now vanished hose—and crossed it entirely out. The poem began to breathe, and I've been in debt to that painting and its secret ever since.

DELIVERED AT THE ROUNDTABLE DISCUSSION ON ROBERT DASH, PARRISH ART MUSEUM, WATER MILL, NEW YORK, APRIL 11, 2015, AND REVISED FOR *HAPPINESS: THE WRITER IN THE GARDEN*, BEINECKE RARE BOOK AND MANUSCRIPT LIBRARY, YALE UNIVERSITY, MAY 5, 2017

THE PYRRHIC MEASURE

IN AMERICAN POETRY

At the beginning of its new century American poetry proceeded in an aftermath of doubt. While the treasury was diverted and the future plundered, while the human body was betrayed—in those years trust leaked from the vocabulary. Words were not what we thought, or, if we already knew that, they were even less. Doubt was nearly the national muse, what vistas were to Whitman. But if you liked the vistas, if you ever thought as I did that the old joke about Whitman (he seemed to believe because a prairie is wide, debauchery is admirable, and because the Mississippi is long, every American is God) was not a joke but a *compliment*, you might think doubt makes a cramped frame for poetry. You might wish not to lose the scale.

Scale can be measured in a poem not just by form but by its effect on the reader. Dickinson's scale is as immense as Whitman's. But from Emerson's *Essays* through *Leaves of Grass*, to Ashbery's "Soonest Mended" and beyond, the big vistas seemed to appear most consistently in big blocks of words, prosy chunks that in their sequential and cumulative effects can be sized up as kin to paragraphs. Some of the more interesting poets to follow Ashbery, including the significant examples of Marjorie Welish and John Koethe, began by writing in allegiance to this paragraphical scale. Yet their subsequent poems looked on the page like a test of that allegiance. Welish took the big block of words and fractured it, while Koethe (pronounced KAty) made it even blockier. Taken together, their opposite responses amount to a kind of diagnosis; as a model for poetry, the paragraph was in need of attention.

Emerson's injunction, that the meter-making argument makes the poem, should indicate what the trouble was. It implied there might actually be an argument, when we had come to distrust the capacity of words to make arguments at all. It implied that poems made from an opacity of words might be transparent, that one could see through them to a planet they accurately described, when we had come to re-gard words as so fully refracted by textual and social constructions that from then on, as Koethe warned in the journal *Critical Inquiry*, poems that neglected to acknowledge their disability would simply fail. Even the poetic inheritance I am invoking could not be named innocently at a time when one person's history, as Welish observed in *Art Criticism*, was another's oppression. By the turn of the century, it was possible for people to look back on a poem of emancipating nobility like "Soonest Mended" and read it as an example of irony, indeterminacy, and distrust instead.

Of course, doubt had come to North America before. In the guise of a skeptic faith it was doubt that arrived here on the ships of the first Great Migration. One of those ships in 1633 brought the Puritan theo-logian John Cotton, who, barely ashore, set out immediately to prevent Walt Whitman from ever happening. It's almost touching, from our vantage, to hear the unassimilated suspicion he urged on his congre-gation: "[T]hat certainly here is this distemper in our natures, that we cannot tell how to use liberty, but shall very readily corrupt ourselves. Oh, the bottomless depth of sandy earth! of a corrupt spirit, that breaks over all bounds, and loves inordinate vastness! That is it we ought to be careful of."

Cotton's worst fears were confirmed, but why? I suppose if we look no further than Emerson or Whitman we could say that their claims of inordinate vastness provided such a useful foil for unimpeded capitalism that the system created them as part of its technology of control; could say after de Tocqueville that each of them in solitude was escaping the fearsome gap between the individual and the democratic mob by leaping directly into the sublime; or say that their vocabulary of ecstatic vista was nothing but a provincial hash of Idealism and Romanticism slung together by excitable young people afraid of going brain-dead and forgotten on the outwash of European civilization. We could say any of these if love of the vast were contemporaneous only with capitalism, or Jacksonian democracy, or Goethe and Coleridge. But what do we say then of Jonathan Edwards—a generation before Kant, two before Goethe, an exact century before Emerson—who, facing the woods of the western frontier, disguised his sense of the vast adroitly as a measure of his sin, but whose thrill in its extent was as audible as if he were already Emerson glad to the brink of fear? "My wickedness, as I am in myself," he wrote, "has long appeared to me perfectly ineffable and infinitely swallowing up all thought and imagination, like an infinite deluge or infinite mountains over my head." *As I am in myself.* He all but boasted it, betraying clearly enough that he was ascribing this stack of infinites ("I go about very often, for this many years, with these expressions in my mind and mouth, 'Infinite upon infinite. Infinite upon infinite!'") not to the almighty but to none other than the human mind incarnate in Jonathan Edwards.

In what was to become the United States there was in those days more space where nobody was than where anybody was. That is how Gertrude Stein, in *The Geographical History of America*, explained the scale of American literature. (Edwards, born alongside it in 1703, would reflect the River of Rivers in Connecticut.) But in her increasingly quoted lecture "Poetry and Grammar," Stein left a still more practicable explanation for the big vistas of her tradition. Poetry, she explained, is between you and the noun, and you do with the noun what you do with a lover. You use and abuse it, want it and lose it, caress and avoid it. You also say its name over and over. "Anybody knows," she wrote, "how anybody calls out the name of anybody one loves." *Infinite upon infinite!* The trouble is, if you already knew the name, or once you have known it for a while, the thrill is gone. In postmodern parlance we might have said the name was mediated. So the poem must rename and unname what it loves, give it private names, or better yet no name at all, to return it to its radical otherness. Poetry is not synecdoche but metonymy. Poetry is replacing the name that no longer does justice to desire.

Since nature is not all there is to nature, the vistas anyone loves will be multivariant, multitemporal, and metaphysical as well. That is what makes it next to impossible to accomplish naming, let alone unnaming, in a single word—no matter how juxtaposed. As far as the subject you love is out of bounds, so will the metonymy you are forced to produce be led by its own logic to increase in scale. My favorite way to think of this is that when you are trying to measure anything that is remote, elusive, and intrinsic all at once, you must build a bigger detector. To see the moons of Jupiter you could look through Galileo's telescope, but to locate cepheids in the Andromeda Galaxy and conclude that indeed it was a galaxy required the 100-inch reflector on Mt. Wilson. To scatter alpha particles and prove the atom had structure you could make do with a sheet of gold foil on a table, but to close in on a bottom quark as bound in the upsilon particle required the proton-smashing energies of a synchrotron four miles in circumference at Fermilab.

To me, those analogies make sense of the scaled-up American poem, some examples and forerunners of which resemble particle accelerators themselves: the philosophical writings of Edwards are hulking, repetitive, and practically unmerciful. Nor was Emerson's leap into the kindlier but still immense energies of his *Essays* much of a surprise coming from a writer raised in the persistent half-life of Puritan journals, sermons, and (since *Freedom of the Will* was in his father's library) the works of Edwards. People like to repeat their received wisdom that Emerson wrote in epigrams, when in fact many of his sentences are breathtakingly long. It should have been predictive to learn from his early lectures on English literature that Emerson praised Chaucer and Shakespeare for their prose qualities, and characterized Milton as a "prose poet" (this was in 1835, twenty years before Baudelaire began the *Petits poèmes en prose*). Likewise, he described the works of Swedenborg as "strange prose poems" during the series of lectures he delivered in 1842 to a New York audience that included the twenty-two-year-old Walter Whitman. It was there Whitman would have heard that rhyme may disappear, because, as Emerson explained, the "sweetest closes and falls are not in our metres, but in the measures of prose eloquence which have greater variety and richness than verse."

And if strange prose poems could provide a sweeter metonymy for metaphysical things, Swedenborgian things, what of democratic things, sexual things?—until it's no wonder Whitman responded. There was more he could suggest by indirection, by furtiveness, in the persuasive democracies of prose. Like the American drawl itself, the lines of American poetry could be lengthened, flattened, and expanded in scale to replace the name of just about anything. They could be written to a dimension I have learned to regard, after the example of Ashbery who has written so many of the best of them, as the pyrrhic measure. The pyrrhic foot is the unsung hero in that tribe of iambs and trochees, dactyls and anapests. It is the unstressed platform of the poem, the opposite of the spondee. (If . / is used to represent the iamb and / . the trochee, then . . is how the pyrrhic would be shown.) Many of Ashbery's finest lines seem to echo a distant alexandrine or sometimes tetrameter that has relaxed into an abundance of unaccented, pyrrhic feet. When he wrote in his poem "And *Ut Pictura Poesis* Is Her Name" that "one must / Find a few important words, and a lot of low-keyed, / Dull-sounding ones," he came close to describing in his own words a prosody built on a lot of low-keyed, pyrrhic syllables marked by only a few stressed ones.

But in case my terminology sounds cavalier, I should reveal that I lifted it in the first place from another Ashbery poem, "Grand Galop." This is a longish poem that hints at its prosodic worries by invoking Wyatt and Surrey, then offers in passing one of those used or abused clichés that can exasperate you or go right to the heart of the matter: "If the victory is pyrrhic I haven't won it." No, he hasn't. The victory was won already by Whitman and Marianne Moore, to name but two. It was Moore who implied slyly, as early as 1916 in a little essay she called "The Accented Syllable," that we have had it all wrong. The *un*accented syllable is the one that is interesting.

A persuasive, if unexpected variant in this pyrrhic tradition has been taking shape in the assured but reaching lines of John Koethe. Certain of Koethe's poems can be read as new examples—some being a kind of pyrrhic blank verse—or as abiding descriptions of the pyrrhic impulse.

301

They come to me alone, at first amorphous and serene, in
Sighs and platitudes against a faint interior refrain . . .
Sometimes they seem to me no more or less than convoluted
Variations on a single mode of being, phrased in narrow terms
Directed by exaggerated feelings splayed across a large
Pretentious canvas on the ostentatious scale of the unseen. . . .

The sustained heft of those lines (they are from Koethe's poem "The
Waiting Game") recalls a stubborn truth about prose and the poetries
that mimic it. Sentences are not emotional but paragraphs are. That
was Stein's distinction, although she chafed at it. As a matter of practice
the distinction is hard to avoid. I think any writerly reading of Emerson's *Essays* will discover, for instance, that even where the sentences
are most epigrammatic it is still the paragraphs that make the sparks
fly. Or, as one of Emerson's would-be Boswells, Charles Woodbury, reported in a popular memoir that appeared the year Stein was sixteen,
"It became plain that Mr. Emerson considered the paragraph for him
the limit of logical expression." And whatever we say about the prove-
nance of *Leaves of Grass* (Whitman himself called it a new Bible, and
remarked on another occasion that it could not have been written without the opera), I can't deny that it, too, first read to me as great paragraphs, not versicles, not aria and recitative. Stein did try for a time
to make her sentences as emotional as paragraphs. Then, after "Poetry
and Grammar," she attempted poetry of a different order. Yet even
Stanzas in Meditation, with its ranks of end-stopped lines, retains the
virtue of paragraphs. When Ashbery reviewed it in 1957 he chose to
praise not its indeterminacy, opacity, or spatial qualities, but its dis-
cursiveness: "the feeling of time passing, of things happening, of a
'plot.'"

As an instrument for naming and unnaming, the scaled-up pyrrhic must seem a perfect measure to accommodate the love of the vast, to convey what Koethe called "the ostentatious scale of the unseen." With their frequently heavy caesuras, their twists and turns like an alexandrine that might drag Latinate weight along, pyrrhic lines can be assembled into an instrument like a supercollider, big enough to detect the remote but intrinsic otherness expressed in all the collegiate and corporate, technocratic, litigious, and grandiose vocables that move or, depending on your point of view, control us from the unseen today. During the presidential campaign of 1992, the wife of the eventually successful candidate [meaning Hillary Clinton, of course] was mocked for what the press called her "fugues" of technocratic prose. She had explained that her husband was motivated to become president because "the country was trending in the wrong direction on so many indicators." I thought that was a fluent and all too accurate phrase, a quickening look at the dangers impending on the unseen scale where human lives are moved like inventory. It was the kind of language Ashbery would seize at once for his unfolding landscape of planetary culture—because, as Ashbery has shown so brilliantly, one could deploy the pyrrhic measure to perform a metonymy on the whole information empire, to rename its aesthetic and theoretical abstractions as things, and reveal as no poet yet had done the landscape of the cosmopolitan mind as if its environing styles and clichés were flora and fauna. Or rivers and mountains.

The more we know about the world the more there is, however, to rename. And there, on the frontier of that expansion, is what keeps po-

etry big. Perhaps too big, because today in our supposed embarrassment of riches, we are inclined to worry that the instrument accommodates too much. We are, according to theory, rendered blank: overwhelmed by an infinite upon infinite of simulacra, a vast electronic
badinage in which once solid ground has become bottomless sandy
earth almost as if John Cotton had risen up to say I told you so. Emerson claimed that day is best in which we have the most perceptions.
He had not seen television, fax, or Button Your Fly T-shirts. [Fax?
He hadn't seen the *Internet*.] "Why can't I find my name in this profusion?" complains Koethe in his poem "Early Morning in Milwaukee," a title that scarcely hides its regard for the modernist composures
of an ordinary evening in New Haven. "Nothing even stays," he continues. "No image glances back at me." And yet anyone, anywhere in
the media empire, must now endure this same shifting profusion of
images that never respond, of names from which the thrill is gone
and even the thrill of knowing it's gone is gone—the insubstantial, indifferent profusion in which it finally feels that he or she can hardly
call out names of their own, but are doomed to reproduce a gossip of
clichés as oppressive as the always arriving surfeit beyond which
there is no longer thought, let alone hope, of an alternative place to
live.

　　Well. Admit the problem and one must admit its challenge to the
pyrrhic measure, the meter-making argument that makes the poem.
On its surface the measure appears to be discursive. But if it is discursive, the question it hasn't answered yet is where, in a culture that
is simultaneously various and isotropic in all directions, and under
whose conditions, does the discourse begin? The question is nearly
an accusation and it explains the popularity of chance; because one
way to deal with an embarrassment of riches and still pretend inno-

cence is to flip a coin. Chance is enriching when the world is rich, the empire expanding, and every import brings us something to desire. John Cage had the "chance" to study with Arnold Schoenberg. This was chance that had prepared itself through a century or two of conquest, capital formation, mayhem, accrued literacy, and forced asylum until it was ready to happen right there in Los Angeles in 1934. An accumulation so rich is not likely to occur just anywhere, and at the moment it is increasingly less likely to happen in North America. When America is shrinking poor and clogged, will chance be so attractive? It will be fun perhaps in Paris or Berlin, or parts of Manhattan, but less so in the industrial aftermath of Flint and Youngstown, to say nothing of deeply betrayed Detroit. People are fond of chance because it pretends they are innocent. But if you flip a coin to choose between readymade names, you get a readymade name. Chance alone is not metonymy.

The true virtue of chance methods is that they demonstrate contingency. What they really propose is attention to the initial conditions, the observing conditions. And since the question for any tradition is where to transmit, just as for discourse it is where to begin, a tradition's best agents will recognize when the answer can no longer be casual. Among poets and artists the insight may in fact be scrupulous, as revealed—most acutely, perhaps—in the ongoing work of Marjorie Welish. The following is from her "Design, with Drawing," an exemplary poem that functions also as a critique of our perennial reluctance to believe in art until it is compromised by interpretations of the sort I just inartfully supplied.

> Why ask the artist? Ask the art:
>> rock-ribbed

breakwater, to mark the hue and cry of forgetfulness
and gray areas.

                    Addressees,

what constitutes evidence in stylistic transmission?
Disbelief "much bigger and faster"

                        or problems corroborated,
in a more efficient axe.

Both Welish and Koethe began their careers by writing poems
shaped in the pyrrhic heritage. Her first book, *Handwritten*, and his,
Domes, proceed in sinuous syntax that winds flush left downward
through stanzaic or stichic paragraphs to leave the writerly signature
of a ragged right-hand margin on the page behind. Welish's "Design,
with Drawing," which appeared in her third major book, illustrates
one way she chose to disrupt the linear expectations of her earlier
form. The poem nearly separates on the page into left and right perceptions. If you squint at it to isolate its shape it may even look like a
Cage mesostic, though with the mesostic letters removed and only the
wing words visible. The wings have a wide span. Refocus, and they resolve in a tease of transitions, a license to proceed. The consequent
trade of energy, between the poem's aleatory look and its discursive
undertow, provides the kind of tension that elevates an artifact from
complaint to art.

Koethe, instead of disrupting the pyrrhic form, would fill it out. (He
once admitted that *The Tennis Court Oath* was to him an essentially
lyric book.) His lines grew more solidly impelled, uninterruptible,
their inertial force being so artful as to confess on sight the deceptions

of discourse, while they advanced with equal candor a model of the discursive ideal at work. The resulting exchange, between doubt as expected and doubt as modified in the poem, can lift the tired thrill of distrust into something like but beyond it—a discrepancy of retrospect that redefines.

Like their modernist antecedents, these two poets have composed their spontaneities with care. So, of course, did Emerson. The truth of his meter-making argument needs to be better understood, in order to make it manageable. It was the way he wished to write, perhaps, or his account of the desired effect but not the laborious composition of his words. Alcott left us a description of Emerson down on his hands and knees among sheets of paper on the floor, crawling between them as in a maze to find a prudent escape from here to there. Woodbury reported how tortured were his drafts, pasted or pinned together, written and over-written until the paper "resembled palimpsest." This was surely the opposite of our New York School conceit that the meter-making interruption should make the poem: the telephone call, the chance noise from the street. Ashbery remarked once that "recklessness is what makes experimental art beautiful," and there is truth to his proposition just as there is truth to the merits of artistic prudence. But what if they were two sides of the same coin all along? Such was the timely, perhaps inevitable resolution posed by Welish in her poem "The Poetry Project," whose final lines summoned a poetry that is still undisclosed . . .

> or lies slumbering with amendments
> as our steps drag behind yours, dropping off
> behind your occupancy. Like rain in shadow
> yet pertaining to you, a song of prudence.

Prudence is a term that has a distinct history in American poetics. It made an early appearance in "The American Scholar," where Emerson with his customary irony identified it as the "commendable prudence" of those who know when to jettison home and habit, to "sail for Greece or Palestine, follow the trapper into the prairie, or ramble round Algiers" in search of inspiration and new material. Whitman drew his own "Song of Prudence" from his 1855 "Preface," where he had described nothing less than "the prudence of the greatest poet" and revealed that he, too, was thinking of new material. The greatest poet won't go to Algiers, of course, but will stay put in These States and entice to himself the present day. But we shouldn't understand Whitman to mean by this anything as comfy as our recent aesthetic of the everyday. It is eternity, he explains, that "is held by the ductile anchors of life, and makes the present spot the passage from what was to what shall be, and commits itself to the representation of this wave of an hour." A prudence so cosmic would entail sympathy as much for the ductile anchors as for the waves that travel them. And a prudence so material would affirm its sympathy for the emotions as ductile anchors, too. Doubt of all resource is as naive as trust. Prudence in American poetry means a wisdom of materials.

Welish has been widely recognized as an art critic and painter, as well as a poet. In her critical writings on Jasper Johns, she once commented favorably on that painter's "cautious mode of address," which permits a viewer of his later paintings to reposition in the mind's eye what might seem otherwise a mere overload of images. One hardly needs substitute "prudent" for "cautious" to recognize that the artist was being praised for wisdom in the application of his materials. It should be no surprise, then, to discover that Welish sometimes configures her poems in differently written sections, much as a painting like Johns's *In the Studio* is configured in differently painted sectors. She might compose one section in a fluent, writerly syntax, another in a deliberately disrupted lineation, and yet another as a reductive alternative in which the materials alone (the nouns, for example) appear as though unmixed on the palette. Seen side-by-side as in a painting, or scanned sequentially as in a poem, her prosodically distinct sections operate less as isolated cells of language than as recursive alternatives that accumulate into something newly defined by the detecting eye or ear.

An early signal of her interest in a recursive poetics appeared in Welish's second book as a kind of virtual sestina, "And Now Such a Shore." The poem opens on a sunset. Mediated and familiar, but still "too deep" for words, this sunset will become a metaphor for a change in style. It is first "secret"; then it is "narrow and pure." In ordinary sestinas, the procession of six stanzas plus envoy is frequently the excuse for a willful transit from one irony to another. Welish's "Shore" hides none of that arch sadism. Its sections are as faithful as the unrealized but propagating alternatives represented in the wave function of a muon. Before the event, any one of them is possible. Once the observation is made, it changes everything:

> In preparation for our reading
> we consent to a future,
> but what comes back from the printers is too flimsy
> for mailing—a sunset—and we have to redo the announcements.
> Or perhaps he thought I meant "postcard-like."

It could be a coincidence that those lines by Welish were published the year following the appearance of *La carte postale*, a book in which

Jacques Derrida drew attention to the sequential bias built into the Western tradition (Socrates before Plato, or, in the present case, sunset before postcard representation of the same). It could be. But as "Now Such a Shore" advances toward its envoy it seems to entertain the case against sequence and, coincidence or no, resolve it recursively. Like the smoke from Niels Bohr's pipe as you see it pictured in popular science books to illustrate entropy, Welish's metonymy does not run backward.

> A sunset is too deep
> It is pure secret.
> It is postcard-like.

If you grant poems the appeal of their words alone, the affair may come apart for lack of trust. Grant them unexamined lyric spontaneity and it peters out in empty sentiment. But if you put a prudent sympathy for the words together with a welcome to their recursive consequence, you get a model for something from which the thrill was nearly gone. You get a model in which the creative implications of choice can emerge almost as palpably as things. When Stein spoke in "Poetry and Grammar" about the poet's renaming things, she was careful to include states of mind among those things. She spoke directly from her tradition. "Brave; for fear is a thing," counseled Emerson, confident that fear, once regarded as a thing, could be placed outside us and controlled. In her own confident and increasingly idiosyncratic sequences, Welish has constructed a metonymy for creative choice that places it, too, practically outside us as a thing. She relocates genius so you might take charge of it.

Koethe, in addition to being a poet, has been throughout his career a respected professor of philosophy. Between his first and second books of poetry, he published in a philosophy journal a tightly argued analysis of what the later Wittgenstein meant by the "criteria" that allow us to talk of mental states. At the center of his analysis was a prescient hypothesis that revealed his motive for worrying about such criteria in the first place. Suppose, he wrote, a community where by sudden mutation the individuals can no longer feel pain. "Suppose that they believe the mutation is only temporary; or that their children, or the occasional foundling, should be taught what pain is (in case they decide to migrate to another community later; at any rate, suppose that they have an interest in *explaining* what pain is, despite the fact that they cannot *feel* it)."

Suppose, indeed. Suppose a postmodern culture so saturated by stimuli that it has lost the capacity to feel not pain but subjectivity. A poet might want to explain the feeling of subjectivity anyway, either in self-justification or in case the mutation proves only temporary. As a philosopher, Koethe argued that this would not be an epistemic problem, not a problem, that is, of whether we can prove such mental states exist. It would be a semantic problem, a problem of naming, of using and abusing the noun. That doesn't make it easier. When we are told to have hope, for example, most of us probably think of something we would be hoping for. But what is hope itself, without its object? In his subsequent poems, Koethe seemed determined to represent such mental states as hope and disappointment without reference to their objects, to present them not in terms of other things but as things themselves. The fact that Wittgenstein found such a project difficult to impossible must make it the kind of dare that philosophers, and apparently some poets, too, are unable to resist.

A notable example of Koethe's determination was his 208-line poem, "The Constructor." The poem begins as a lament for the modernist fictions we now know to distrust. It ends as an invocation to fictions we haven't yet described. Along the way, its emotional logic is achieved not by denying distrust, but by testing it, with a tenderness both to distrust and the persons forced to harbor it. If we are not persons, for instance, if there is nothing personal prior to language, then "Why must there be so many ways to disillusionment, of / Coming to believe that no one else can feel and that / One really *is* alone?" By the end of the poem, the constructions of the modernists have been turned by use and abuse into those added by the philosopher-poet himself. His "Constructor" becomes a metonymy to offer readers the sense of being sounded that they once expected from "Soonest Mended" or the "Final Soliloquy of the Interior Paramour." Welish has made creativity visible; Koethe makes subjectivity visible. The vistas he names over and over are those of emotions and mood, those fiercely subjective things that render persons unknowable and desirable, both to others and themselves.

By describing our mental states as if they were things, Koethe also shows us ourselves as strangers (and provides a new insight, perhaps, into what Stein really meant when she said she wrote for herself and strangers). In his long poem "Mistral," he inscribed a portrait of this stubborn stranger-ness in which anyone's subjectivity is visible only as a reflection.

> a condition beyond certainty, in which nothing changes
> And it remains alone, in an oblique kind of happiness,
> Bathed in the furious transparency that separates it from
> Another person's dense, unimaginable interior reality.

Those are lines that went to the soul of our distrust. Having assumed that subjectivity issued from the personal depths we had no choice but to doubt it, because we rightly doubted the depths. We were an easy mark. Subjectivity never came from the depths at all. Transparency is what made us individual. Transparency is the barrier that forecloses intimacy, not because you aren't there—you seem dense and unimaginable—but because I am not there. People understood this in America once before and it made them radical. Others are lenses, Emerson told his listeners, and without them you simply cannot focus your own mind. "Each man," he continued, "seeks other men, and the *otherest*." And still this was no skepticism. It is our furious transparency that provides us with the otherness to save each other, is therefore most to be protected, and is proof at last of the necessity to defer to the subjectivities we love as we would to any other materials of the poem, because they are things.

Every so often a critic decides to expose charlatanism in American poetry and begins by ridiculing the dictum of Williams, no ideas but in things. The critic should not be taken seriously. Insight, explained Emerson in the nineteenth century, will always "ultimate its thought in a thing." Edwards, in the eighteenth century, was imperative (the italics are his): "The child should be taught to understand *things*, as well as *words*." Stein in the twentieth was ingenuous. "And then, something happened and I began to discover the names of things, that is not discover the names but discover the things the things to see the things to look at." No, the real question for a critic who has done the reading is why a tradition so stubbornly focused on things should continue to produce writing that is, for the most part, outscale and abstract. The answer seems to dwell in the things themselves. Isolation is not what they have in mind. "Gravitation and chemistry cannot content them," said Emerson of the stars. "These beautiful basilisks set their brute, glorious eyes on the eye of every child, and, if they can, cause their nature to pass through his wondering eyes into him, and so all things are mixed."

Tradition is most persuasive when it comes to a barrier, and leaps. The two poets I have been considering in this essay chose opposite approaches to get the pyrrhic measure clear of doubt, yet in the work of each the tradition has landed on its feet. I am tempted to say it landed with its transparent eyeball intact. ("That meant new terms of transparency," writes Welish, "or, rather, that meant we were transparent to everything—.") And as long as humans are transparent, it will be things at the surface that count. Truth is not isolated in sensation for Nominalists nor in theory for Realists, but skates as Experience teaches in cross-correlations of the two. We should not be surprised that the tradition turned out to be more than metaphor. When Bohr said it didn't matter what quantum mechanics was about as long as it worked, he could have been testifying on behalf of our native pragmatism. "It is 'about' correlations in our experience," he said, "what will be observed under specified conditions." You can hardly sense unaided, for instance, the character of a muon. It has a mean lifetime of 2.197×10^{-6} seconds, and a spin of ½, but there is nothing there that is really spinning. The muon may exist beyond language but it comes true only when mixed in human media and named. One could even say the skeptics have had it backward, and it's no proof of skepticism that our words don't live up to nature. It's proof of optimism that our words are the best that nature has.

Sometimes when people discover the infidelities of words they react as if personally betrayed. They press their case as if justice could be done. Who will do it? Our hopes like our physics evolve in cross-correlations of media and its users, media and the altering otherness that confronts and teases us. Even Edwards had some powerfully mediated language to confront as he prepared to rename the immensities before him. When in 1716 he entered Yale at the age of thirteen he had access to one of the three copies of the *Principia* (this one the gift of Newton himself) then in America. The first philosophy Edwards undertook to write, when he was sixteen, was backed by an addendum of his speculations on gravity made thick in its initial pages with the same Newtonian word over and over: *infinite*. From the very start, the tradition thus made its pyrrhic scale in the cross-correlation of things and, as Koethe observed in an early poem he called "Partial Clearance," what things are like.

> Why is it supposed to be so important to see things as they actually are?
> The sense of life, of what life is like—isn't that
> What we're always trying so desperately to say?
> And whether we live in between them,
> Mirror each other out of thin air, or exist only as reflections
> Of everything that isn't ours, we all sense it,
> And we want it to last forever.

The trouble is, the mind that sees muons sees mass mailings, too, and it would be a sad trick to preserve in poetry a tradition that can only mimic the stimulus overload we blamed for our populist accidie in the first place. Transparent to everything, won't the pyrrhic measure end as the ultimate parody of Whitman's lists? The serious answer is that things have been for sale in America for a long time and we are not the first to notice it. Poetry, for this is what else Stein said, is also *refusing*. "Poetry is doing nothing but using losing refusing and pleasing and betraying and caressing nouns." Whitman's famous lists did not pick up on every offering. They included certain classes of everything: things of birth, evolution, and death; things of exploration, expansion, and contraction. They did not specify the early sensationalist merchandise of our long dawning day. People forget that Whitman was first an editor. The test of literary composition, he explained in *Democratic Vistas*, was "Nature, true Nature, and the true idea of Nature." You will read in vain for cherubim and seraphim, or nightingales. "Make no quotations and no reference to other writers," were his instructions to himself when he was living at 99 Ryerson Street in Brooklyn and writing the new Bible that would become *Leaves of Grass*. "Take no illustrations whatsoever from the ancients or classics ... nor from the royal and aristocratic institutions and forms of Europe." Can anyone wonder what Whitman would think of ideas by Gucci, theory by Sony, poetics by Hermès? The inexpungible *Leaves of Grass* is evidence not so much of inclusiveness as of a passionate partiality.

The diction of Koethe's poems has been as unique in contemporary poetics as if he had admonished himself in formulas the way Whitman did. Make no flippant reference, suggest no surrealist insincerities. His sentences are notably dispossessed of the swank ironies and preening sarcasms we seem to regard as our birthright and grave responsibility. Sometimes poets parody the clichés. Koethe writes as if already forward of their inevitable decay. His response has been to use, abuse, and forgive nouns mediated so long that their very familiarity calls attention to their being summoned home, as in his "Argument in Isolation," to make poetry.

> I think the truest language is the one translated by the leaves
> When the wind blows through them, and the truest
> Statement is the one asserted by the sun
> That shines indifferently on loneliness and love;
> And that neither one is bearable.

Ashbery, asked once how many types of diction he was aware of incorporating in his poetry, answered, "As many as I can think of." The retort might appeal to Koethe, but could not apply; the dictions anyone can think of were purged from his palette in order to isolate the argument itself. But to return at this date to the most familiar of nouns for your semantically sophisticated project is to make use in public of a long poetical history. The classic diction that Koethe employs to frame his skepticism paradoxically implies an atemporal confidence, which both summons and requires the optimistic evidence of his style.

Welish announced even more overtly an aesthetics of partiality. The title of her poem "A Full Hand" would be suggestive on its own. Owing to my private interests it made me think immediately of a remark by Red Jacket, the Seneca chief Emerson quotes so approvingly. To someone who had complained of not having enough time, the chief replied, "Well, I suppose you have all there is." With like wisdom, Welish acknowledges in "A Full Hand" that every artist must confront the task at hand with the only hand there is.

I cannot imagine myself free-standing, only occasioned
and partial . . .

Still, I hereby affirm
the pen is on the table, the draft is pure surface.

Welish in those lines was as much a moralist as Marianne Moore. It would be a dim petulance to decide, because you can't know everything, that you will write nothing; as dim as deciding, since you can't live forever, that you won't live at all. The desperate need to reference all data—on bond issues or celebrities, recherché literatures or rival software; the need to be in the know, itself—is of course an envy. Unsatisfiable, it makes us easy to manipulate. The reassurance Welish builds into the very structure of her sequences is that the part doesn't envy the whole. When she places one configuration against another, one pattern against another, she testifies that the pattern, like DNA, not only contains the whole but may even be its point. Like the genes that transformed the cultural landscape of the earth, the part is as immense as its possible planet in both act and memory.

Many, often divergent flora are in delicate competition
and a little published,
as when a phrase I speak awakes as yours.

By transforming the gestures of the pyrrhic paragraph, Welish and Koethe have shown the way to an effective preservation of its scale. Put these now dissimilar poets together and this is what they say. *He*: we act as a site of transparency, an impressionable thing that mirrors words on a surface that desires them. *She*: those words are inevitably poetic, and when we sequence them we act as the thing once known as creativity. *Together*: change happens through us, though we as the sites of transparency are never changed. There remains, then, a necessary role for the agent of subjectivity which Welish warily identified in an essay as the "poststructuralist contemplative," and Koethe cautiously described in a poem as "the genius of reflection / Imprisoned in its self-consuming enterprise that still / Continues to reverberate throughout the universe." Each of these exacting poets preserves that scale where choice and the unwillingness to choose operate from a desire, understood as the conscious limits of the world, that wants no limits but those it sets itself.

Eventually, the success or failure of a poem will depend on your opinion of what poetry should do. If you think it should assemble and sustain a coherent self and society, you will be disappointed. If you think it is a way to use and abuse, and so fleetingly to devise a universe that no one otherwise could inhabit, you may regard it as evolution's gift and a bravery to transmit beyond the self in trust. As a species, we have been misled by advertising and religion to believe we have some inherent lack in ourselves. We have been led to believe that this lack can be supplied if only we will spend the rest of our lives on getting something. But subjectivity as a capacity doesn't change. It stares unblinking as a sphinx, no more or less immortal than when it started out. The advantage is, it entertains our questions in the sequences we bring to it. The idea was not for you to be made more significant by things. That would be specist. The idea is for things to be made more significant through you. There is the morality of metonymy. I am sorry Emerson ever revised the wording of his advice in "Self-Reliance." He had it right the first time: do your *thing*.

Desire respects things in their absence, and it makes us reach. The genius of the pyrrhic measure—in line, scale, motive—must be proved in a reach that justifies doubt as one more state poetry lived through, one more state in the infinite vista of states. This is not mere faith. If there are pyrrhic victories, the kind it is wise not to win, then there is pyrrhic defeat of the kind it is art to lose. Decomposition is metonymy, after all, and yours is what the universe wants. Things stand apart to tease us, and language that takes them for granted is not what things have in mind. You wanted them true forever? That is how through desire, anybody repeating the name of anything one loves, through desire as always, nature gets the job done.

1992

THE APPLAUSE OF SCIENCE

Voyager I was still closing in on Saturn when the *New York Times* wondered in an editorial what a poet would say, what Auden in particular would say, about the encounter. "We wonder," wrote the *Times*, "—and with due respect to all poets past, present, and to come—we don't. Because the words we've read in the news reports have the kind of poetry, the poetry of fact, that occasionally surpasses art."

It wasn't true, unfortunately, about the words, but there was something to consider in this editorial all the same. I used to think only poets, and then only the nuttiest, most ambitious poets, actually took it as a matter of course that it was up to them to provide the tropes and metaphors we humans need to hook the new cosmology, to haul it home into the human memory. Yet here in the paper was an opinion writer who, despite some mild bard-bashing, plainly assumed that the wide universe would inevitably get its poems. Since I believed then, and still do, that civilization implies a poetry to ratify Hubble and Heisenberg as much as Newton, Darwin, or Galileo, I thought the writer's assumption was, well, touching.

All this came back to me when I was reading a new volume from the Yale Series of Younger Poets, *Terms to Be Met*, the first book of the poet George Bradley. On the cover is a photograph of M31, the Andromeda Galaxy, and in the contents are poems called "Antimatter," "About Planck Time," "The Life of Stars"—enough to suggest that the author is one of those poets to come, already making the new universe his enterprise. Except, as he decently acknowledged in his title, Bradley has a problem. Where once the poet of nature hoped to encounter facts, there are now "terms" to be met instead.

321

Of course, writers have always faced a factual estrangement, the secondhand way our species has of knowing things by name. As a poet of the new cosmology, Bradley has a further problem, however, in what we should think of as practical poetics. Emerson observed the distinctive shape of the Dumbbell Nebula in Vulpecula through an Alvan Clark refractor, one of the high-tech instruments of its time. Milton, in *Paradise Lost*, described features of the lunar landscape with such discovery that it would be nice to think he inspected it himself, having seen it (Milton then still had his sight) through a telescope of Galileo's during his visit to the old astronomer in Fiesole in 1639. But Bradley cannot see the features of a quark. Even if he went to Fermilab, he could not see a quark. And he cannot inspect the features of a quasar. At the national observatory on Kitt Peak, or at the Very Large Array of radio telescopes in New Mexico, he could expect only the grossest image of quasar morphology. At Kitt Peak he must wait for the image to build up on emulsion or silicon; at the Very Large Array, for computer images to be mapped from radio wavelengths to which he is simply insensible.

Yet no one doubts anymore that quasars (quarks, too) are real, and the mind regards them with longing. Maybe they do represent the extremes, in an explosion of scale that we can comprehend but never apprehend. No matter, the mind still longs to expand with them, to be big enough to hold even one idea that will remain, as Bradley puts it in his title poem, valid through all extremity. It doesn't seem, though, to be working out that way. The quarks and quasars leave us behind, "at the margins of the mind, where we must live."

To the long tradition of epistemological regret, this poet thus adds a more immediate lament. And if it is really true that the state of blessedness rests on the act of vision (which is what Beatrice told Dante) then Bradley has something to be sad about for sure. Like the rest of us, he lives in a cosmic precinct that scientists tell him is more immense but more measurable than anyone ever thought, and at the same time he is reduced to perceiving it by their terms: quasar, quark, and worse, intermediate vector bosons and black holes.

Words like these compound the poet's troubles. If you try to use them they are likely to confound the poem, not because they are awkward but because they are so proud. Worked up for a paper, invented for a conference, they are aimed to convince, awe, charm, or simply to bludgeon the skeptical into agreement. They are words that make you try to remember exactly what a boson is and how it is different from a meson; and if you are remembering, said wise Gertrude Stein, that is what a masterpiece is not. They are words used also to display possession—of knowledge, status—and it was maybe this usage that suggested to Bradley the appealing remedy he deploys against them. In *Terms to Be Met* he demonstrates that one good way for a poet to meet the new cosmological terms is to humble them, and be humble about your possession of the cultural capital they stand for.

Humility is not a practice most people associate with poetry. The *Times*, in its Voyager editorial, clearly believed that when poets got hold of Saturn they would make it more poetical. Many writers who popularize science seem likewise to believe that to excite an audience you have to embellish the science with poetic license. The astronomer Carl Sagan was eager to emphasize how we trace our roots to the dispersion of heavy elements from exploding stars, and before that to the fashioning of those elements by fusion within the stars, and still before that to the appearance of hydrogen and helium from the precise mix of elementary particles that obtained at the first hundredth second of the Big Bang. All this he summarized when he called us humans "starfolk." It was sophisticated in its way, just right for television. And yet, though it was exactly what the majority mean by poetic, it is difficult to hear this proud expression fitting into even a postmodern poem.

The irony is that it's the poet, not the scientist, who turns out to be the more matter-of-fact. The first poem in Bradley's book could not have been written without the standard model of cosmic evolution, the very one Sagan celebrated. "The composition of many particulars / Held the broad promise of our beginning"— this is the abstracted way the poem begins. So welcome to the lecture, you say; only it's a lecturer who is well along in the poet's project of not quite remembering. That precise Big Bang ratio of a billion photons for every one nuclear particle has come back in the poem as mere "particulars." And as the poem ends, its almost clandestine terms suggest, but don't quite remember, the settling into this planet of those elements that would twist themselves up into starfolk. The cosmology is there but its terms have been humbled, just right for a poem though not nearly poetic enough for public TV.

In another way, however, this poem of Bradley's tallies perfectly with the expectations people have of poetry. It doesn't seem to be about what it seems to be about. Ostensibly, it isn't about stellar evolution or anything like that, but about crossing the Verrazano Narrows Bridge. And, since it proceeds by a formal conceit meant to suggest a bridge, it could even be about structure. James Merrill, who as judge of the Yale Series selected Bradley's book, pointed out in his introduction that the end words of the poem enact a "little triumph of engineering" as they ascend toward mid-poem and, in reverse order, descend. You pass them like pylons on the way down. If you watch them, they divert you all the more from the subdued astrophysical terms in the background of the poem.

There will be scientists who wonder why anybody has to review their cosmology so indirectly. They should consider that poetry is scaled to a human receiver, and think back to a time when scientific observation was scaled the same. Even today, if you are trying to find a faint star with the naked human eye you will be told to search for it indirectly, out of the corner of your eye. It works, too, because the rods at the outside of the retina are more light-sensitive than the cones in the center. The point is, something similar happens when one is looking at a poem. If I'm going to be convinced, it's because I've read it there slantwise for myself, not because I had it pounded into me. So poets plan for the corner of your eye, and that is why they tell truth slant. It also explains their efforts to get you to look away from the main event. Think of *The Changing Light at Sandover*, Merrill's epic at the Ouija board, where the Ouija board serves to divert you from the truly audacious project of the poem—writing an ethic for the cosmos meant to be valid, as Bradley himself perhaps read it, through all extremity.

But the unavoidable reason that contemporary science must inspire a poetics of indirection is still the practical one: you can't directly describe what you cannot see. The real surprise will come as poetry meets this problem in ways that might have appalled us when we were modernists. Young poets, who haven't learned to hoot at the gaucheries of the pathetic fallacy, are apt to discover that the discredited techniques have become plausible again. After all, if you can't even see the plain and leafy fact that Ruskin told you to describe, what's wrong with a pathetic fallacy? Or remember the scorn we were supposed to feel for poems that drew a moral? Then Bradley's poems will be cause for wonder, because they thrive on allegory. They also flirt with the forbidden fallacy—so successfully in a poem about our neighbor galaxy, "M31 in Andromeda," that Bradley seems to be inventing a variant: the galactic fallacy. What makes this fallacy different is that *human* pathos is not its main concern. The main event takes shape in the background. The reader can question the correspondences, but it is established meanwhile that the galaxy in Andromeda is really here, as continuously part of the mental landscape as Bradley's other subjects, Kansas City and Monument Valley, Galileo's abjuration, or the Alexandria library on the day it will catch fire.

By reopening Ruskin I am not trying to suggest, because quarks are bound and quasars thirteen billion light-years off, that we must endure an onset of anthropomorphic black holes or squalid moralizing. The civility, the Lucretian gravity that characterize Bradley's lines in "M31 in Andromeda" seem to demonstrate that we can look to postmodern poetry for its own high standards. Maybe it is scientifically absurd to ask a poet to apprehend directly the plain and leafy fact of quarks and quasars, but we can still ask if his or her trick of indirection is acquainted with what we know from science to be true about the world. Yes, this is dangerously substantive. In unsubtle hands, inquisitorial. But it is just not enough to judge poems on their technical facility. In the long run, we *expect* them to be well written. What distinguishes a poet, what makes us name her Bishop, him Stevens, is the poet's attitude.

Stevens thought a poet's attitude was itself an analogy, an analogy to mediate the reality that is not ourselves. I think he was right, and we are permitted to judge attitudes just as we would judge any other analogies or tropes the poet uses to write a poem. Stevens also believed that the supreme virtue for a poet, in regard to how he or she fashions such an analogy, is humility—"because the humble," he wrote, "are those that move around the world with the love of the real in their hearts." Based on motion and love, this is no formula for meekness, but for active practice. As Bradley employs it, knowingly or not, it is the formula for an active democracy of consideration: a kind of one-fact, one-vote respect for things that are real.

Most real things are still discovered on earth, or from it. So the poet's perspective, at least for now, will have to be planetary. But what an advance that perspective already is. In *Terms to Be Met* there is a poem, named for El Niño, in which a violent perturbation of climate can be read as an allegory written by the planet itself. Seen as allegory, the violence El Niño does to the earth corresponds to the violence done by all the human perturbations, economic and religious, which also distribute the wealth and divide the blessings, which move things around because they have "tired of this world and begun to dream / Another dream of how this world should be." In contrast would be the figure who presides over a poem Bradley sets in Assisi, a town identified in the poem as "dedicated / To a man who managed to love what was around him." El Niño dreams of an ideal world, and his missionary dissatisfaction threatens to rupture the living cell of this real one. In Assisi, the saint of Assisi manages to dream only of Assisi. You may find the attitude that draws such a contrast to be deeply conservative or radical. It will depend, perhaps, on whether your frame of reference is the study of man or of the earth.

It is unfortunate, but the love of things as they are, whether on earth or in its real heavens, comes no easier for poets than for the rest of the species. In the seventeenth century, George Herbert wrote an unpleasant poem, his first "Vanity," which condemned astronomers along with chemists and pearl-divers for preferring facts to faith. In the nineteenth century, Whitman stooped to an instant chestnut, "When I Heard the Learn'd Astronomer," the burden of which was he'd rather look in ignorance at his stars, thank you. Still another century after that, and Auden was doing just what Whitman did. In fact, the reason the *New York Times* speculated on how Auden would respond to the Saturn encounter was that he had responded to the first moon landing with a poem even more disagreeable than Herbert's or Whitman's. "Unsmudged, thank God, my Moon still queens the Heavens"—that is what Auden wrote, if you can believe it. I wonder how far that truly differs from the sentiment of Vicki Frost, the plaintiff in a federal court in Hawkins County, Tennessee, who complained that her rights were violated by a seventh-grade textbook that suggested her children consider themselves a part of nature. "Our children's imaginations must be bounded," complained Vicki Frost. She might as effectively have said "unsmudged."

All four cases—Herbert's and Whitman's, Auden's and Vicki Frost's —reveal a preference for ignorant fancy over reality. The fourth case, Vicki Frost's, reveals why it matters. Poets and parents may wish themselves out of evolution, but somewhere is a boy or girl who will want to join it. Since no one knows the whereabouts of that boy or girl, our best bet as a species is to look after the probabilities that most favor the random achievement of what Bradley calls a mind of "optimum content." It's our best bet, because . . .

                                    although no one
Seriously believes it of himself, all of us are born
Equal to one another more than we know and equal
To little else, neither the love of women, held
In the tremulous hands like something fragile, nor
The love of language, words turned on the tongue;
And thus the poem arises out of a chance accumulation,
Out of a mind that perhaps achieved optimum content
Months or even years ago, say one morning in winter
When the sky was so blue and steam rose off the ocean
Into the other element of air.

What does poetry have to do with the evolving cosmological content of the human mind? Poetry does not occupy most minds for very long. But it gets them sometimes when they are in love, or when they are in school—attentive moments in the life of a mind. Whitman said it when he had his wits about him: poems are the final applause of science. Maybe poets don't legislate, but when the mind is prepared it may hear how a poet applauds. The poets ratify.

THE NATION, 1986

DEBORAH ROSENTHAL'S

ART OF DEEP TIME

Time is the great secret pleasure of poetry, not time recaptured but time opened and free of constraint, time the pervasive vista, and a proposition to be discovered in the abstractionist work of Deborah Rosenthal is that time, so perceived, is the secret pleasure of painting as well. The art historian E. H. Gombrich, who once judged abstract art a failure, would not have agreed. Painting, he explained, lacks the dimension of time—a perhaps hasty dictum that serves mainly to remind us that abstraction as a continuous tradition was in his day barely begun, and is today still in its youth.

Klee, having noted that a distinction between temporal and spatial art was "an academic delusion," went on to locate time in the line. Delaunay saw vastness in color. And as heir to both insights Rosenthal has refined them in metaphoric solutions that are now wholly her own. Each of her paintings, by excluding perspective, foreshortening, or other recessional illusions, insists on the integrity of a *line* that evolves but can never vanish in the surface geometry. Each, then, is a vision of time not to be circumvented by mere entry or passage. Meanwhile, her always transitive *color* (the artist herself has called it "hyperbolic") is likewise released from representation. Allowed to extend its own dialectics, her color responds in a plenary membrane of forces, making a bold analogy to the fabric of this universe where the farther we look the more time we see.

The analytical cosmology implicit in her work was confirmed by

Rosenthal's dramatic painting *Landscape with Lovers*, first seen by many when it was reproduced in *Modern Painters* in 2004. Yet no one, not even seeing that painting, could have predicted the sustained creativity that would produce a series of such lovers and continue by adding, with uninterrupted energy, an astonishing second series that calls to mind the asterisms long seen in the constellation Orion. The viewer does not have to wonder what combination of personal circumstance and motive demanded these two series in order to appreciate that they are metaphors driven by the artist's creative fate. They constitute two *pendant* series, whose meaning intensifies logarithmically when they are viewed together in one room.

The body-like figurations of the great *Landscape with Buried Lovers* are daringly frontal, not only contained in their Prussian blue medium but sustaining it, as if they were quantum persons raised from the well of probabilities and about to collapse back into it. They must be Paolo and Francesca, "summoned by desire" as Dante described them, "with wings poised and motionless," bound together in this painting by the passionately torn blaze that links their erased—or are they white-hot?—heads. Perhaps their still buzzing thoughts radiate from beyond the normal spectrum, can't be revealed, and they are really our template parents, Adam and Eve, about to discover free will and where to choose. Or maybe it's better to regard them as pure emblems of binary balance—desire and repose, the equals sign, chromosomes—borne by a medium that might be the web of gravity, tradition, genetics, or even the inescapable history of art. They are binaries of mutual support, protection, and (one has to conclude this from the Orions that follow them) they may mutually engender, too.

How satisfactory, then, that Rosenthal's striding, youthful Orions not only comprise the space they approach but alter it as they go. Her allusive image could be Poussin's blind Orion, the mythical giant in search of light. But our knowing that the constellation of that same name is in reality the site of an immense star-forming nebula—the nearest such nebula to earth—means that *our* Orion is in itself a source of light. So the figure in Rosenthal's spectacular *Orion Sharp and Emphatic,* with its subtly Vitruvian proportions and shining nimbus, could as likely be a metaphor, as was Blake's *Albion Rose,* for an ambiguous, if undeniably beautiful and prescient grandeur.

Rosenthal has been called a metaphoric abstractionist. Labels are always mistaken, but this one has the virtue of bringing the artist's affinity for Byzantine mosaics, Romanesque altarpieces, Gothic stained glass, and illuminated pages like those of the Morgan Library's ninth-century Beatus manuscript into a focus that makes perfect sense. "The wall and the page, the carved stone doorway and the glass mirage, all haunt me," she has written. "History, homage, have nothing to do with it!" Her interest is the metaphor. And the very shape of her paintings may prove it. Three of the Orions mimic the narrow dimensions of a predella, the lowest section of an altarpiece, while *Landscape with Buried Lovers* suggests a horizontal relief in the tympanum above a Romanesque doorway. In a previous show, certain of her paintings recalled pages in an illuminated manuscript.

To this observer, however, her images of evolving line and hyperbolic color recall just as vividly those false-color composites that come back from the infrared or X-ray satellites whose sensors are trained on the remotest events of cosmic history. They are called "false-color" not because infrared and X-ray wavelengths are unnatural but because the image must be enhanced to distinguish signals our species can't otherwise see. You might say the color is hyperbolic but there is nothing anti-naturalistic about it. In the same way there is nothing antiquarian or nostalgic about Rosenthal's affection for pre-Renaissance art. She is no more transfixed by the remote past of predella and tympanum than the astronomer is transfixed by the remote past of quasars and exploding galaxies. Hers is another example of the artist's mysterious intuition as it leads to the exact metaphor that will express for the rest of us a reality we can't afford to misapprehend. To be in the same room with her unexpected Lovers and pendant Orions is to be alive in a perceptually expanding universe, and sense how, with world enough and time, we might inhabit it.

ANNOUNCEMENT ESSAY, *LOVERS / ORION*, AN EXHIBITION BY DEBORAH ROSENTHAL AT THE BOWERY GALLERY, NEW YORK, SEPTEMBER 30–OCTOBER 25, 2008

THE CIVIC METONYMY

OF MICHAEL SCHIAVO

Michael Schiavo's supercollider of a poem, *The Mad Song*, appears at first glance to have returned a universe of fractured aphorisms. It has produced, in other words, exactly the results you might expect if you could load the familiar expressions of civic wisdom, fashion, and popular belief like protons into a giant accelerator ring and hurl them in opposite directions to collide at nearly the speed of light. The ensuing shower of particles—the verbal omegas, taus, and upsilons—would resemble the bursts that have been recorded in the stanzaic paragraphs of Schiavo's poem. Measured separately, his lines have the bite of epigrams. Taken together, they lope with the erotic generosity that proceeds from all the best unions of high and demotic culture. They represent in shards the "bittersweet village," as Schiavo calls it, a structure one might democratically imply, or reassemble, from "the scrapyard of knowing" and "the amorous dell."

Or perhaps not. The English poet W. H. Auden maintained there was no such thing as a democratic aphorism because an aphorism could never be written in a democratic style. Its wisdom was by nature aristocratic, and any writer that pretended otherwise was a coward and a hypocrite. Of course, if this were true it should make us suspicious of aphorism, not democracy. Americans, at least, might answer from the example of their literature that wisdom comes rather from a common store; that the writer retrieves it for others who could as easily gain it for themselves if they, too, had been afforded the preparations for the trip. This was, in fact, a perspective shared by the more encouraging American poets, and it was formulated to perfection by Gertrude Stein, who thus countered Auden beforehand with an aphorism of her own. "The important thing," wrote Stein, "is that you must have deep down as the deepest thing in you a sense of equality." The proposition, we remember, was supposed to be self-evident. So it is more than satisfying—it's a relief—to discover the same radical sympathy ennobling Schiavo's poem and ready in a new form to be passed forward once again.

One wants to believe that American poetry will always have room, like the Fourteenth Amendment, to expand toward voices that faithfully call on it. There will be servile justices, of poetry as of law, who try to restrict the franchise. But the logic of the literature is against them, and the great principle returns to extend its formal and experimental reach. In this latest instance, an alert prosodist would see that our poet has conceived his poem in the form of a flag. Unless we're totally nuts it scans as a flag. Why else the thirteen sections like thirteen stripes or the original stars? And why otherwise five stanzas per section like the five points of a star? Granted, it isn't the flag on your lapel or the one over the ballpark, and it's certainly not the shock-and-awe prop they station in ranks behind the candidate on the platform. It's the radical pennant within: a constituent of perception and organization as intimately registered as any of the metrical drumbeats and prosodies to which, by this poem, it is now formally compared.

On the other hand, my scansion could be madness itself, as I'm all too aware. Years ago, having explained to an analyst how depressing it was to feel day by day the diminishment of our national prospects and liberties, I was gently informed that it is considered a personality disorder for the boundaries to be so fragilely perceived between the nation and the self. The analyst, however, was not a product of these United States. He had not internalized Whitman and wasn't schooled in the heart—as the author of *The Mad Song* so clearly must be—by that Emerson who observed once of the Union that the crime of dissolving it would diminish the importance of every person that lived.

Because of its form, *The Mad Song* is sure to be labeled a prose poem. The label functions customarily as a polite denial. There are clever definitions that compare prose with poetry and attempt to dodge the snobbery by blurring the distinction. A more useful approach might be borrowed from the ever-helpful Stein, who preserved the distinction in a way to illustrate why *The Mad Song* is poetry through and through, and not some cousin of the art. Prose, she pointed out, is an affair of verbs, adverbs, prepositions, and articles. Poetry is an affair of the noun. By this she meant to indicate that prose describes while poetry renames. Likening the poet to a lover, she reasoned as a good pragmatist not from the prosody but from the behavior that makes a poem. "Anybody knows," she wrote, "how anybody calls out the name of anybody one loves." The problem, as anybody also knows, is that the name may prove inadequate to the passion, too soon get stale, be rendered ineffective or insupportable. And that's just people. Imagine if your anybody encompassed the nation itself, democracy, the environment, or even the flag. In a time when rumor and perjury arrived as if from the infected air, when evil, having escaped its bottle, perverted your own name as well as the one you love, who could bear to recite the foundational name? The answer, as Stein concluded and Schiavo would demonstrate, is to recite the name over and over, try new ways of reciting it, in the fervent desire to reinvent its effect. Poetry thus defined is not description, it's metonymy.

Perhaps my scanning *The Mad Song* as a metonymy of the flag was not so disordered, after all. Schiavo does seek to restore, and the solution he adopts is the one of alternative recitation. Necessity would be the muse, therefore, of the inventively varied diction that evokes in the course of his poem Stein herself, *Star Wars* and Shakespeare, Dylan and Dickinson, Robert Johnson, Thomas Jefferson, Jeff Tweedy, and more. The presence of Jefferson, as the stylist of the Declaration of Independence, is diagnostic: the Declaration, too, was a cry of unrequited love. It expressed for the colonists their aggrieved love of country and baffled frustration at being denied its protections and liberties. Indeed, the abiding pain of broken trust that animates the Declaration is distant only in time from the emotion we ourselves may feel when forced to watch silently as a justice of the Supreme Court offers on television another sophistical brief for trashing the Bill of Rights, or when we wake after a holiday to learn that the executive has sneaked out a new finding to permit strip mines in Yosemite or asbestos in oatmeal. The familiar perfidies may explain why the temper of a mad song appealed to Schiavo in the first place. The anonymous seventeenth-century verses ascribed to Tom of Bedlam (i.e., a deranged indigent, scorned in love, who is turned out of the asylum and must beg for sustenance) convey an adaptive mix of injury, anger, pride, resilient affection, sarcasm, and sullen lucidity which could hardly be better attuned to the plight of the average citizen rendered invisible by a banal and condescending oppression. Schiavo's saving insight was to import the intensely personal sense of betrayal from a mad song into the vastly impersonal optimism of his native romantic pragmatism. If it seems an unlikely combination, he has nonetheless effected it seamlessly, and his own *Mad Song* is simultaneously sobering, heartening, and pertinent as a result.

The main current of American poetry has never fully accommodated the disabling deficit its readers would sustain when betrayed by their own country. There have been outcries, *Democratic Vistas* and *Howl*, whose places in the tradition remain unsettled. And yet poetry, no less than political society, needs to recognize the measure of its injury in order to continue as a credible agent of cultural transmission. Schiavo's prosodic achievement, which arrived with a spontaneous authority that may be harder won than he knows, resizes the necessary wisdom to a lyric dimension that still doesn't impede the exercise of what can only be called a transcendental citizenship. His refusal to be diminished by the country—the refusal to let the country diminish itself—is ultimately a kind of devotion. One thinks naturally of Hart Crane. But we might also recall the original instance of a patriot's adopting the persona of a mad Tom. That was Edgar, the betrayed heir of Gloucester in *Lear*. Outlawed, hunted, while arguably the sanest character in the play, Edgar chose to wait out his fate in disguise and is notable for not fleeing, plotting, or collapsing in despair. Imitating a madman, he preserved the abused fragments of society as they came into his charge (in the person principally of his blinded father) until the transition could be made from anarchy to a legitimate, albeit damaged peace. It claims much for poetry, though not more than anyone should demand, to observe that poetry in a similar disguise may likewise further a transition. "Let go of the land," writes Schiavo in a haunting, aphoristic line that goes on to signal conditionally why this shouldn't be our wish at all. "Let go of the land if not for the odd." By preserving the fragments of the civic litany that came into his care, by reciting them in a metrical coalition that seeks to reinvent their effect, Schiavo has created in *The Mad Song* a metonymy for the requited citizenship one might have enjoyed in a country that loved its citizens as much as they love it.

FOREWORD, *THE MAD SONG,* **2008**

APERTURES ON

A VIRTUAL FIELD

Michelle Jaffé remarked once of her room-sized installation *Wappen Field* that it asks us to consider "what we, as human beings, share in common instead of focusing on what divides us." On the evidence of the installation itself, which I saw in 2012 at the Bosi Contemporary Gallery in New York, she couldn't mean this as the blameless sentiment we think. It certainly wouldn't describe my reaction as I turned from the sidewalk to the glass-fronted gallery and was there confronted by a phalanx of twelve impassively gleaming helmets, suspended at face height, and seemingly locked on the whites of my eyes. Instead of our common humanity, I was impelled to consider in haste how we as a species are alien—to others, each other, the planet, and ourselves. In the game plan of those helmets, I didn't register even as an impediment.

They made a deep phalanx, too, in staggered ranks of five, four, and three helmets each, such that an end run was inadvisable. In short, I was toast.

In the meantime, they sure were beautiful. High-tech but Homeric, faces both of fashion and terror, they presented the innocent art-goer with a perfect occasion to reflect on the distinction between things beautiful and things sublime. That distinction, which properly refers not to the objects but to the experience they elicit, has become respectable in art discourse again. You can raise it without fear of hyperbole, and this, too, no doubt encouraged me to my thought.

Of course, they weren't really helmets, not even if Jaffé's title prompts us to think of them that way. The German *wappen* (she pronounces it with the "v" and not a "w") means coat of arms, which naturally would inspire a visitor to parse the English as a field of battle. One might interpret it as any contested territory, I suppose, or as the expanded field that sculpture has long since won. A diagnostic essay on site-specific art, published by Rosalind Krauss in 1979, was called "Sculpture in the Expanded Field." But the truth is, battlefield or abstract territory, the objects that confronted me weren't really helmets. They were fire extinguishers. It took Jaffé nine years of directed patience to bring *Wappen Field* from conception to its exhibition at Bosi, although the work was substantially complete a year earlier when it was installed at the Urban Institute for Contemporary Arts in Grand Rapids, Michigan. She had been far along in its creation when she learned that the helmet-shaped objects of her design would cost more to manufacture than she could budget for the entire project. The fire extinguishers were a sudden insight. Each empty canister was refashioned into the minatory shape I could now see, and the effect was made the more fearsome by her decision to have the resulting objects chrome-plated. Economy aside, they certainly looked expensive. They were all polished indifference. They betrayed nothing of an interior being, but amassed their effect by sequence, one gleaming object after another. In such manner these helmets (for now that I've made the point of their facture, we can call them that again) revealed their impeccable minimalist lineage.

In early minimalist work the sequence itself had to supply the dynamic that keeps art interesting. Today, we might reason that repetition increases the probability of an emergent order. Complexity theory has pointed the way. Once I regained my nerve, for instance, and had penetrated the front rank of helmets in *Wappen Field*, I could see the others advance or shift position to intercept me from the periphery. More dramatically, I could see that the forbidding, convex shapes that first confronted me were, on their reverse, vulnerable and concave. They were vacant, ready to try on. Each helmet, recognized more accurately as the visor part of a helmet, featured a narrow aperture horizontally incised at eye height. It would not be long, to judge from my experience, before you as a visitor put your head inside, eyes at the aperture, there to exchange your observer's overview for the restricted squint of one of the visored guard. Outside the convex, you were threatened. Inside the concave you are the threatener. This polarity, which remains unresolved, was enough all by itself to make *Wappen Field* a minimalist success.

There was a time when a minimalist success, especially in music, was a liberation so extended one could hardly want to go beyond it. Judd's boxes were thrilling, but *Music for Eighteen Musicians* was meant to free the bound quarks. The repressions that too soon intervened—the social, ideological, and informational enormities—made the style seem optimistic, too innocent perhaps to be believed. It had come to seem, as John Ashbery once observed, "as quaint as a Shaker rocker." So the post-minimalist response was to counter skepticism with information, to add allusive content (helmets, rather than boxes) while reducing the redundant assertions of form. One might also add media. Some sculptors added light or sound. Michelle Jaffé adds both.

I say she added them, when it is obvious from *Wappen Field* that this was not the case. The thin shields of light she projected on the floor beneath each helmet were there to counteract our sense of gravity, which otherwise might weigh the helmets down to earth. One perceives immediately the shields of light and only later the chaste rods that suspend the helmets from a framework at the ceiling. Photographs, by collapsing space, collapse the timing of this perception. On site it's the shields (perhaps they are the *wappen*) that seem to hold each helmet aloft, as if on a column of invisible memory. And because Jaffé's light toys this way with gravity, because it alters the perceived mass of her installation, it is clearly sculptural. It was not an add-on; the work would not survive without it.

When you put your head into one of the helmets you also discover that Jaffé has sculpted in a similar way with sound. The helmets, though they betray no interior life from without, are all commotion within. As your visual field narrows to the visor-like aperture, your auditory field expands. It expands in an onrush of unintelligible vocables—unintelligible, that is, as discourse, while perfectly intelligible as prelingual emergencies of being. Among them I could identify anxiety; but also anger, surprise, relief, erotic chatter, gutturals such as those that betoken wisdom, reverence, grief, and even prelingual pretense.

The sounds were not off-the-shelf, either, nor adventitious. Jaffé worked with composer Ayelet Rose Gottlieb to create vocal sound events, which were performed and recorded by Gottlieb and six other vocalists. Jaffé and the software artist David Reeder then reconfigured the recorded events by means of the open-source program SuperCollider. The resulting sonic flux was routed through the suspending rods to speakers in each helmet. Because the sound is algorithmically spatialized and recomposed, no two persons in separate helmets will hear the same thing at the same time. Most visitors, who seem instinctively to recognize this separation, move from one helmet to another, their sound plane shifting as they change position.

The contrast posed by the serene visage of each helmet and the visceral unrest within is frankly spooky. Once you have seen the serenity, once you have heard the internal chorus of mammalian aspiration and complaint, you might wonder all over again what humans share in common that the other species don't. The query must have been there from the start. Conceptually, it was one of Jaffé's mediums and she sculpted it in. She has always been interested in what she calls "the pre-cognitive." In fact, she qualified that statement of hers, the one about *Wappen Field* and our shared humanity, by referring immediately to the limbic brain that drags us into repeated conflict. Apparently, what we share in common is that we are fatal to one another.

The field I encountered at Bosi Contemporary was thus a reminder of all those interminable fields where the vanished bodies leave only secrets for us to listen to. The allusion was intensified at the gallery by the placement, beyond the helmets, of silent works that resembled cast-off armor: namely, codpieces. Sensuously realized by Jaffé in anodized aluminum, these outsize jockstraps called to mind the proud equipment that is discarded on the field, or seized for trophy after the slaughter is done. More fatefully, they were that same armor in resplendent storage, silently building up pressure for the war to come. I'm indulging the distant perspective (you can almost hear "Taps") when it's just as plausible the armor was funded by Homeland Security; it will be deployed by the officers in the helmets to crush dissent. Here, then, was an exemplary use of gallery space. The anodized artifacts functioned as evidence that what you had just experienced in *Wappen Field* was imminent as well as historical.

In your position at any helmet, the limbic experience that registers in the brain was not only personalized, it was frequently isolating. Thanks to SuperCollider, the sounds come according to an indifferent flux, rising sometimes from the field, approaching sometimes from the back or sides, but continually stretching or contracting your apprehension of the field. Sometimes—a deeper surprise—the groans seem to emanate from you yourself. You have become the alien, trapped in this alien phalanx on a planet where you never intended to be born. Jaffé, having changed your apprehended space by means of sound, was making it clear that sound is a sculptural medium, too.

She is certainly not the first to make the point. Max Neuhaus always insisted that sound was a spatial medium and this has been the traditional way to think of it in three-dimensional sculpture ever since. The question is whether three dimensions are enough. Christoph Cox, a pacesetting philosopher of sound who began his career with a book on Nietzsche and progressed from there to a critique of sound art, argues that sound as used in sculpture is indeed more than spatial. He thinks it adds a fourth dimension of time, not clock time, but time as a kind of temporal sublime. He also maintains with earnest, perhaps unwitting charm that sound art is "under-theorized."

It seems impossible there could be anything left in art that needs more theory; but I'm willing to believe that Cox is right. Deploying an amalgam of Nietzsche and the currently rehabilitated Bergson, he aims to reconceptualize sound by separating it into two categories. One is actualized sound, the attentional sound of a musical composition, lecture, or even a poem. The other is virtual sound, the unceasing, unattended sonic flux we thought was noise until John Cage offered us an aperture for its appreciation in his famous silent piece, $4'33''$.

Sculpture, when it advanced on the expanded field, did so partly in search of analogues for Cage's breakthrough. One of those analogues was Walter De Maria's *Lightning Field*, installed in 1977 on a high plain in western New Mexico. The irony of *4'33"* had been that it required a concert setup, complete with seated audience and David Tudor at the silent piano, to frame the virtual sound that one might otherwise hear by simply listening. The irony of *The Lightning Field* was that it required a grid of four hundred stainless steel poles, placed two hundred and twenty feet apart on a remote plateau, to frame the planetary weirdness of our planet, which, but for lack of attention, one might observe anywhere nearby if not anywhere else. Jaffé brought those two ironies of framing together in a single installation, *Awakening*, exhibited at Sylvia Wald & Po Kim Gallery, also in 2012. In that work she used Cage's idea of virtual sound to rescue De Maria's virtual space.

The plan of *Awakening* was breathtaking in economy, as economical in its way as *4'33"*. Jaffé traveled to *The Lightning Field*, which is notoriously difficult to visit. It admits annually no more than eleven hundred visitors, six at a time. Those six must stay overnight together in the single cabin. Photographs and videos are not allowed. The well-known photos you've seen are authorized. Perversely, although it was meant to reveal a dynamic tapestry of light, dark, and atmosphere when visited in person (it is said to be glorious at dawn), *The Lightning Field* has become for most of us a static postcard. Jaffé turned her attention to its sound. She recorded what you might hear there during twenty-six minutes and twenty seconds after dawn. At the gallery she placed seven fluorescent tubes, fixed horizontally to the walls at a height ten inches above the floor. On the floor she left two pillows so visitors would take the hint and sit. The gallery's lights are dimmed, the tubes glow thin-atmosphere blue as if on a high horizon, and with the assist of strategically positioned speakers, the dawn begins. Coyotes yip and wail, the wind drones, insects chitter, the ravens croak, and one raven takes flight with wingbeats so percussive you are inclined to duck.

In a travel essay published the same year Jaffé made her recording, the writer Geoff Dyer described his own experience at *The Lightning Field* as intense. He described its light and dark and distance; but he never mentioned sound. Not a yip, wail, croak, or buzz. So perhaps sound is under-theorized, after all. I can certainly attest that the allusive playback of Jaffé's *Awakening* did for my static image of the famous field—and by extension any field on the turning earth—what 4′33″ once did for noise. It opened an aperture on unattended space by framing that space in the sound of time.

According to Christoph Cox, the difference between actualized sound (such as a composition or a poem) and virtual sound (such as Jaffé brought back from New Mexico) will correspond to the distinction in Nietzsche between being and becoming, or the distinction made by Bergson between quotidian time and duration, *les temps* and *la durée*. To my mind, there is something beguiling about that latter distinction, *la durée*: rather too beguiling, like finding out there really is an eternity. Cox is confident, however, that there is nothing essentialist at its base. More to the point, then, I would like to know how he would distinguish the sounds, composed but algorithmically reconfigured, which emerge from the helmets of *Wappen Field*.

I think I can guess. There is good minimalist authority for linking the flux of perception that precedes a work of art to Bergson's concept of durational time. None other than Donald Judd cast his appreciation for the paintings of Pollock and Barnett Newman in just such terms. The thought and the emotion of their work, said Judd, was "underlying, durable, and concerned with space, time and existence. It's what Bergson called 'la durée.'" But Cox has gone beyond Judd. He implies that the installation artist can actually sculpt with duration the way Cage composed music from duration, not by process of analogy but by providing in the work itself an aperture that opens directly onto durational time. Cage and the post-minimalists, he writes, "posed a notion of time as duration and proposed an infinite, open process in which presence and completeness are forever deferred, a boundless flow that engulfs the auditor or spectator in a field that he or she can never totalize."

Well, there you have it: the answer I was looking for. That boundless, engulfing flow is not a bad description for the unintelligible commotion that issues from the concave interiors of the helmets in *Wappen Field*. Once again, it appears they weren't really helmets. They were portals, through which I could overhear the virtual, sonic field of a species whose emergence was but one possibility in durational time. By the same token, the fluorescent tubes of *Awakening* weren't blue-fingered dawn. They were foils to bewitch the eye and focus the ear, transports to the alien sonic events that occur as this oddest of planets spins, and accomplishes unacknowledged what should stupefy us every day with disbelief.

A boundless, engulfing flow is not a bad start, either, toward a description of the sublime. In the nineteenth century, if you wanted to confront the sublime you stood on a pinnacle of the world and looked into the abyss of geological evolution. Time flowed boundlessly to your transparent eyeball. You were "glad to the brink of fear," as Emerson said. People once got this thrill in the Catskills. The fortunate, who can afford the price of admission and travel, may get it still at Marfa, *The Lightning Field*, or *Spiral Jetty*—although these are increasingly destinations of privilege. Imagine the carbon track entailed. Nor are they under-theorized, which must eventually compromise their brink of fear.

Jaffé's models of the sublime, by contrast, are each transportable. *Awakening* can be set up anywhere, like a tent. And *Wappen Field*, as we know, was installed initially in Michigan, where it was popular with the art-going public and featured on local Fox TV. Now, I don't doubt that Fox TV can compromise the sublime. But it would be nihilism in the extreme to deny that a free quotient of Michiganders, perceptive beyond the media, could discover in art more than enough of wonder to redeem their state.

Wherever it goes, one thing that will be said of *Wappen Field* is that the helmets are beautiful. They seem too beautiful, almost, to be sublime. Regarding their ranks from the front, or recollecting in tranquility from the back, you can always take the distant view. It's a comfort, that view, the way "Taps" is comforting. It elevates you above the fray, and visitors who go through the installation in a hurry can probably preserve the elevation. On the field itself, brought to attention inside the helmets, their sense of comfort would begin to fall away. In place of the visually serene order they would hear the ceaseless, reconfiguring field of vocal skirmishing. It was inevitable that someone, if not this writer, would compare that field to the philosopher's concept of durational time or the composer's virtual sound. But there was another comparison we could make to the same effect. We could approach *Wappen Field* as a field in quantum physics, and conceive its sound as the unrealized events that are propagating there as waves. Seen, or rather heard like that, the vocables one registers through any helmet become the constituent elements that someday may evolve— or fail to evolve—a star, a particle, or a species. They are those elements before they actualize as language or collapse back into inanimate entropy. To listen through one of the helmets is to hear back in time, the way a telescope looks back in time when focused on a distant nebula.

When we express our fate in terms of such grandeur we are still, of course, indulging the distant view. We are regarding it *sub specie aeternitatis*, as the philosophers used to say, "under the aspect of eternity." This, too, is a comfort, since it presumes we are still here and our fate has been a success. Knowingly, or because she couldn't help it as an artist, Jaffé removed the safety of that beautiful view. She made sure our view would be limited, as it is in life, by the armor that protects us. She approached the sublime not by making us grander, but by inserting each passing visitor as an alien—inarticulate, helmeted—in the indifferent flux she defined by sound. I call it indifferent because, thanks to SuperCollider, you can never rely on what is coming next. There will be no time-out for "Taps." Caught even momentarily in that field is to be sonically subject to a sentient but thoughtless universe, not even grist in its evolutionary will to power. It would be only human to resist.

One can make a case that the traditional sublime, the view from the mountaintop, influenced profoundly the art and science of its time —probably the politics, too. In the guise of romanticism, it was widely perceived. People haven't widely perceived the evolutional sublime.

You don't climb a mountain to see it. Because it comes to us in private, because our bodies are familiar to ourselves and lovers, because we measure it in blood pressure, orgasms, sonograms, and exiguous decades, it seems only *our* birth, *our* death, *our* fever. We measure it in policies and negotiations as if it were *our* war and *our* climate change, rather than what it is, the indifferent thunder of evolution in anonymous flesh. There is the new abyss.

The thing is to confront it. That is why these works by Michelle Jaffé matter. She is never strident; her installations refuse to give up their subtlety. She can sneak their effect right past the media. Whether in the immersive dimensions of *Wappen Field* or the exquisite chamber work *Awakening*, she has opened apertures on the sublime that render it visible, audible, and imminent.

A PUBLIC SPACE, 2012

INTRODUCTION TO

A LONG POEM BY

ROBERT C. L. CRAWFORD

Critics frequently ask the kind question of a poem. They ask how it was written when the rest of us might more radically wonder why. We know school can produce an agreeable how, as can influence, but some crisis in lived experience seems to be required before the poet can summon a convincing why. The logic of the requirement verges on trite. Times change, while the unavoidable anxiety for poets and readers alike is repeated in each generation and is always the same. Ethically, practically, emotionally, *how shall I live?* Opinion lags, and only experience can match the anxiety to the times, possibly to resolve them. That is the possibility Rob Crawford has proposed in "Euangelia," his audacious, spiritually epic poem in seven parts, the first two of which I'm introducing here.

I was tempted, given the title of his poem, to announce that Crawford has finished the job and we can all relax. *Euangelia* (you-anGELL-ia; it's plural) means good messages, good news, which does seem to promise optimism. The promise must be provisional, however, as it's not entirely borne out by the news that arrives in the first sections of the poem. Here, in metrically intuitive but unfettered lines, the reader will encounter a somewhat ominous mix of aims, admonishments, nourishing loveliness, and abject reversals—which, taken in sum, make a plausible analogue for the ambiguous profile of our times.

There is no doubt an excess of pride in believing we are uniquely compromised by the times, yet many can imagine with more than a shudder how we will rate in retrospect. "All had espionage in the blood," observes Crawford in the poem. "And it is sure this can never be repaired!"

Of course there is room for praise, in even a dreadful age. "The quail is nesting, and the vibrant jay," he reports, and the mere sighting of something so joyous can still make you feel like kissing the air. Meanwhile, especially if you are young, tugging against your will a coercive debt and expecting no sinecure, let alone inheritance from the 1 per cent, there can be no evasion, no elsewhere, no ethical flinch. Your daily work, as Emerson once advised, is to learn the secret of your time. Never quaint, he also identified an exacting program for learning it. The source of your information to unlock the secret of the age, he said, is your love of it.

Defined like that, love is an instrument. As a means of discovery it could account all by itself for the sweeping, restless embrace of Crawford's poem, each section of which resembles at intervals a kind of enraptured deposition taken by counsel for the plaintiff spirit. Because the title is plural (the singular is *euangelion*) the sections can be read as multiple messages, compound evidence that collects in the space of just a few lines or in a single allusion. The poem opens, for instance, on a vista of arrival and accumulation as if seen from a promontory, which is here called West Rock. The actual West Rock is a ridge of Jurassic basalt that rises in the outskirts of New Haven, Connecticut. From its south crest one can see much of that city, including Yale. Famous once as the hideout of Puritan regicides, West Rock was the subject of an early work by Hudson River School painter Frederic

Church—his breakthrough painting, because it abandoned the usual foreground of rocks and trees in favor of a frontally abrupt expanse. Crawford's momentary allusion to this particular compound of geology, history, art, and atmosphere might recede from view if I hadn't selected it for attention. It's an instance of his setting the scene as life does, in a nonstop if discontinuous sequence of image, subject rhyme, and sound. You can't live it all. But from the discontinuities one inevitably selects markers, for a reason the poem makes perfectly plain: "for one must / Prepare, comprehend where one stands, below the shifting starlight."

The most dramatic of markers to be seen in Crawford's poem is its sheer prosodic mass, an allusion to Milton and, closer perhaps to contemporary interest, the Ashbery of "Clepsydra" and just after. It is a release of pleasure (innocent pleasure, by the way) to follow the capitalization at the head of each line as it proceeds without embarrassment down the page; the effect is as bracing to the eye as the fused pillars of basalt on the face of West Rock. Not everyone finds the fashion for lower case soporific. But any who do will appreciate the way the confident capitals hold the disrupted syntax of contemporary poetry taut. Their procession down the page marks, like a conductor's downbeat, the time counting out in the poem and running out in the life. They are units as useful as minutes, hours, and days—days such as Crawford describes near the close of his second section: "Whose sensual power we feel though they later end / And in the end leave a record less real / Than the lives they helped to bring." Not the least message of "Euangelia" is that it assumes the reality of those individual lives. In its very prosody it reminds us that poetry may have great aims, even when eminent voices continue to discount great aims as if they were still fighting the battles for reputational space begun long ago in their youth.

Crawford must be the first poet to use the word *soteriology* in a poem. He uses it only in passing, but on reflection it's surprising not to have encountered the word in poetry until now. Having looked it up, I can report that Soter was the mythological spirit of safety, i.e., the savior, and as a title the name was applied to Zeus and to other gods. By analogy, Caesar was styled Soter Augustus and the early Christians seized on the term as their own. Soteriology becomes thus the study of salvation. Not even Ashbery, as far as I know, has used the word, although absent a digital search I grant you I couldn't say for sure. We all remember from "Self-Portrait in a Convex Mirror" his famous apophasis that "the soul is not a soul, / Has no secret, is small." Crawford's reformulation, whether in response to "Self-Portrait" or not, can be isolated in two syntactically upfront lines. "The soul, seeing its own death, cries out for a savior / And, there, cries the birth of the true, eternal soul."

You or I may balk at that, as perhaps would Ashbery, but Crawford too has complicated the hypothesis. He has done so in a way that once was heresy. Paraphrased, his formulation reads like this: that the soul, even if not a soul, resembles one at the moment it wishes it were. It's a kind of soteriological pragmatism. Something like it was there in varying degrees in Whitman and Dickinson; in modernists Eliot and Moore; in Susan Howe, John Koethe, and of course much of Ashbery. Perhaps it's the subject of the great American poems. Perhaps the writing of poetry—the why of it—is soteriological. Until Crawford, I hadn't thought of it just this way.

One doesn't have to parse a poet's soteriology to enjoy the how of a poem any more than you need to embrace the Congregationalism of Frederic Church in order to admire the breakaway bold mass and attendant details of *West Rock*. I can admire "Euangelia" as I would the painting, without reducing it to an exegesis that confines. There are sweet details to be read in the edges and middle distance. I was an easy target for the poem's idiomatic line "It brought a tear to my eye to see, so real was each thing," because of the way it recalls the heart-stopping *sunt lacrimae rerum* (there are tears in things) spoken by Aeneas at Carthage. It may not be immediately clear how such a detail relates, or why some lines are disjunctive while others obtain the lyric elevation of Crawford's final lines in his section two. But one knows from traditions of the long poem that a line at the outset can resolve when it returns in variation at the close, that the andante of one part is justified by the allegro of another when heard in the overall score. It is necessary to both hear and read, close up and at a distance, and all preferably at the same time. We have long since learned to see a painter's brushstroke resolve at a distance into a single compelling field. Likewise, one can hear the syntax of "Euangelia" resolve, feel its anxiety melt, into the kind of sustained tone Crawford has described elsewhere as "its stately fearful ambience."

Crawford has a liturgical ear, as does Ashbery. He can deracinate a sentence, as might a Language poet. Such strengths are the effects of lineage as well as influence, and they can be used to reconstitute poetry's aims as well as its language. Crawford has taken them over for spiritual ends, much as Church redeployed his artistic inheritance to suggest in *West Rock* a beneficent spirit of nature in the American nation. In "Euangelia" the reader will find a memorable phrase for that kind of successful overhaul; Crawford calls it a "translate depiction."

Reading his ambitious and finally hopeful poem, one realizes how many things natural and cultural must in fact be translated to survive. There was a time, as pictured in *West Rock*, when hope itself seemed to create the good news. It appears the good news of poetry must now create the hope instead.

PRELUDE, 2015

MARK MILROY

PAINTS MY PORTRAIT

People should wait to be famous before having their portraits painted. It's only polite. Although in that case how does one account for certain memorable examples of the postwar era, including Fairfield Porter's early portraits of poets James Schuyler and John Ashbery? They weren't famous then. I suppose they wanted to be, which raises the question: Is it sheer vanity that motivates a sitter?

The predictable answer is yes. The English critic Michael Archer, author of *Art Since 1960*, wrote once that the very mention of portraiture made him snort with derision. If we must have portraits their subjects should at least be famous—the celebrities painted by Elizabeth Peyton, or morally didactic figures re-imaged by Gerhard Richter—subjects that arguably elevate an artist's work to the status of history painting. Better yet would be a video feed of random pedestrians in Trafalgar Square. But for an individual sitter, warned Archer, to have your portrait painted was a "preposterous bit of self-aggrandisement," and the artist who functioned as a "jobbing portrait painter" had nothing at all to do with contemporary art.

Behind a sneer, of course, there is usually fear. Surely I felt a kind of fear when Mark Milroy announced he should paint my portrait and showed me a postcard reproduction of his work. I hesitated. Or perhaps my preposterous vanity hesitated, because this Milroy didn't look like the Porter portraits I admired. For one thing, I had no idea who it was. Proud, handsome, the subject was nonetheless anonymous to history. Later it would be possible to construct a genealogy of the portrait's style, but my first attention stumbled on its unexpected visual heft. It was more material than virtual, as if Porter (to say nothing of Peyton and Richter) could be placed lovingly in the pantheon, there to be acknowledged without being followed.

Something in the pose of the anonymous subject also implied that sitting for one's portrait was not the same art event for the sitter as described by the critic. For the sitter it was perhaps an investigation—an individualized instance of conceptual art—which promised to succeed despite the fear of self-aggrandisement. Or indeed because of it. Aren't you supposed to go in the direction of your fear? In fact, it suddenly occurred to me that deciding not to sit for your portrait because portraits are an exhausted tradition would make no more sense than deciding not to have sex because your parents and grandparents have already done it. Besides, it would get me admitted again to an artist's studio.

By the time he proposed my portrait, Milroy was painting from his studio in a nineteenth-century barn in northeast Pennsylvania. For a dozen years he taught drawing at the National Arts Club, while his work appeared in independent galleries in Brooklyn, Manhattan, and Sag Harbor. Living in Manhattan, raising one son and expecting another, but facing a merciless rise in rent, he and the writer Kelly McMasters decided to move their family full-time to the farmstead they had purchased earlier to have a place in the country. The township where they would now live was twice the area of Manhattan with a population of 656, or fifteen residents per square mile. From the porch Milroy added to their farmhouse, you could hear, on a cold autumn night, more coyotes than that.

The romance of the place did not disappoint me (it might have been *Home in the Woods* by Thomas Cole), although I wondered as I parked the car and Milroy came forward from his studio in the barn if I had disappointed him. His face fell, just for an instant. I had been told to wear whatever was comfortable, and since I spend the better part of my life in nearly identical work shirts had worn one of those. Comfortable it was, but no doubt austere compared to the striped crimson vest worn by the subject on his sample postcard.

As we entered the barn my confidence recovered. Milroy was converting the structure himself and had chosen to emphasize its dramatic lift of space. There was a window where the hayloft door would have been, and the north light fell from a great height to suffuse this distant workplace with its uniform glow. Since our first item of business was to agree on the portrait's size, I was invited to look at several finished canvases: a richly hued head-and-shoulders of New York publicist Lauren Cerand, an ambitiously scaled portrait of a mother and daughter, *Anita and Nora*, and the perfectly sized, three-quarters view of slouching choreographer Stanley Love, whose posture betrayed the resting energy of a feral cat.

It was an intimate exhibition, curated for an audience of one. But it set in motion the kind of experience you can have at a crowded retrospective when the aesthetic on view locks suddenly into place as if you'd been preparing for it all your life. These weren't the faces of restrained transport one sees in Porter's latter-day transcendentalists. Nor were they faces of anguish, apathy, or incipient necrosis as rendered by the expressionist and realist artists to whom Milroy is sometimes compared. Placed next to those previous examples, the individuals in his paintings would appear to inhabit, as the saying goes, another planet. If the paint was expressionistic, the faces were not. They had the fated caution of animals, making me think I had entered not so much a studio as a cabinet of specimens at some alternative stage in our natural history.

Sitting for your portrait is said to be a collaboration, or a contest of wills. The painter Michael Wishart likened sitting for his friend Lucian Freud to undergoing delicate eye surgery (this was before lasers). Milroy favored the collaboration approach, explaining several times that we would work together to make the portrait a mutually satisfying event. I'm afraid I suspected on the spot that his words were rehearsed. It's true I was consulted. We had no sooner got started than he asked what color were my eyes and I thought, *huh*? This guy can't distinguish the color of my eyes and I'm going to let him paint me? Until on the instant I had to suppress a smile, remembering the orthopedic surgeon who, as he directed me to remove my jeans so he could examine a trick knee, asked gravely, "Are you wearing underwear?" Each was creating a record: the surgeon against a harassment charge, and Milroy, not against getting the color wrong but against insulting my untaught sense of color. He must have had subjects who believed their dim eyes were blue, or dishwater hair blond, before they saw otherwise in the finished portrait.

Martin Gayford, whose book *Man with a Blue Scarf* was about sitting for Freud, made the interesting observation that to sit for a portrait is like returning to youth. It affords the luxury of long hours in which to trade ideas, jokes, and stories. The appeal of such a luxury perhaps varies with the personalities involved. The feminist writer Naomi Mitchison, sitting in the 1930s for Wyndham Lewis, remarked that she would have sex with him so she didn't have to listen to his opinions. Schuyler recalled that Porter rarely spoke. Milroy, however, talked freely and did his best to make me reciprocate. We compared tastes and shared complaints. On one occasion he looked out from the easel, brush poised, and asked did I look more like my mother or father? Since he had never seen either of those individuals, I hardly believed the answer could help him. Father, I replied, although alas I have my mother's smirk. She would try to smile and all she could do was smirk.

"I think I've got the smirk," he said in wicked triumph.

But no matter how animated the conversation, it was still not a collaboration. I took a plaid shirt to the second sitting, thinking to make up for my monochrome first impression. Milroy wasn't interested. Apparently he had accepted my mail-order wardrobe as a challenge. This was all as it should have been. I wasn't standing over his shoulder to create a self-portrait by proxy. I wasn't staging a self to be portrayed.

The genteel skeptic will interject that there's no self to be portrayed, anyway. It is customary now to believe that consciousness is contingent, fragmentary, multiple, to the point that the individual is less a reality than a social construct. The curator Donna De Salvo reflected on this changed perception prior to an exhibition of portraits she installed at the Parrish Museum. "Portraiture is an incredibly complex topic," she said. "A lot of it doesn't even have faces in it anymore." And that was 1995. The self has hardly recovered its authority in the meantime.

Artists and critics seem oddly proud of this devaluation of their subjective being. Some have been pleased to discredit the self as a way to discredit expressionist painting, or lyric poetry. For a while they discredited it so forcefully one could be forgiven for wondering who was the enemy and where the argument. Had they never read "Self-Reliance"? Or were they so taken in by secondhand intelligence they didn't realize that the notorious essay with the ironic title is a lesson in how to evade self-interest and rely, instead, on our common origin. Ashbery is the poet who has restated the lesson most usefully for our time. "We must learn to live in others," he writes; "they create us."

How simple and beautiful that formula is, and hard to follow. Stating it, however, one begins to understand why sitting for your portrait can become an individualized instance of conceptual art. One sits for a portrait as for a translation. One sits to be othered. *Je est un autre*, your portrait will say, as before your eyes it escapes its occasion.

David Hockney maintained that portraiture is an instinct. "It cannot be taught," he wrote. Others believe it's a fallacy to imagine that a painter can reveal the complications of a subject. If we think it possible, so the argument goes, this is only because we've learned to read the conventions of the craft. An abundance of paint means intensity, tangled paint means complex emotions, and so on. The Neo-Expressionists of the 1980s gave this kind of art a bad name—they were proof positive of the "expressive fallacy"—and no one, unless it is disguised as ceramics or ropework, has dared to like it since.

I suppose that is why Milroy's work first caused me to hesitate. He uses a lot of paint and rarely thins it; his canvases become as physical as you sense his perception of the sitters must be. One never finds in his work the flat, affect-free surface meant to glorify the mechanically reproducible while remaining aloof from the mess of human biology. His colors slip and accumulate, often right to their edges. Yet none muddies the color adjacent. In this way his paintings reflect the temporal slippage of lived experience, but without dissolving into any skeptical disregard of the boundaries that inhere, sometimes sternly, in physical fact. One might expect from the expressive physics of his surfaces that Milroy flings himself at the canvas. That wasn't the case. He painted intently, but with an air of directed husbandry. You could imagine him leveling a door. At the same time, the man did love his paints. Turning *ut pictura poesis* on its head, he once spoke to me of the lure of writing. "Often I wish I could write," he said reflectively. "But then I know I would just want to be in the studio with my paints; it happens with everything." The dedication was shared by the whole family. At a later sitting his two-year-old son, Angus, selected one of the costliest sable brushes from its place on a painting table, brought it carefully across the studio, and handed it to me. When I thanked him he removed his Yale baseball cap and solemnly offered me that, as well.

A fear of painting is not new. Tom Hess, the admired editor of *Art News* in its glory years, anticipated the aversion as long ago as 1953. "Ever since Van Gogh," he wrote in the renowned Paints a Picture series published by his magazine, "sentimentality has been the curse of the painters, who took the liberty to distort." Hess was writing about de Kooning, and his thesis was that de Kooning had found a way around expressionist self-pity by rendering the contorted figure with his broadly gestural brush. Porter, somewhat later, was said to find a way around realist exhaustion by realizing the vision of Vuillard through de Kooning's handling of paint. Milroy, according to this approach, can be said to outflank expressionism by containing its intense choreography in the diagnostic grace of the neglected English painter Cedric Morris.

Given the forthright sympathies of their work, it should be no surprise that Milroy discovered an affinity for this earlier painter whose portraits occasioned a near riot when they were exhibited in London in 1938. "Humans I regard as an unpredictable species of animal," Morris once said, which no doubt explains why his portrayals provoked the outrage. Like Milroy's, his subjects neither seek nor expect pity. Their self-containment is expressed in their forward attention, a pose traditional for gods and emperors but familiar as well to anyone who was ever stared down by a cow or cat. The same pose is favored by Milroy. In his early *Joan Hornig*, the subject appears in a nimbus of hat and flowers as if she were a detail from some contemporary *Primavera* of the goddess Flora. Fate in such an image replaces motive. On his iPhone, Milroy showed me the abrupt frontality of Morris's fiery portrait of the novelist Mary Butts, remarking with approval, "Doesn't she look like something from outer space!"

Discreet friends will secretly want to know if I paid Milroy a commission for my "individualized instance of conceptual art." Others will ask outright. So the answer is yes, I certainly did. But this subject of commissions is vexed, and it invites hypocrisy. Gayford confided in his book that Freud found commissions so distasteful he refused them, when of course that painter received from Gayford exactly the compensation he had in mind, which was lasting publicity. Porter's dealer, Tibor de Nagy, claimed that Porter wished only to paint his friends, when in fact that painter undertook portraits of his friends because he hoped the examples would attract paying clients. One client who commissioned a portrait by Porter was the young Andy Warhol. Twenty years later, Warhol was turning out portraits himself. At his peak, he could accommodate fifty sitters per year at forty thousand dollars each. The resulting two million in annual fees must have made him one of the great jobbing portrait painters of all time.

Confront it with facts, and the epithet "jobbing" thus shrinks to snobbery. Why not accuse the artist of living over a shop? The irony is almost poignant when the charge issues from someone who believes art should resist global capitalism. Everyone knows the engines of the art world are coupled to capitalist excess at its most egregious. So how can principled people, the same ones who are likely to favor sustainable agriculture as practiced and consumed on a human scale, regard with disdain a private transaction made on behalf of sustainable art? We ought to reflect on what the commission truly represents in an art-world context. Artists paint portraits their clients are buying to keep. Surely, artworks meant to be loved and kept represent a practical, attainable strategy for circumventing the detested market.

Being the object of Milroy's perception, hours at a time, convinced me meanwhile that the infamous "male gaze" may be no fiction. If anybody had it, Mark Milroy did. "The human being in front of you has complications," he once told an interviewer for *Dan's Papers*, the Hamptons weekly. "I want the complications." My plan was to stare back, fully aware that my image could be caught wide-eyed like a Mary Butts from outer space. I assumed I was prepared. When I was finally allowed to see the portrait my immediate impulse, however, was to laugh. Since the painting (shirt included) was brilliant, since Milroy was regarding me quizzically and McMasters, too, was present, I managed to hold it down to a chuckle. But my old friend Chris Cox had been proved right. Years earlier, Chris wrote in passing in the *Soho News* that I was "as tall and thin and preacherly as a character out of Washington Irving." At the time I was too young to laugh at myself. Now, after decades of striving to correct my fate, I had lived long enough to be amused.

Portraits are aesthetically intensified perceptions, and intense perception makes people nervous. They defend themselves in the case of a portrait by calling it a caricature. Critics who are ill-disposed toward portraits as a genre describe them as "verging" on caricature. They probably shouldn't use the term at all, verging or no, because a portrait can be a caricature only if you think it is a depiction rather than a painting. One never hears that Cézanne's hills are caricatures of hills, or Braque's guitars of guitars. Nor was Milroy's portrait a caricature of me. He had perceived a figure in paint, no more capable of avoiding its fate than a mink, a rabbit, or a wolf.

However intense the artist's perception, one still has to wonder if it can be keen enough to portray fame, as some apparently think it should. The critic Arthur Danto was expressing the same good taste as Michael Archer, albeit from a different direction, when he made fun of the rich who sought portraits by Warhol that would make them look as famous as Marilyn Monroe. Danto was a philosopher before he was an art critic. So I presume he was making a casual jest rather than asking us to conclude, as a matter of philosophy, that Warhol indeed had rendered the fame of Monroe in paint.

Either way, his remark should indicate the presence among us of another fallacy—not about expressionism this time, but about fame. The fallacy can be detected by considering, as a kind of thought experiment, how we might match different attributes to our view of an imaginary portrait. Imagine it's the portrait of a face we are seeing for the first time. "Look at that portrait," we say. "Look at how beautiful she is," we might justifiably add. Look at how thoughtful, look at how sad.

But imagine I said of the same portrait, "Look at how famous she is." It sounds nonsensical, but why? The attribute doesn't fit the category. Where on the human face did I see the fame, in what cast of eye or lift of brow? It doesn't inhere in the physical person. It is only reputational, and it is a reputational fallacy to believe that portraits of the famous portray their fame.

This is not to say, of course, that a painter can't add the indexical signs. That's what the pearls, swords, globes, and sunglasses are for. Among the reproductions I saw pinned to a bulletin board in Milroy's studio was one that made explicitly this point. It was the portrait by Morris of Paul Odo Cross, an art collector of Native American descent, whose background in the painting so much resembles an ancient petroglyph it could be a Gottlieb gouache before the fact. Likewise indexical roles have been assumed in Milroy's work by the rooftops of Hell's Kitchen that appear behind his subjects *Glen and Kelvin*, the chihuahuas held by his sitters in *Portrait of Pam and Josh*, even the light-flecked scurf that prefigures the emergent being of his *Christopher Wolf*. Wrote publicist Cerand, who posted on her blog the first of two portraits Milroy painted of her, "Also the background is inspired by Van Gogh's The Postman, which he didn't even know *that I love*."

My own response would be a lot like Cerand's as my eyes coursed over the painting that was to bear my name. In the background were distant hills, beneath an overcast sky that suggested summer haze or, nowadays, the unseen CO_2. One hopes it wasn't methane, for these were the shuddering hills of northeast Pennsylvania. I was surprised to see them as part of my portrait (bookshelves might have been the obvious indexical choice), especially surprised since Milroy couldn't know I had just made a pilgrimage to one of those hills, north of his studio by only half an hour. That was Kingsbury Hill, elevation 1,818 feet, which affords from the pioneer cemetery near its summit one of the more stupendous views across the Delaware Valley to the east. Silence, even at that height, magnifies distance. The early settlers, who were from Connecticut, must sometimes have stood here half hoping to see all the way back home.

Because Frank has Kingsburys in his family tree, we drove up to the cemetery to have a look. The silence at the summit had been displaced by the thrumming tower of an exploratory well, the Hammond 1V, drilled by the Hess Corporation in anticipation of fracturing the underlying shale to capture natural gas. This, of course, would be fracking. At the end of that year there were five thousand shale wells active in Pennsylvania, and another twelve hundred waiting for connection to a pipeline. A major line crosses the Delaware, traverses New Jersey, and connects to a spur that dives under the Hudson to enter Manhattan at Gansevoort Street. By the following spring, thirteen hundred buildings in the city had made the conversion—mandated, by the way—from oil-fired boilers to the cleaner-burning gas now flowing in from Pennsylvania. Those buildings were soon joined by others, including the one where Frank and I have long had our apartment. We were assessed for the conversion. The subject Milroy portrayed, the one bearing my name, could protest fracking in Pennsylvania and return home to a hot shower in Chelsea fueled by the fracking he hates, and subsidizes.

Milroy's portrait of me was thus like a portrait in fiction that tracks ahead of time its subject's fate. I had become the Dorian Gray that made it possible to recognize what troubled and fascinated me that first day in the studio. The portraits I saw were not what I had in mind. The faces, as Milroy had perceived and painted them, were those of a species that must choose to live, if not in its own demise, then in the demise of those other species that have made its life on earth seem human. This will be life by enforced hypocrisy. In the long tradition of portraiture, the change in registry will of course be subtle. It is also complete.

Emerson asked in his magnificent essay "Fate" what he thought was a rhetorical question. "If, in the least particular, one could derange the order of nature,—who would accept the gift of life?" He could not have known that the question would come to sound naive. The familiar portraits of expressionist, realist, and our more recent didactic art have all implied that it matters whether the subjects portrayed once suffered, cared, or inflicted evil. Being deviations from a standard, they all but begged for the correction that would redress their fate. Milroy's subjects could have no such expectation. They were, to borrow a term, hauntological: haunted not by the deficient past but by a shameful future. In his remote studio in this imperiled place, Milroy was painting the faces of the first geological age to be initiated by a species that knows what it has done. The portraits he showed me—mine now belonged among them—were portraits not of fame but fate, which made them history paintings after all.

TETHER, 2015

IN THE EMPIRE OF THE AIR

The appearance in print of the collected poems of Donald Britton is an affront to cynicism and a triumph over fate. When Donald died, in 1994, it was sadly reasonable to assume that the influence of his poetry would be confined to the few who had preserved a copy of his single book, the slender, deceptively titled *Italy*, published thirteen years earlier. As the few became fewer it seemed all but certain the audience for his poems would disappear. Donald never taught, so there were no students to mature into positions of critical authority. There was no keeper of the flame to incite publication, no posthumous foundation to subsidize it, not even a martyrology in place to demand it out of sentiment. The survival of his work would have to come about, instead, as a pure instance of "go little booke"—an instance that must now warm the heart of anyone that has ever believed in poetry. It was the poems in *Italy* themselves, free of professional standing or obligation, that inspired the successive affections of two remarkable editors and the confident publisher of a new collection. Donald, who despite his brilliance was a modest and self-effacing person, would be surprised.

I met Donald on New Year's Eve, 1978, at a crowded party hosted by Michael Lally in his loft on Duane Street in the section of Manhattan later called Tribeca. The first thing one noticed about Donald, having registered already at a distance that he was blond ("dirt blond," he once corrected me), was the beauty of his high forehead. His eyes were blue, or 298U in the Pantone matching system (he informed me of that, as well), familiar since as the color of the Twitter logo and known sometimes as Twitter blue. But the arresting feature was the forehead, a placid expanse that seemed the emblem of intellect and imparted to his face an overall composure that persisted through even the most animated moments. The effect could be misleading. It defeated the initial efforts of painter Larry Stanton, whose portraits of Donald's friends Brad Gooch, Tim Dlugos, and Dennis Cooper are eerily ideal to anyone that knew them, but whose attempted likeness of Donald, as part of a triple portrait with Tim and Dennis, resembles the demented hitchhiker of your worst nightmare. The forehead has distorted the face, and each fix Larry applied—he even changed the haircut—made the image less satisfactory. A subsequent effort, the double portrait of a noir Dennis and beatific Donald, was dramatically more successful. Larry was so pleased he kept this second painting a secret until its exhibition at a private gallery in the East Village, where Donald would see it for the first time the night of the opening.

Born in San Angelo, Texas, in 1951, Donald went first to the University of Texas then got his doctorate in literature from the American University in Washington, D.C. When he moved on to New York he was following the example of Tim, who likewise had followed a trail blazed earlier by Michael Lally. In Washington, Michael was a founder of the Mass Transit reading series that gave Tim and other now prominent poets their initial audience. By the time Donald lived in Washington, Mass Transit had been succeeded by the equally influential series sponsored by Doug Lang at Folio Books. Here Donald found his own early audience. In those years, whether in Washington or New York, one's circle of poet friends was fluid, social, and embraced a heady mix of Language-centered writers and latter-day disciples of the New York School. You could meet Bruce Andrews at a party and not fear you had compromised his aesthetic. Donald thus took for granted that there was more than one way to articulate the times, and he respected any poetics that would approach the task seriously. That he himself approached it seriously is apparent from his work of this period: "*La plus belle plage*," with its careening nouns that nonetheless verge on narrative, or "Notes on the Articulation of Time," with its observation that "We need / these narratives, we want them." One might conclude he had thereby chosen sides, as Kenward Elmslie was to imply in a blurb for *Italy* claiming Donald as a "super-Ashbery-of-the-Sunbelt." But if that was humorous then, it is misleading today. The early "Serenade" (which I hadn't seen until Philip Clark obtained it from Donald's correspondence with a friend) is a reminder of a moment in our poetry when it was possible to conceive of uniting Eliot and Hart Crane, under the tutelage of Mallarmé and perhaps the wary eye of Pound, and so make an end run around Ashbery altogether. If Donald came out sometimes at the place Ashbery was to occupy a week later, well, this made the result no less worthy and gave him an insight, meanwhile, into the reproducible strategies of genius.

Taking up residence in New York put Donald in contact with a wider circle of writers and artists, many of whom still basked in the glow generated by Ashbery and the other poets known originally as the New York School. Dennis Cooper, who was to live in the city from 1983 to 1985, described in a later interview the excitement of being introduced to that circle by his friends. "I'd go to a party with Tim and Donald and Brad," remarked Dennis, "and there would be slightly older writers like Joe Brainard and Kenward Elmslie and Ron Padgett, and then the established greats like Ashbery and Schuyler and Edwin Denby, and nonpoets too, like Donald Barthelme and Alex Katz and Roy Lichtenstein and just an incredibly multigenerational group of artists, gay and straight, who felt some kind of aesthetic and personal unity." That unity was more than notional. The figures named (all male, but there were women at those gatherings, too) shared for the most part a faith in chance and daily experience, a faith that whatever came through the open window would be redemptive and nourishing, or else no worse than a disappointment, which would be nourishing as well. Tim and Eileen Myles adapted this faith to liberating effect. Eileen tagged it accurately as an aesthetic of "exalted mundanity." But Donald had his doubts. He had acquired a good dose of skepticism from his Language-oriented colleagues in D.C., internalized the skepticism of Shakespeare while performing the plays at the University of Texas, and probably learned, long before, the survival skepticism of the wise child who grows up in a provincial town. Tim occasionally wrote parodies of his poet friends and the one he dedicated to Donald, "Qum," already captured Donald's growing unease with the poetics of exalted mundanity and Language both: "Wanting people to desire us / we (meaning you and I) wear a bright veil / of language (meaning words) before which pale / the mundane elements of waking life."

Considering the dual spell of spectacle and diminishment which had begun to fasten its grip on New York and the rest of the country, a degree of unease was justified. The proposition that chance would always be nourishing appeared less obvious, for instance, as social and economic prospects were being hollowed out. Meanwhile, there was the spectacle. With momentous timing, Donald's first year in the city had turned out to be the year the band Blondie released their chart-topping single "Heart of Glass." A New Wave lyric aloft on a disco sound, "Heart of Glass" was regarded by some as a sellout and by others as a vindication of downtown. Donald and his friends favored the downtown clubs, but anywhere one went—bars, restaurants, the drugstore—this was the song most played. Viewed today the video may look quaint, but Debbie Harry never will, and the pulsing 24-track mix as one awaits her perfect lip-sync of the words "pain in the ass" should demonstrate what an overwhelming experience the club scene was. Donald's preferred moment in the lyrics was "mucho mistrust." It was a diagnostic delight on his part even then: because disco, whether maligned or meant for the young and free, offered a taste of spectacles to come whose design was to stun the individual spirit, not augment it. Personal history might be "annihilated, ground / Into a very fine talc," to use Donald's words from the poem he titled, inevitably it seems, "Heart of Glass." Since his poems possess, as he did, a kind of intimate reserve, they are likely to be read as if they lived on literary allusion alone, without reference to politics or popular culture. But the distant allusion to Rimbaud in Donald's "Heart of Glass" (especially the "Parade"-like twist at the ending) and a possible allusion to the Herzog film of the same title, only lend depth to the poem as the meditation on spectacle it is. To read it with the clubs in mind is to be present in the strobe lights as inside a Venetian bead, on the dance floor as the little threshing floor of earth, and better prepared for the indulgent but unsettling ending in which the awed hero "elated at the portrayal of things beyond his ken / Shouldered his people's glorious future." In a manner consistent with the best work of his maturity, Donald's "Heart of Glass" has the uncanny effect of having been our history, written ahead of time.

Donald never discussed at length, at least not with me, the theory behind his poems. For an explicit quotation one has to rely on his published statement in the anthology *Ecstatic Occasions, Expedient*

Forms. But with "Heart of Glass" in evidence, I can safely testify that he intended his poetry to enable, rather than disable language, in the belief that poetry so energized was the ideal vehicle to move us beyond "mucho mistrust" to the usable illusion of discourse. The alternative idea that he might divest himself of language and repossess it once it was purged of injustice would have seemed, as the years went by, quixotic if not credulous. How long did one have to wait? The blunt truth was that you articulate the narrative of your time or someone of another party will articulate it for you, and you don't have all day. One of Donald's endearing habits in this regard was to mark the temporal narrative of our lives by planning his own birthday celebrations. For his thirty-first birthday he arranged dinner at a Tex-Mex restaurant from which we could walk afterward to the piano bar Marie's Crisis, where Tim drove us nuts belting out from memory the show tunes he all too clearly loved to sing. For his thirty-third birthday he picked a trendier restaurant, this time more Tex than Mex, on West Fifty-Fifth Street. Frank and I discovered on arrival that we had to ring the buzzer as if for a private club. Being several years older than Donald and his other friends, we felt privileged to be included. Upstairs we found Brad and the director Howard Brookner, the most electrically beautiful couple we knew; Chris Cox, writer and photographer, who when we first met him was the lover of Edmund White; Dennis and Rob Dickerson, whose upturned face appears in a photo by Chris on the cover of Dennis's novella *Safe*; and Donald and David Cobb Craig, who had been Donald's partner for about a year and would remain so to the end. Tim wasn't there. He had dated David first and at the time of this party regarded Donald as a treacherous thief.

A knowing reader may suspect today that Donald's plan to let language follow its own initiative was equivalent to the supposedly hope-less search for a safe passage between "parataxis" and "hypotaxis," that is to say, between the Scylla of nothing but upright nouns and the Cha-rybdis of seductive syntax. I remember it instead as an instinctive be-havior that permitted him to proceed as if the dilemma didn't exist, as it probably doesn't. Donald intended his poetry to be impersonal, or "non-personalized," as he put it; but he expected it to issue all the same from personal encounters with friends and life, affairs and be-trayals, necessities and emergencies. That was the point of the birthday dinners, my retelling and his planning them in the first place. There wasn't much talk of prosody at those events. Criticism was communi-cated by an eye roll, groan, laughter, or shared enthusiasm. And yet it was Donald who insisted with enthusiasm that we read, and better yet get to know, Marjorie Welish; he once planned her birthday dinner, too. Their subsequent friendship, given Marjorie's observed rigor and his apparent romance, warrants a second look at both. And it was Don-ald who insisted we attend a lecture at Cooper Union in which Tim analyzed the art of Larry Stanton, Joe Brainard, Bill Sullivan, and Tre-vor Winkfield (who did the black-and-white cover art for *Italy*). By then Donald had his heart set on acquiring a Winkfield of his own and was thrilled, years later, when he was able to buy *Landscape with In-terior* direct from Trevor's studio. The abstractions he took from such personal encounters were compressed deep in Donald's poems: the homage to Joe's *I Remember* hidden midway in "Italy," a bow to Mar-jorie's recursive disciplines in "Masters of Self-Abuse," a recovery of Bernard Welt's prose outcrops in "The Lake Evening." There was even a gentle dig at my own preoccupations in "Disappearing Mountains." By no means, however, was there indiscriminate approval. Because he had asked me once if he shouldn't "do more for his career," I suggested we make a raid on the 92nd Street Y, the primary venue in New York at that time for poets of grandeur. I must have thought any event would do. The reader that night was Robert Penn Warren, which was grand indeed, and Donald's dismay as we sat trapped in the auditorium through the interminable reading was palpable. Having made it to the end, we decided to brave the reception, hypocrites on the make. But Donald was soon ready to flee. "Awful," he told me. "Dismal." Those were his words. He never asked what to "do for his career" again.

The language Donald achieved in his poems was frequently so ravishing that one could virtually feel the pleasure of his mind as it coursed over the emerging syntax, a kind of pleasure he identified indelibly in his poem "Winter Garden" as "the ever-skating decimal's joy." Some theorists have complained, of course, that a poetry of obliging syntax tends inescapably to nostalgia for fantasies that could never exist. A happy decimal must be a case in point. Donald himself was sympathetic to the charge, which is why he acknowledged in his statement for *Ecstatic Occasions* that he might be accused of an untutored belief in the language of flowers and voiceless things, *le langage des fleurs et des choses muettes*. (It's Baudelaire, from "Élévation," and Donald did know French.) Still, it is peculiar that poets of all people should apologize for an attempt to express things inexpressible, or speak for things that cannot speak. I suppose an opinion in this regard depends on where one locates the working surface of a poem. If one assumes the surface is coterminous with the visible page, then it's only natural to be interested in the physical look of words alone. If you assume that the working surface of poetry is time, then it's equally natural to be interested in the invisible, voiceless precincts beyond the page. Such a distinction would account for the sense of scale—one might call it the intimate vast—which Donald embraced in even his shortest poems. It will account, too, for the apparent prescience in his work, as in the hauntingly titled "In the Empire of the Air," written after he had met and fallen in love with David. Suddenly, he seemed to anticipate the dissolution of his body and its dispersal from the art he would leave behind. Perhaps he feared, already, that he had the virus. Who didn't? He found his title in a sixteenth-century French poem translated into English as "The Amorous Zodiac." Witty but sexless, as witty art tends to be, "The Amorous Zodiac" conveys the poet's regret that he can't stay forever in contemplation of his love, but must be dissolved by nature into the empire of the air, the water, or the earth. Donald's poem was certainly not sexless. Owing to its erotic charge one is driven to think of the embodied individual, blond with a high forehead but since dispersed, who conceived and wrote it. "Think of me," Donald wrote, "in the empire of the air / Or on the street, or with white sails / Stiff against the wind / Whistling far out over the water."

We had first heard of a mysterious illness among gay men in May 1981, only two months after *Italy* appeared, but the first friend Donald or I knew to actually die was Larry Stanton, the painter, in 1984. After that, one lived with the certain apprehension that the friends who defined your life might suddenly wither, suffer, and disappear. The critic David Kalstone, a source of wisdom and encouragement to many of us, was hospitalized the next year and died at home on West Twenty-Second Street in 1986. Tim tested positive in 1987 and Donald the month after he moved to Los Angeles in 1988. Howard Brookner, who stopped taking the debilitating drug AZT so he could complete his first feature-length film (*Bloodhounds of Broadway*; it stars Madonna), was moved into an apartment in Frank's and my building and died there in 1989. Tim and Chris Cox died in 1990; Joe Brainard, then Donald, in 1994. We say "died," but of course they were killed, by a threat they never could have foreseen. It's true that Donald didn't write much after the march of death began, although his heart-trapping "*Zona Temperata*" is sufficient by itself to stand for the suspended aspirations of his final years. He would not have dramatized his situation and, as one can tell from his poems, didn't consider the individual case to be that interesting. More to the point was the brute fact that his living tradition had been traumatically taken away. The infrastructure he relied on for a roll of the eyes or hoot of approval was simply in ruins. Because that infrastructure was by its nature private, even secret, I can describe Donald's situation only through an example of my own. One day Howard called unexpectedly (he was so glamorous I was shocked he knew my name) to announce with wicked delight that he hadn't read my book but Brad had taken it to the bathroom, which meant it must be important, and "Congratulations, dear." It was the funniest, finest accolade one could receive. I am sure Donald knew similar moments of surprise support and I hope some of them came from me. But when that spontaneous network of trust is gone, you are not so much redefined as returned to a state of undefined entropy, such as you endured as a child. There is no way to repeat the young adulthood during which poets, like others, make their lifelong friends. People who survived, or were never even in danger, shouldn't crow about the superior longevity of their careers.

Donald's posthumous success in inspiring the publication of his collected poems, coupled with the undeniable failure in worldly terms of his career, is occasion to wonder if the career is ever the same as poetry itself. From time to time a critic will imply that Hart Crane's suicide, for example, or Joe Brainard's decision to stop making art, may be regarded as proof that the artist realized what his admirers don't, that the work was a failure and the career could not be sustained. The critic doesn't quite dare to draw the same conclusion from the abjuration of Rimbaud or the suicide of Sylvia Plath, which reveals of course that the logic in the first case was as opportunistic as it is preposterous. Someday, a critic will do us the service of disentangling poetry from the standard map of a professional career. The map is a convenience to committees, but meaningless to the future reader—the twelve-year-old boy or girl in San Angelo—the very reader poets must hope to have. What is useful to that boy or girl is sometimes no more than a phrase, perhaps a book or a poem, amounting to a style of mind in which to escape or dwell. I recognized such a style of mind in Donald Britton and it made us friends. The first time I heard him read his work in public was at the Ear Inn in New York, the afternoon of March 7, 1981. Blond as ever, he was in that environment an apparition of nervous grace. I can't say he connected with the audience; he certainly didn't flatter it. He conveyed, perhaps too clearly for the occasion, his sense of an audience beyond the room. One got the feeling he expected to reach across time and elicit a response composed of the same respect for intellect and desire that we had there, in the Ear Inn, that Saturday afternoon. Donald's poems were not lessons or anecdotes. They are invitations to the unending contemplation of ourselves, and things beyond us, that makes the human species a window on creation.

AFTERWORD, *IN THE EMPIRE OF THE AIR*, **2016**

NOTES

PREFACE

P. XII. *the words of Alfred North Whitehead.* I am indebted to Kylan Rice
for drawing my attention to this quotation. Whitehead taught at Harvard
from 1924 to 1937 and his process philosophy, though not currently a focus
of mainstream American philosophy, was a topic in certain intellectual circles through the middle of the century. He was a major influence on
Charles Olson, who called him "the great master and companion of my
poems." Duncan's interest followed Olson's. In the context of this book it's
perhaps significant that Fairfield Porter took Whitehead's course at Harvard in 1926 and continued reading him throughout his life. "He told us
that the artist doesn't know what he knows in general," recalled Porter, "he
only knows what he knows specifically," a summary that suggests for Whitehead a continuing influence on the aesthetic of Porter, Schuyler, and possibly others of the New York School. Readers of *The Autobiography of Alice
B. Toklas* may recall that Toklas, said to know she had met a genius when
she heard a bell ring, met three authentic geniuses in her life. They were
Stein, Picasso, and Alfred North Whitehead.

ON AUTUMN LAKE

P. 9. *sat down . . . to write the poem.* In the last stanza of "On Autumn Lake"
it was David Kermani who was upstairs studying Persian and Aramaic, and
Thomas Spence Smith who, in the kitchen fixing dinner, was "distilling /
Weird fragrances out of nothing"—though metaphorically I suppose we
were all doing that.

P. 10. *his last email to me.* Ashbery's brief but pertinent message, which arrived late the night of August 30, 2017, was transcribed and sent by his assistant, the poet Emily Skillings. The day before, as she notes in her edition of his unfinished longer poems, *Parallel Movement of the Hands*, he had dictated seven pages of such correspondence. No doubt each message was as tailored to its recipient as the one meant for me.

A VOICE LIKE THE DAY

P. 14. *fact checker at the* New Yorker. Schuyler was not pleased by the *New Yorker's* policy against printing dedications. After the poem "Yellow Flowers" appeared in print, he presented Frank with the original proof sheet from the magazine. The dedication *for William Corbett* had been carefully added in his own hand.

P. 27. *Jimmy's ashes were buried that fall.* The funeral, however, was held April 16, 1991, at the Church of the Incarnation in New York. Tom Carey delivered the eulogy and John Ashbery, Raymond Foye, Eileen Myles, and Darragh Park each read a poem. The Rev. J. Douglas Ousley officiated.

MAKE IT TRUE

P. 29. *éminence grise in* that *house.* The story of Frank O'Hara's remarking that Schuyler was the éminence grise in the Porter household was so quotably perfect that I feared, even at first writing, it might be too perfect and I'd better check it out. Boldly, I contacted Barbara Guest, who told me the story was true. So I was more than caught off guard when an aggrieved Jane Freilicher called immediately after the essay appeared in print to complain that Frank would never say a thing like that. What could she mean, I wondered, as she hung up the phone; it sounded just like the

O'Hara we have all heard described. Only later did I learn that Porter and Schuyler had been having an affair, perhaps there in that house under Anne Porter's nose. No wonder Jane thought O'Hara's remark too cruel, even for him. I have rewritten the paragraph to indicate more clearly why the remark was insightful, and perhaps as unobjectionable in context as it seemed on my first hearing it. Throughout this collection I've tried to correct other such errors, adjust anachronisms, and minimize repetitions to protect the reader from the embarrassments of my younger self. I gave up on the repetitions.

THE POET'S SO-CALLED PROSE

P. 36. *first ball of the season*. At least one reader objected that Dodgers fan Marianne Moore must have thrown out the first ball at Ebbets Field, not Yankee Stadium. But the Dodgers left Brooklyn in 1957. During her *Paris Review* interview, Donald Hall asked Moore if she missed the ball club and she replied, "Very much, and I am told they miss us." Since the Dodgers had deserted her, and since she seems to have been an untiring moralist, perhaps she meant it as a moral lesson (i.e., "Don't look back") when she did in fact throw out the first ball at Yankee Stadium in 1968. According to Elizabeth Phillips' *Marianne Moore*, "she kept her pitch low."

P. 45. *a very different stylist*. Moore was reviewing *The Geographical History of America*, by Gertrude Stein.

A SCHUYLER BALLADE

P. 54. *stolen it direct from Jimmy*. The structure of this essay and its title are indebted to Schuyler's own quotation-piece, "The Fauré Ballade." The poems quoted are of course his.

P. 56. *our turn to respond*. Not one but two editions of Niedecker's poems appeared in 1986. I reviewed them in the essay that follows. Neither was the definitive book her readers were waiting for. It would be another sixteen years before publication of her *Collected Works*, edited by Jenny Penberthy.

FREE AND CLEAN

P. 57. *didn't know enough about her*. In fact I'd been as naive about Niedecker as I was about Porter and Schuyler. She did more than correspond with Zukofsky; she slept with him. She first traveled to New York to stay in his apartment at 41 West Eleventh Street in 1933. After an interval of returns to Wisconsin and reappearances in New York she became pregnant in 1935. She agreed to an abortion, returned again to Wisconsin, and four years later Zukofsky married Celia Thaew; their only child, Paul, was born in 1943. Nor was Niedecker's marriage at age sixty her first. In 1928, at age twenty-five, she married a neighbor who was four years older and moved with him to a house he built in nearby Fort Atkinson. In 1930 the couple lost the house to the Depression and returned to live separately with their parents. They saw each other for the last time in 1934, although Niedecker did not obtain a divorce until 1942.

P. 58. *her best known poem*. Bertholf printed this poem, as he did others, with a variant line. I've corrected all variants to agree with the texts established by Penberthy in the *Collected Works*.

P. 64. *talented child of six*. The child addressed in "For Paul" turned out to be the young Paul Zukofsky, which has confounded the critics and prevented them from reading the series as addressed to any American child of six. Zukofsky himself insisted in a letter to Cid Corman that Niedecker couldn't base durable poems on his son's childhood. "It becomes sentiment of the affections," he complained. Readers today are accustomed, however, to the practice of Frank O'Hara as described in his not-so-mock manifesto, "Personism." O'Hara was careful to distinguish his practice from mere sentiment of the affections. "It does not have to do with personality or intimacy, far from it!" he exclaimed. The idea was to divert "love's life-giving vulgarity" into the energies of a poem rather than expend it in pursuit of an actual person. On the evidence of her series itself, there could hardly be a better description of Niedecker's own practice as a poet in "For Paul." If only she had given it another title: *For Jim*. For Larry.

P. 64. *constituent poems in eight groups*. The first two groups of "For Paul" were published intact but in her attempts to publish the others Niedecker encountered resistance from editors and opposition from Zukofsky. She dismantled the series, scrapping some poems and rearranging the rest in a new manuscript, *For Paul and Other Poems*, which she hoped would overcome the objections. It didn't, and likewise went unpublished. But because it survived in the Zukofsky archives this diminished version is the one that now appears in the *Collected Works*. For an approximation of the original we are forced to rely on the imperfect presentation in *From This Condensery*. In that book you would read groups one through four, skip backward to read as group five the bracingly angry poem that begins on page 37 and continues through 42, then return forward to page 65 and read groups six through eight. The latter groups are incomplete and may never be authoritatively reconstructed. If they were artfully reconstructed, or even left unfinished, it wouldn't be the first time a major work of art reached its audience in tantalizing but still rewarding form.

P. 64. *no match for the manuscripts*. The truth is that the editor underperformed at best and the book he produced, *From This Condensery*, was a disservice to a great poet. I was reviewing the poet, however, not a consumer product, and decided it was important to praise the poetry rather than risk a negative impression of Niedecker among general readers who wouldn't be buying the book anyway. Given that so few had heard of her, I think the decision made sense. Elizabeth Pochoda, the literary editor of the *Nation*, had the further idea of including a tiny anthology of Niedecker poems scattered through the issue in which the essay appeared. We learned later that this was indeed the way some readers first encountered the once neglected poet who is now recognized as a major American voice of the twentieth century.

NIEDECKER AND THE EVOLUTIONAL SUBLIME

P. 72. *the notes Niedecker made.* This essay was effectively complete when I discovered that Niedecker's notes on Lake Superior had survived. Her neighbors Gail and Bonnie Roub preserved them after her death. So I was relieved, and a little gratified on reading the notes to find they confirmed facts and conclusions I'd already inferred from the poem itself. It made the poem seem all the more uncanny. The notes, my essay, the poem, and certain supporting materials are reprinted together in the Wave Books volume *Lake Superior*, edited by Joshua Beckman. For the initial favor of quoting the notes and poem I remain indebted to Cid Corman, the first literary executor of Niedecker's estate.

P. 85. *Lake Superior was the shining Big Sea Water.* If by some remote chance Niedecker had not read *The Song of Hiawatha* before she met Louis Zukofsky she would have learned of it from him. By the time he was seven years old Zukofsky could recite the poem from memory—in Yiddish. He was sometimes cornered on the street by older boys who refused to release him until he recited enough to earn his freedom.

P. 103. *paraphrase a naive sonnet.* The sonnet, "High Flight," was written by John Gillespie Magee, Jr., an American pilot who volunteered for the Royal Canadian Air Force and was killed in the defense of Britain on December 11, 1941. At the time of his death he was nineteen. The quotation was placed in the president's remarks by speechwriter Peggy Noonan.

NATIVE GENIUS

P. 126. *Fat, brainy, Jewish, lesbian.* My fond caricature of Gertrude Stein marks the only time my words were censored by the *Nation.* I was not allowed to say "fat." I wish the vigilance had extended to my use in the same essay of a quotation from Robert Frost. The character of the United States, said Frost, depends on its living traditions such as the Declaration of Independence and the English language—"which is not," he added wryly, "the language spoken in England or in any of her provinces." Not until I saw that quotation in print did I suspect it could be taken at first glance to mean English only. In fact I meant it, as I believe Frost did, to remind us that the American language is not a colony of English, nor of the English, and should not be judged by English standards. This will become only more obvious as the language is further influenced by Spanish. Whitman predicted as much in the nineteenth century. I quoted his prediction in my commonplace book, *Amerifil.txt,* but it bears repeating here: "As to that composite American identity of the future, Spanish character will supply some of the most needed parts. Who knows but that element, like the course of some subterranean river, dipping invisibly for a hundred or two years, is now to emerge in broadest flow and permanent action?"

LINES FROM LONDON TERRACE

P. 127. *January 1, 1987.* Frank and I moved into our apartment in London Terrace in November 1974 and I began keeping a journal shortly thereafter. These excerpts from 1987 were published later in a special edition of the *Seneca Review*. Because journal entries are provisional when made, and should be regarded as provisional even when published, I have in this instance left the embarrassments intact.

P. 129. *generational persuasion from 1939.* It turns out that Susan Howe was born in 1937, but her name belongs here by inference if not by fact. It would belong here even if this list were revised, as no doubt it should be.

THE LEFTOVER LANDSCAPE

P. 133. *our appreciation of landscape.* In perhaps the last art review he wrote before he died, William Corbett provided for painters and poets who need it a functional justification for their interest in landscape. After noting that the abstract paintings of Thomas Nozkowski had changed in response to that artist's habit of hiking in the Shawangunk Mountains, Corbett suggested why this might be so. "The shapes we encounter in landscape," he wrote, "are all impractical since they serve only themselves and are endless in their variety." The shapes were useless, in other words, which made them well suited to that perfectly useless concentration that Elizabeth Bishop identified as both desired from art and necessary for its creation.

P. 139. *doesn't transcend its limits.* The suggestion that Emerson meant the human species as either individuals or societies to transcend the limits of nature represents a common misapprehension of his thought, based on the kind of incomplete reading that stops at "Circles" and "Self-Reliance." "The idea of right exists in the human mind," he observed in a later essay, "and lays itself out in the equilibrium of Nature, in the equalities and periods of our system, in the level of the seas, in the action and reaction of forces. Nothing is allowed to exceed or absorb the rest; if it do, it is disease, and quickly destroyed. It was an early discovery of the mind,—this beneficent rule."

AN OUTSIDER'S INTRODUCTION TO EMERSON

P. 154. *Emerson's frame . . . was the paragraph.* Anyone who turns to the secondary literature will soon discover that my understanding of Emerson's practice is not shared by most contemporary scholars. The biographer Robert D. Richardson countered in 2009 that the sentence, not the paragraph, was for Emerson the "main structural and formal unit." Phillip Lopate, three years later in the Harvard *Annotated Emerson*, emphatically agreed. "Emerson's basic unit of structural composition *was* the sentence," he wrote. But to define the unit of prose composition as the sentence seems to me, if not simply a tautology, then at least otiose. Emerson's sentences ride on their context; they wait to be refracted by the sentences that follow them, sometimes as distantly as the second half of the essay. His essays, like the sermons from which their form descends, have no meaning or rhetorical logic without their arrangement in paragraphs. On November 28, 1839, Emerson wrote in the journal he labeled *E*, "Poetry makes its own pertinence and a single stanza outweighs a book of prose. One stanza is complete. But one sentence of prose is not." I can only conclude that the scholars are sight-reading line by line rather than listening broadly to the modulations of each essay as a whole.

THE PROPHETIC ASHBERY

P. 167. *let me offer a proposition.* The donnish manner of this early essay was deliberate. I had been asked in 1976 to teach for a year at the University of Rochester, where I discovered that my new colleagues were bemused by my candid assumption that Ashbery's work was of the first importance. Having never had colleagues before, I must have taken it as my obligation to bring them up to date on the poetry of their time. The amiable Joseph Summers, a scholar of George Herbert and friend of Elizabeth Bishop, proposed that I write a paper to persuade them. This essay was the result. One professor who read it, James Rieger, responded dryly that what he liked best was my send-up of faculty prose. I pretended not to be surprised.

P. 171. *"terminally sophisticated" society.* The quotation is not from a poem but from Ashbery's dust-jacket description of the society portrayed in Edmund White's first novel, *Forgetting Elena.*

P. 197. *literature on pathological narcissism.* The authority at the time was Otto Kernberg's *Borderline Conditions and Pathological Narcissism.* The possibility of an analogous disorder in the culture at large was a popular topic in the late 1970s among people I was trying to convince.

P. 204. *the exploded context Americans live in now.* This essay was written before the election in 1980 of Ronald Reagan. It should go without saying that the context of American life is no longer what it was then. And for critics who thought the attitude described here would lead inevitably to political disengagement, it shouldn't have been necessary to point out that politics, in a public theater for action, is itself a form of serious play.

JUSTIFIED TIMES

P. 207. *the mind of Ronald Reagan?* Ashbery said later that my comparing his line "the blackboard is erased in the attic" to the mind of Ronald Reagan had made him laugh. I asked if he approved of the essay itself. "It's what I'd want everybody to think about my work *all the time,*" he replied brightly, without indicating that he thought it even marginally valid. The title "Justified Times" was supplied by the *Nation*; it unnerved me but I got used to it.

P. 217. *namesake Tibor de Nagy*. One sees a variety of phonetic spellings (tee-bore d' NAJH, NAJ, NAZJH) but the gallery's name is normally pronounced to rhyme with collage. A rough American approximation of the Hungarian might have been nodge. Friend of the gallery Roland Pease recalled his amusement whenever de Nagy in the early 1950s wearily answered the gallery's phone, "tee-bore da NAGGY." In Martina Kudláček's documentary *Notes on Marie Menken*, the painter Alfred Leslie in fact pronounces it that way. But Ripley, who was versed in Magyar, left a memorable mnemonic: "Naggy? No, no, pronounce it nodge. / He's a sweetie, not a stodge." The French "de" is phony, of course, and was inserted in the gallery's name to add cachet.

P. 218. Evolution with Mushrooms, Bud, and Pineapple. This Ripley drawing was reproduced by the Guggenheim Museum in *Peggy Guggenheim & Frederick Kiesler: The Story of Art of This Century*, edited by Susan Davidson with contributions by Francis V. O'Connor, Don Quaintance, and Jasper Sharp.

P. 219. *aesthetic influence on the painters and poets*. Katy Siegel suggests persuasively that Ripley's influence was one of sensibility. See her introductory essay, "Contextually Boundless," in *The heroine Paint: After Frankenthaler*, published by the Gagosian Gallery in 2015. Ripley's verse play "Beach at Amagansett" was printed for the first time in *The heroine Paint*, while three of his satirical poems on art appear, also for the first time, in the Library of America's anthology *Art in America 1945–1970*, edited by Jed Perl.

P. 219. *first poem-paintings seen at de Nagy.* Two such Ripley drawings returned to the Tibor de Nagy Gallery for its sixtieth anniversary exhibition in 2011. Two were also included in the exhibition *Pretty Raw: After and Around Helen Frankenthaler*, curated by Siegel for the Rose Art Museum at Brandeis in 2015.

A HIDDEN HISTORY OF THE AVANT-GARDE

P. 222. *Hartigan's painting held between them.* Barr had previously taken three of Hartigan's paintings to his office for consideration but rejected them. When he chose *The Persian Jacket*, he held it, too, for consideration. Eventually he asked Hartigan to come to his office to repaint a portion of the picture before he decided the museum should keep it.

P. 223. *her sale was received as unprecedented.* In 1944 a work by Irene Rice Pereira, *Composition in White*, was sold directly from a show at Art of This Century to the Newark Museum.

P. 242. *Greenberg was selecting a group exhibition.* One reads repeatedly in art histories that *New Talent 1950*, Kootz's first such show, was selected by Greenberg and Meyer Schapiro both. This is not correct. "Clem Greenberg picked the first, then collaborated with Meyer Schapiro on the second," Kootz told Jay Jacobs of *Art in America* (November–December 1966, p. 109). Perhaps, as Greenberg's reputation clouded, the artists sought to make the story of their selection more palatable by seasoning it with a less controversial figure.

THE DRAWINGS OF DWIGHT RIPLEY

P. 255. *"fabled Dwight Ripley."* The reader will notice that there's a lot of Dwight Ripley in this book. Painters and composers are permitted, even expected, to return obsessively to themes on which they produce variations. We aren't so tolerant when writers repeat themselves. In my case it's

even worse than it looks in these pages, since Ripley and his lifetime partner, Rupert Barneby, are also the subjects of the biography, *Both: A Portrait
in Two Parts*, which I published in 2004. Their story was exemplary and
their contributions to art and botany in America were critical, yet no one
knew of them. After Barneby's death, Frank and I found ourselves entrusted with their remaining archives. Here was an authentic history, not
further opinions, impressions, or sensitivities, and by an accident of fate I
was the one poet in the world who might keep that history from vanishing.
I took it as a moral imperative.

THE NEW YORK SCHOOL REVISITED

P. 266. *a magazine called* View. The young Robert Duncan did not share the
enthusiasm for *View*. In a scathing review first published in 1947 he argued
that the magazine was aimed at rentier dilettantes ("refugees from their
million dollar sense of uselessness") and was cynically designed to exploit
their boredom by providing the illusory thrill of participation in a trans-
gressive avant-garde. It was a magazine styled to flatter the wealthy in the
same way *National Geographic* was styled to flatter the middle class retiree.
Since the New York School poets were all middle class in origin, Duncan's
insight makes it possible to regard their subscriptions to *View* as a kind of
social climbing. At the same time it's amusing to note that Duncan himself
published an early poem in *View*, but after a falling out with the editors
his further submissions were rejected. It was then he wrote the review.

THE ENDURING INFLUENCE OF A PAINTER'S GARDEN

P. 282. *can still see in my mind.* The images that accompanied my talk at the
Parrish Museum can be seen in a video online at the time of this publication
at *vimeo.com/132469924.*

P. 287. *poems hung on the wall.* The gallerist Elaine Benson adapted this practice for the exhibition *Some Poets and Painters of the Hampton Landscape*, held at her gallery in Bridgehampton, New York, in 1977. Instead of collaborative works she hung one painting per painter and one poem per poet. The paintings were all 30 × 36 inches and up, while the poems were 8 × 10 or 8½ × 11. At the crowded, smoke-filled opening, Jane Freilicher asked, "Which poem is yours?" Nervous, proud, young, I pointed through the cigarette smoke and over the elegant heads of the guests to the distant shape of my poem on the opposite wall. Jane looked quickly in that direction, turned back to me, and said, "Oh, it's *lovely.*"

THE PYRRHIC MEASURE IN AMERICAN POETRY

P. 296. *beginning of its new century.* This essay was requested for an anthology that never materialized and it remained unpublished until it appeared in my earlier selection of essays, *Lines from London Terrace.* Sometime in the interim I must have changed the tense of the piece to reflect that the century had in fact turned.

P. 313. *ridiculing the dictum of Williams.* Donald Davie, who was consistently hard on Williams, called no ideas but in things a "sloppy and shallow slogan."

THE APPLAUSE OF SCIENCE

P. 328. *a poem even more disagreeable.* Because I thought my environmentalist sympathies were obvious in this essay, I was surprised when the *Nation* received an outraged letter from Edward Abbey condemning the "idolatry of science" and demanding to know what I could mean by calling Auden's moon poem disagreeable. The Auden poem, "Moon Landing," begins by proposing that "It's natural the Boys should whoop it up for / so huge a phallic triumph, an adventure / it would not have occurred to women / to think worth while." It continues by denigrating the work of scientists, the value of technology, the beauty of desert landscapes, and finally sports the awful schoolboy pun, "Unsmudged, thank God, my Moon still queens the Heavens." I stand by the reply I made to Abbey at the time, that I couldn't think of saving reasons for lines so sexist, so smug, so puerile, when those lines are so disagreeable to the ear.

THE CIVIC METONYMY OF MICHAEL SCHIAVO

P. 338. *harder won than he knows.* Schiavo, who published *The Mad Song* using an Espresso Book Machine at the Northshire Bookstore in Manchester Center, Vermont, was quick to point out the influence of Lyn Hejinian's *My Life* on the shape of his own poem-paragraphs. The lineage makes his work only the more encouraging, as an example of the way content can infuse and alter the impact of a form it admires. Priority is not fatal. The same might be said for Hejinian's title *My Life*, which before it was hers was the title of a well-loved and prosodically much different poem by Michael Lally, as well as being the title before that of autobiographies by Leon Trotsky, Alfred Russel Wallace, and who knows how many others.

MARK MILROY PAINTS MY PORTRAIT

P. 368. *reputational fallacy.* I meant to write, as may be obvious, that fame is a category mistake. In deference to a friend who wanted that term for an essay of his own, I came up with reputational fallacy instead. Perhaps either term works.

P. 369. *gas now flowing in from Pennsylvania.* The progressive citizens of New York congratulated themselves and praised their governor when he banned fracking in their state. No one seemed troubled that the ban had become politically convenient because the state's metropolis was now supplied with gas produced by fracking the shale fields of less fortunate Pennsylvania. In February 2021 the Delaware River Basin Commission, a regional authority whose voting members are the governors of New York, New Jersey, Delaware, and Pennsylvania, plus the North Atlantic division engineer from the U.S. Army Corps of Engineers, imposed a permanent ban on fracking in the area on both sides of the river under its jurisdiction. That area includes Kingsbury Hill. The four governors who voted to impose the ban were all Democrats. Two Republican state senators from Pennsylvania, joined by two counties and two townships in that state, had already filed suit in federal court on the grounds that the regional commission was usurping the state legislature's authority to govern its natural resources. The suit by the state senators was dismissed for lack of standing, but the plaintiff counties and townships were invited to refile if they could better demonstrate their own standing to challenge the permanent ban.

IN THE EMPIRE OF THE AIR

P. 371. *two remarkable editors*. Britton's poems were collected initially by Reginald Shepherd, but Shepherd died before he could enlist a publisher. The project was taken up by Philip Clark, whose expanded collection of Britton's work was accepted by Stephen Motika for Nightboat Books and published under Britton's own title, *In the Empire of the Air*.

ACKNOWLEDGMENTS

Trevor Winkfield urged me for years to collect these essays and it's a pleasure to acknowledge him in print where he can't think better of his advice.

It is likewise a pleasure to remember those who encouraged the essays in the first place. I am indebted to Elizabeth Pochoda for her confidence in my contributions to the *Nation*, Henri Cole for the occasion to address in public my interest in Emerson, Jenny Penberthy for indulging my need to write on Niedecker's "Lake Superior" when she intended to write about that poem herself, Eric Brown for suggesting I explore the art and life of Dwight Ripley, Stephen Motika for the idea of exhibiting Ripley's impact on the New York School, Philip Clark for the chance to recall the genius and friendship of Donald Britton, and Alicia Longwell for inviting my reflections on the work and influence of Robert Dash. For similar encouragement I am grateful to Joan Abrahamson, Alexandra Anderson-Spivy, Andrew Arnot, Matthew Bevis, Brice Brown, Carlos Carrillo, Rowland Collins, Deborah Garrison, Brigid Hughes, Jacquelyn Kallunki, David Kalstone, Paul Kane, David Lehman, Tod Lippy, Erroll McDonald, Joseph Parisi, Ian Pople, Donald Revell, Deborah Rosenthal, Alejandro Saralegui, Nancy Schoenberger, Richard Sennett, Thomas Spence Smith, Joseph Summers, Deborah Tall, Brian Esparza Walker, Alex Wagner, and Timothy Young. For their ongoing wisdom I'm grateful to Miles Champion, Lynn Chu, Alan Felsenthal, Maxine Groffsky, Glen Hartley, Andy Hughes, Martha Kaplan, Jed Perl, Matthew Zapruder, and, of course, Frank Polach. And I am indebted always to the late William Corbett, founder of the small press Pressed Wafer, who published an earlier selection of my prose. Bill would be gratified as I am to see the complete essays, envisioned and now published by Nightboat Books.

My debt to Nightboat, the publisher also of my collected poems, cannot be overstated. It is a great and unexpected satisfaction to find one's fortunes joined with those of younger poets, writers, and editors who care so deeply about the future of literature. I've been especially fortunate in this regard to work closely with Lindsey Boldt, Gia Gonzales, Caelan Nardone, Lina Bergamini, and Nightboat's director and publisher, Stephen Motika. Their dual commitment to innovation and perseverance has been an inspiration. I am likewise fortunate in their choice of a designer whose instinct was to unite my two collections, the essays and the poems. The words may be mine, not to mention the errors, but their physical appeal as they rise from the page is the work of poet and book designer Jeff Clark. He is the author of their visual success just as Nightboat is author of their presence in the world. I could not be luckier in friends and colleagues, and it's an abiding pleasure to acknowledge them all.

INDEX

410

son, 97, 100, 151, 300; on Emerson, 96; inclusiveness of, 177, 207; *Leaves of Grass*, 114, 118, 154; Niedecker and, 59, 64; paragraphic scale, 296, 302; partiality of, 316; on prudence, 308; pyrrhic measure and, 301; "Scented Herbage of My Breast," 17; on science, 328–29; "Song of Myself," 115; on Spanish in American identity, 391; vastness in, 297–98; vistas of, 129, 134, 136, 141; "When I Heard the Learn'd Astronomer," 328

Williams, William Carlos, 55, 116, 264, 313; Davie on, 130, 398; on Moore, 37; Moore on, 39–40; Niedecker and, 63

Willis, Patricia, 36

Winkfield, Trevor, 20, 377; *Cottage Industries*, 238; at Dash's garden, 15, 46, 284, 286

Wisconsin: The Badger State (WPA Guide to Wisconsin), 71, 73

Wittgenstein, Ludwig, 311

Woodbury, Charles, 302, 307

Wordsworth, William, 69, 92

Wyatt, Thomas, 163, 190, 301

Zukofsky, Louis, 57; and *Hiawatha*, 390; Niedecker on, 78; Niedecker to, 64, 70; as Objectivist, 61, 63, 65; objects to "For Paul," 388–89

DOUGLAS CRASE is an independent poet and essayist. He was born in Michigan in 1944, raised on a farm, and educated at Princeton. A former speechwriter, he has been described in the *Times Literary Supplement* as "the unusual case of a contemporary poet whose most public, expansive voice is his most authentic." His first book, *The Revisionist*, was named a Notable Book of the Year in 1981 by *The New York Times* and nominated for a National Book Critics Circle Award and a National Book Award in poetry. His collected poems, *The Revisionist and The Astropastorals*, was a finalist for the Lambda Literary Award and named a Book of the Year for 2019 in both the *Times Literary Supplement* and *Hyperallergic*. His dual biography of influential aesthetes Rupert Barneby and Dwight Ripley, *Both: A Portrait in Two Parts*, was nominated for a Lambda Literary Award and named a Stonewall Honor Book by the American Library Association. He has received a Whiting Writers' Award, a Guggenheim Fellowship, and a MacArthur "genius" award. He lives with his husband, Frank Polach, in New York and Carley Brook, Pennsylvania.

NIGHTBOAT BOOKS

Nightboat Books, a nonprofit organization, seeks to develop audiences for writers whose work resists convention and transcends boundaries. We publish books rich with poignancy, intelligence, and risk. Please visit nightboat.org to learn about our titles and how you can support our future publications.

The following individuals have supported the publication of this book. We thank them for their generosity and commitment to the mission of Nightboat Books:

Kazim Ali
Anonymous (4)
Abraham Avnisan
Jean C. Ballantyne
The Robert C. Brooks Revocable Trust
Amanda Greenberger
Rachel Lithgow
Anne Marie Macari
Elizabeth Madans
Elizabeth Motika
Thomas Shardlow
Benjamin Taylor
Jerrie Whitfield & Richard Motika

This book is made possible, in part, by grants from the New York City Department of Cultural Affairs in partnership with the City Council and the New York State Council on the Arts Literature Program.